The Wealth Inequality Reader

4th Edition

Edited by Sam Pizzigati, Linda Pinkow,
and the Dollars & Sense *Collective*

DOLLARS & SENSE — ECONOMIC AFFAIRS BUREAU
BOSTON, MASSACHUSETTS

The Wealth Inequality Reader, 4th Edition

Edited by Sam Pizzigati, Linda Pinkow, and the *Dollars & Sense* Collective

ISBN: 978-1-939402-00-4

Published by:
Dollars & Sense
Economic Affairs Bureau, Inc.
One Milk Street
Boston, MA 02109
617-447-2177
www.dollarsandsense.org

Research assistance: Sam Osoro
Illustrations: Nick Thorkelson
Design and layout: Linda Pinkow
Production assistance: Chris Sturr
Cover: David Gerratt, www.nonprofitdesign.com

Printed in the United States

CONTENTS

SECTION II   THE CONSEQUENCES OF INEQUALITY

PREFACE

BY CHUCK COLLINS
November 2012

Wealth inequality is making us sick. And that's just one of its harmful consequences.

The dizzying disparity in America's wealth is undermining our democratic institutions, destabilizing our economy, trashing our planet, and tearing communities apart. It is wrecking all that we care about.

This new edition of *The Wealth Inequality Reader* could not be more timely. The first edition, published in 2004, served as an essential primer about the data and dangers of economic inequality. But outside of a few academic journals, the first *Wealth Inequality Reader* came at a time of political silence about the issue.

In the ensuing years, public awareness about the negative consequences of wealth inequality has grown. In the fall of 2011, the Occupy Wall Street movement—"We are the 99%"—galvanized a dramatic shift in the U.S. conversation about wealth inequality. And other social movements around the world, including street protests and rebellions across the Middle East and Europe, have put a spotlight on global inequality.

The U.S. public, as opinion research and election results indicate, is waking up to the dangers of excessive inequality. Before 2008, public opinion polls reflected that a majority of Americans, while troubled by growing inequality, believed that our economic divisions resulted from varying degrees of individual merit. In other words, people's economic status reflected their "deservedness"— their hard work, intelligence, and effort. Most people were not troubled by the small sliver of Americans growing fantastically wealthy. These fortunes, most of us believed, posed no problem—as long as these rich people had fairly attained their wealth and others had the same opportunity to become rich themselves.

But since 2008, public attitudes have shifted. The middle-class standard of living has imploded, with once-stable families now experiencing economic insecurity. And intergenerational mobility—the promise that children will likely live more comfortable lives than their parents—now runs lower in the United States than the level of intergenerational mobility in other industrialized countries. A greater percentage of the American public now believes that our lopsided distribution of wealth definitely does pose a problem. More people today view great fortunes as the result of the wealthy 1% rigging the rules of the game in their favor.

In the last decade, an outpouring of research has detailed how extreme inequalities of wealth are undermining much of what we hold dear. This research from multiple disciplines has revealed how too much inequality worsens public health, slows social mobility, and subverts democratic institutions. A 2012 report from the International Monetary Fund, for instance, argues that extreme wealth inequality in the United States acts as a drag on economic growth and undercuts productive investment. And as a number of articles in this reader document, the adverse consequences of these inequalities are compounded for women, people of color, and young adults.

How did our wealth inequality become so savage? This new *Wealth Inequality Reader* edition includes some of the best analysis we have about the causes of inequality. One basic explanation: A small segment of the top 1%—with an organized base in Wall Street's financial institutions—have worked over many decades to rig the rules of the economy to favor the 1% at the expense of the 99%. The rules have been tilted in favor of those who own large amounts of assets at the expense of wage earners. These rules range from government policies related to taxation and global trade to matters of regulation and levels of public spending. All these rule changes, taken together, have led to massive imbalances of wealth and power that jeopardize peace and prosperity across the globe.

Not everyone in the top 1% is responsible for rigging the economic rules. Within the 1% are people who have devoted their lives to building a healthy economy that works for everyone—affluent men and women who have helped build movements for a more fair and equitable world. The focus of our concern and organizing should be on the "rule riggers" within the 1%, those who use their power and wealth to influence the game so that they and their corporations can gain ever more power and wealth.

But even as public concern over inequality grows, national policy debates in Washington, D.C. remain disconnected from the real concerns of ordinary Americans. The right wing-dominated House of Representatives, for example, remains fixated on fiscal austerity and our national debt—and essentially ignores unemployment, home foreclosures, corporate tax dodging, and the collapse of the middle class.

The seeds of a new political realignment, fortunately, are now being sown. The underlying conditions that gave rise to the 99% movement—joblessness, economic insecurity, bloated CEO pay, mushrooming student loan obligations, grinding poverty, and collapsing middle-class livelihoods—are not going away. Our current political system, dominated by the concerns of the top 1% and captured by a small segment of global corporations, is incapable of responding to demands for greater shared prosperity. And so the pressure will continue to build for real change.

This emerging movement to reduce wealth inequality seems to have several basic principles. The economy should work for everyone, not just the richest 1%. The rules of the economy should not benefit the 1% at the expense of everyone else. We should have a level playing field between global corporations and small businesses.

This reader chronicles a broad vision of potential strategies for change, everything from strengthening our social safety net and establishing "WPA-style" jobs program, to making the minimum wage a living wage. The book also includes proposals to tax concentrated wealth, share the wealth of the commons, and directly close the racial wealth divide with asset-building initiatives.

We can reverse the inequality trends that plague us. We can change the unlevel playing field that is worsening inequality. Indeed, we did this once before, in the last century after the first Gilded Age, as explained in the article, "The Rich Don't Always Win." Throughout U.S. history, social movements have pushed back against organized private wealth, and sometimes they have won significant victories.

In the last year, policy initiatives that were "off the table," such as a Wall Street financial transaction tax or eliminating subsidies for fossil fuel industries, have become subjects for serious debate. Political leaders in Washington, D.C. didn't raise the profile of these initiatives. Grassroots advocacy—from a growing movement of people touched by the adverse impact of inequality—did.

The movement to address economic inequality cannot wait for President Obama or any elected leaders to lead on these issues. That's our job, our responsibility. We need to find the pressure points that open up the political system to rule changes that ensure we can build an economy that works for everyone, not just the 1%. ❏

WEALTH INEQUALITY BY THE NUMBERS

Not since the Gilded Age has this country seen such a profound gap between the very rich and the majority of the population. Global wealth disparities are even larger. The following pages capture this polarization with an array of facts and figures on the distribution of wealth in the United States and worldwide.

Illustrations in this section by Nick Thorkelson

The Wealth Pie

The wealthiest 1% of households own more than a third of the nation's household wealth. The top 10% claim a total of 76.7%, while the bottom three-fifths make do with the crumbs—holding a meager 1.7% of total net worth.

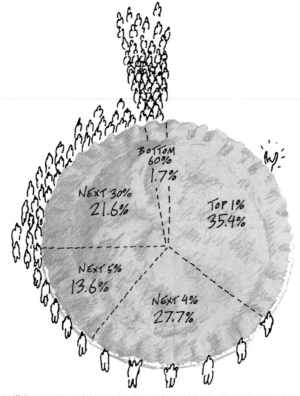

Source: Edward N. Wolff, The Asset Price Meltdown and the Wealth of the Middle Class (Russell Sage Foundation 2010 Project, forthcoming).

WHAT IS WEALTH?

A family's wealth, or net worth, is defined as the sum of its assets minus its debts. In other words, wealth is "what you own" minus "what you owe." Assets are all the resources that a household holds in store—the bank of reserves a family has available to invest in its members' futures. Many assets grow in value and generate income. Asset wealth also provides a cushion, protecting families from the fluctuations of the business cycle. Families can draw down wealth assets during periods of crisis—a job loss, for example.

Financial assets include savings, bonds, certificates of deposit, stocks, mutual fund investments, retirement pensions, and the like. Nonfinancial assets may include homes, other real estate, vehicles, ownership in a privately held business, and all sorts of other property—from rare baseball card collections to jewelry or hobby equipment. Debts are liabilities—credit card balances, mortgages, and other loans that we owe.

How does wealth differ from income? Picture wealth as a pool of resources, much like a pond. Income, by contrast, flows like a stream. Most adults receive an income stream from a variety of sources, such as paychecks, Social Security and other entitlement payments, child support, or pensions. This income stream pays for housing, health care, food, clothing, and all our other expenses. If any trickle of income remains after paying these expenses, we typically set this surplus aside as savings—which then becomes wealth.

People with large "ponds" of wealth receive streams of income from the assets that fill the pond—in the form of interest, dividends, and rent. The very wealthy among us have considerably more than "ponds" of wealth. They hold veritable "lakes" of assets, and out of these assets spring substantial "rivers" of income.

Looking at information about wealth can tell us a great deal about people's lives, more than we can learn from income statistics alone. In 2010, for example, the poorest one-fifth of U.S. households had a mean net worth of negative $2,750. In other words, an average family in the bottom quintile carried a debt burden greater than all of its assets combined. Such a family most likely does not own a

Different researchers use slightly different definitions of wealth. Some exclude those retirement pensions that an individual cannot currently access, while others include the estimated present value of pensions. And some scholars consider automobiles a form of wealth, whereas others exclude the value of automobiles from their calculations.

Data on wealth are far scarcer than data on income. The primary source of information on private wealth in the United States has been the Federal Reserve's triennial Survey of Consumer Finances, which collects household-level data on assets, liabilities, income, use of financial services, and other household financial behavior.

home, but if they do, all of its value has probably been mortgaged or has declined to the point where the borrower is "under water" (the family owes more on the mortgage than the house is worth). If such a family owns any asset, it might be a car that they had to borrow money to purchase.

By contrast, families in the middle three quintiles are likely to own their home, as their largest asset, while families in the top quintile usually own not just one or more homes, but also stocks and other financial assets.

Most discussions of economic inequality focus on income, not wealth, for the simple reason that data on income are more readily available. But wealth has its own dynamic, and its distribution has unique causes and consequences. More than income, wealth both tells us about the past and foretells the future. A family's wealth today reflects the asset-building opportunities open not only to this generation, but also to parents, grandparents, and great-grandparents. Likewise, parents use their wealth to position their children for future economic success in countless ways—moving into an excellent school district or giving an adult son or daughter money for a down payment on a house, for example—that are out of reach for those who may earn a middle-class income but have few assets.

For nearly 30 years following World War II, both government and organized labor acted to limit wealth inequality. Building on the legacy of the New Deal years, a range of government policies and a relatively stable business-labor compact moderated the excesses of the capitalist system, and as a result, a broad swath of Americans shared, at least to a degree, in the prosperity of the time. But since the mid-1970s, determined efforts by conservatives and corporate executives

PERCENTAGE OF WEALTH OWNED BY THE TOP 1%

Year	%
1917	36.7
1924	44.2
1926	33.3
1934	36.4
1940	25.8
1944	27.1
1948	31.2
1960	34.4
1962	33.4
1964	34.4
1967	29.1
1969	34.4
1971	34.4
1974	19.9
1976	20.5
1978	24.8
1981	30.9
1983	31.9
1987	37.8
1987	37.2
1990	37.4
1992	36.5
1995	37.2
2001	38.5
2007	33.4
2010	34.6
	35.6

Source: Edward N. Wolff, "The Asset Price Meltdown and the Wealth of the Middle Class" (Russell Sage Foundation 2010 Project, 2012).

have succeeded in dismantling much of the New Deal legacy and weakening the labor movement. Since then, the rich have become substantially richer, the poor poorer, and the middle has been squeezed.

The Super-Rich

Since the early 1970s, the richest 1% (as ranked by income) have accrued a growing share of the nation's private wealth. When the Forbes 400 list of the richest Americans was first published in 1982, the poorest person on the list held a fortune worth about $75 million. Today, every person on the list is a billionaire.

From 1992 to 2007, the average wealth held by the nation's wealthiest 400 people more than quadrupled. The wealthiest among these 400 people saw the largest gains. Throughout the 1990s, the top 1% held a larger concentration of total household wealth than at any time since the height of the "Roaring '20s."

THE WEALTHIEST 400 PEOPLE IN THE UNITED STATES
Wealth by Rank and Average Wealth (in millions of 2012 dollars)

Wealth by Rank in the Forbes 400	1992	1999	2000	2002	2005	2007	2009	2012
1st	$9,393	$108,796	$77,996	$51,370	$61,846	$71,547	$53,388	$66,000
10th	$5,218	$21,759	$21,047	$14,216	$18,675	$20,615	$17,084	$25,000
50th	$1,864	$5,120	$5,818	$3,822	$5,093	$7,640	$5,018	$6,600
100th	$1,193	$3,072	$3,218	$2,150	$3,032	$4,244	$3,203	$3,900
400th	$395	$800	$897	$657	$1,091	$1,576	$1,014	$1,100
Average Wealth	$1,136	$3,312	$3,707	$2,605	$3,411	$4,669	$3,385	$4,212
Number of billionaires	92	278	301	205	374	400	391	400

Source: Calculated from 2012 *Forbes 400*.

The top percentile's wealth share declined somewhat during the 2001 recession, thanks to falling corporate share prices, but then resumed its climb, reaching 34.6% in 2007. When asset values dropped during the Great Recession of 2008-9, the wealth of America's top 1% remained relatively steady, increasing to 35.4% from 2007 to 2010.

The Owning Class

Upwards of 90% of people in the United States make their living by working for a wage or salary. A far smaller number gain their incomes from the ownership of property. These large-scale property owners may have jobs—usually high-paying ones—but they do not *have* to work for a living. They own businesses, which yield profits; stocks, which yield dividends; real estate, which yields rent; and money, which yields interest. Unlike the houses and cars that comprise the primary assets of average Americans, these forms of wealth typically yield income and, when their value increases, capital gains as well. They also give their owners, in varying degrees, some control over the nation's economy.

HOUSEHOLDS WITH NET WORTH EQUAL TO OR EXCEEDING $10 MILLION

The number of households with net worth of $10 million or more (in constant 2010 dollars) exploded from just under 93,000 in 1989 to 664,200 in 2007. After the Great Recession, the number of these households decreased to just over 500,000 in 2010.

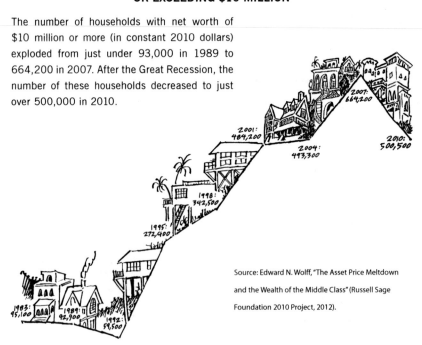

2001: 484,200

2004: 443,300

2007: 664,200

2010: 500,500

1998: 342,500

1995: 272,400

1983: 45,100

1989: 92,900

1992: 59,500

Source: Edward N. Wolff, "The Asset Price Meltdown and the Wealth of the Middle Class" (Russell Sage Foundation 2010 Project, 2012).

Some of the 90% also own these same types of assets: a rental property or a small stock portfolio, perhaps. But ownership of income-generating property is even more highly concentrated than ownership of wealth overall. The income from such property can be considerable. In 2011, private property income—profits, interest, rent, and the like—accounted for 31% of gross domestic income.

PRIVATE PROPERTY INCOME AS A PERCENTAGE OF NATIONAL INCOME, 1959-2012

Source: U.S. Dept of Commerce, Bureau of Economic Analysis, Sept. 27, 2012

Profits and other private property income have ranged between one-fourth and one-third of U.S. national income over the last 50 years. This variation may not seem like much, but when the private-property share of national income declined sharply in the mid-1960s, as a result of high employment and rising worker militancy, U.S. capitalism went into crisis. The "recovery" beginning in the early 1980s coincided with property ownership garnering an increasing share of national income, as attacks on unions and social welfare programs eroded workers' bargaining power. Mainstream economists deemed the economy to be "improving" when the owning class started grabbing a bigger share of the national income.

The distribution of America's financial assets—especially stocks and bonds—is far more skewed than the distribution of wealth overall. A home has long been the single largest asset for most American families who have any wealth at all. Most other kinds of assets are heavily concentrated in the hands of the wealthiest few percent of families. The following chart shows the distribution of the nation's stock ownership. The richest 20% owns over 90% of all stock; the bottom 40% owns less than 1% of all stock.

CONCENTRATION OF STOCK OWNERSHIP BY WEALTH CLASS, 2010

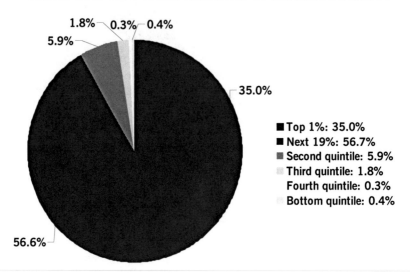

Note: Includes direct ownership of stock shares and indirect ownership through mutual funds, trusts, and IRAS, Keogh plans, 401(k) plans, and other retirement accounts. All figures are in 2010 dollars.

Source: Edward N. Wolff, "The Asset Price Meltdown and the Wealth of the Middle Class" (Russell Sage Foundation 2010 Project, 2013).

The Median and Its Variance

The wealthiest Americans continue to enjoy a rising tide, even in the aftermath of the Great Recession. But is that tide, to quote a common political cliché, lifting all boats? Does growing wealth help everyone grow?

Median wealth grew relatively slowly but steadily from 1962 to 1989. The recession of the early 1990s caused median wealth to fall by 17% from 1989 to 1995, but then median wealth made a strong recovery, rising by 39% from 1995 to 2001. After a slight decrease due to the 2001 recession, median wealth grew by about 20% from 2004 to 2007. Then the Great Recession sent median wealth back to its level of the late 1960s, in inflation-adjusted dollars. Between 2007 and 2010, median wealth plunged by 47%.

MEDIAN WEALTH, 1962-2010 (IN THOUSANDS, 2010 DOLLARS)

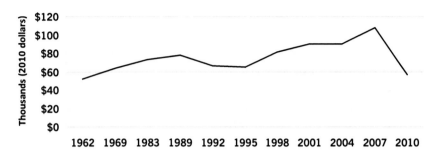

Source: Edward N. Wolff, "The Asset Price Meltdown and the Wealth of the Middle Class" (Russell Sage Foundation 2010 Project, 2013).

PERCENTAGE OF TOTAL WEALTH BY WEALTH CLASS, 1962-2010

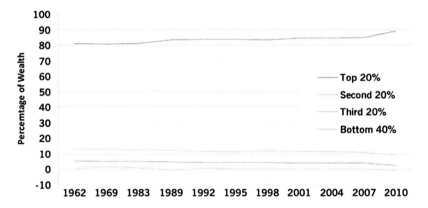

Source: Edward N. Wolff, "The Asset Price Meltdown and the Wealth of the Middle Class" (Russell Sage Foundation 2010 Project, 2012).

MEDIAN OR MEAN - WHAT DO THEY MEAN?

There's an important difference between "median" and "mean" wealth. The mean is the average, calculated by adding up all net worth and then dividing by the number of households. The median is the amount halfway between the top and bottom of the wealth distribution; half of the households have less than the median and half have more.

Wealth statistics are usually expressed as medians rather than means because the mean is distorted by concentrated wealth. The disproportionate wealth of the 1% skews the average upwards and misrepresents the true "middle."

To illustrate the difference: the Federal Reserve Board's 2012 Survey of Consumer Finances found that the U.S. median family wealth in 2010 was $77,300, while the mean family wealth was $498,800.

MEAN NET WORTH BY WEALTH CLASS, 1983-2010
(IN THOUSANDS, 2010 DOLLARS)

	Top 1%	Top 20%	Next 20%	Third 20%	Bottom 40%	All
1983	$9,599.0	$1,156.5	$178.7	$74.2	$6.3	$284.4
2010	$16,439.4	$2,061.6	$216.9	$61.0	-$10.6	$463.8
% change	71.3	78.3	21.4	-17.9	-269.7	63.1

Source: Edward N. Wolff, "The Asset Price Meltdown and the Wealth of the Middle Class" (Russell Sage Foundation 2010 Project, 2013).

When we look beyond the median figures, however, it becomes clear that only the people at the top of the class structure have benefited from the overall growth in U.S. wealth. The average net worth of the top 1% increased by 71.3% from 1983 to 2010. In comparison, the average net worth of the bottom 40% of households dropped from $6,300 in 1983 to *negative* $10,600 in 2010—a change of about –270%.

The wealth of the nation has been growing, the wealthiest households have been taking an increasingly large share of it, and the middle and lower classes have been losing ground. Some boats are rising while others are sinking.

CHANGE IN WEALTH GROUPS' SHARES OF TOTAL WEALTH, 1983-2010

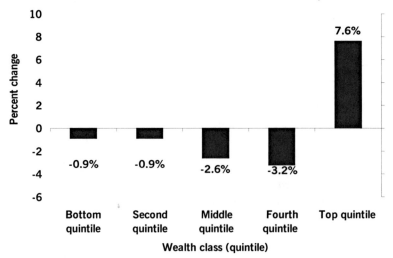

Source: Edward N. Wolff, "The Asset Price Meltdown and the Wealth of the Middle Class" (Russell Sage Foundation 2010 Project, 2013).

The Wealthless

The share of Americans with no wealth or negative wealth was larger in 2010 than in 1983. In 2010, more than one-fifth of U.S. households had zero or negative net

HOUSEHOLDS WITH LITTLE OR NO NET WORTH, 1962-2010

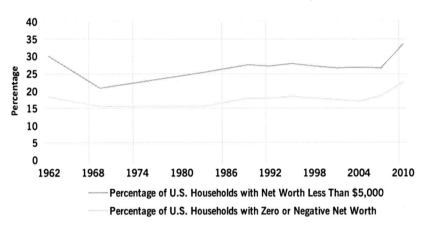

Source: Edward N. Wolff, "The Asset Price Meltdown and the Wealth of the Middle Class" (Russell Sage Foundation 2010 Project, 2013).

THE STRUGGLE FOR THE BOTTOM THIRD

worth, and one-third of households had net worth less than $5,000.

The U.S. Census Bureau determines the national poverty rate based on food costs, inflation, and size and composition of families. The poverty threshold for a family of four in 2011 was $23,021. The official poverty rate in 2011 was 15%, with 46.2 million people in poverty, up from 39.8 million in 2008. According to the Census Bureau, 6.2% of married-couple families, 31.2% of families with a female head of household, and 16.1% of families with a male householder lived in poverty in 2011. The poverty rate for children under age 18 was over 20%. The rate for people aged 65 and older was just 8.7%, thanks in part to Social Security.

Many people live in or near poverty even while they hold down jobs. About one-fourth of workers earned poverty-level wages in 2010. With insufficient income, the poor have little chance to build up any wealth, which puts their children at a distinct disadvantage for future success.

The Squeezed Middle

In a society that prides itself on having a robust middle class, the middle class only controls about 10% of U.S. wealth. Most forms of wealth in the United States belong almost entirely to the wealthiest. For members of the middle three quintiles,

**COMPOSITION OF HOUSEHOLD WEALTH (PERCENT OF GROSS ASSETS)
FOR MIDDLE THREE WEALTH QUINTILES IN 1983 AND 2010**

Component	1983	2010
Principal residence	61.6	66.6
Liquid assets*	21.4	5.9
Pension accounts	1.2	14.2
Corporate stock, financial securities, mutual funds, and personal trusts	3.1	3.1
Unincorporated business equity and other real estate	11.4	8.9
Miscellaneous assets	1.3	1.3
Total assets	100	100
Debt/equity ratio	**37.4**	**71.5**

* Liquid assets = bank deposits, money market funds, and cash surrender value of life insurance

Source: Edward N. Wolff, "The Asset Price Meltdown and the Wealth of the Middle Class" (Russell Sage Foundation 2010 Project, 2013).

their home comprises two-thirds of their wealth. When home values dropped by an average of about 25% during the Great Recession, the net worth of our middle class declined dramatically. This in turn contributed to a dramatic increase in their overall debt/equity ratio, which grew from 37.4% in 1983 to 71.5% in 2010.

Class Mobility

The best way to enjoy high net worth in the United States is to get yourself born to wealthy parents. Only 7% of children born to parents with family wealth in the top 20% grow up to have incomes in the bottom 20%. Likewise, just 8% of children with parents in the bottom income quintile join the top wealth quintile as adults.

CHANCE OF CHILD ATTAINING WEALTH LEVEL AS ADULT, BY PARENTAL WEALTH

	Child's Wealth Quintile as Adult		
Parents' family wealth quintile	**Top 20%**	**Middle 20%**	**Bottom 20%**
Top 20%	41%	16%	7%
Middle 20%	17%	26%	15%
Bottom 20%	8%	17%	41%

Source: The Pew Charitable Trusts Economic Mobility Project, "Pursuing the American Dream: Economic Mobility Across Generations,"July 2012.

The Racial Wealth Gap

We have seen how wealth inequality is perpetuated by the inheritance system that passes accumulated advantages and disadvantages from one generation to the next. People of color, and especially African-Americans, have endured a long history of discrimination, which has severely limited their ability to amass wealth. The racial wealth gap in the United States far exceeds the racial income gap. The median net worth of nonwhite and Hispanic families is just a small fraction of white wealth.

This wealth gap persists even during periods of economic growth—in the 1990s boom, the median wealth of families of color actually fell.

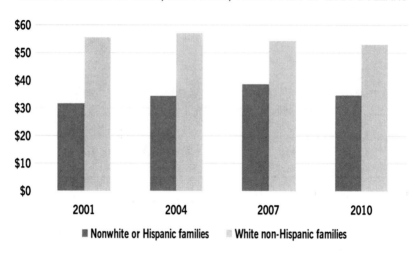

MEDIAN INCOME BY RACE, 2001-2010, THOUSANDS OF 2010 DOLLARS

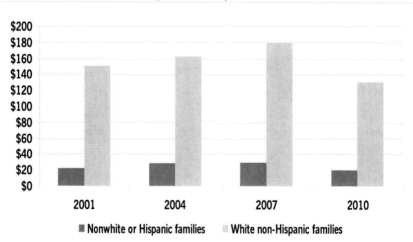

MEDIAN WEALTH BY RACE, 2001-2010, THOUSANDS OF 2010 DOLLARS

SOURCE: Jesse Bricker, Arthur B. Kennickell, Kevin B. Moore, and John Sabelhaus, "Changes in U.S. Family Finances from 2007 to 2010: Evidence from the Survey of Consumer Finances." Federal Reserve Bulletin, vol. 98, no 2, (February 2012), pp. 1-80.
http://www.federalreserve.gov/econresdata/scf/scf_2010.htm

We can find racial disparities across all categories of asset ownership. For nearly every kind of asset, whether financial or nonfinancial, white families are more likely to own the asset in any amount *and* have larger median holdings in the asset, as the following table shows.

FAMILY HOLDINGS OF SELECTED ASSETS BY RACE, 2010

Types of assets:		Certificate of deposit	Savings bonds	Stocks	Pooled investment funds	Retirement accounts	Primary resid-ence	Privately-held businesses
Percentage of families holding selected assets	Families of color	6.5	6.3	7.9	2.6	58.1	50.6	15.6
	White families	15	14.8	18.6	11.6	34.4	75.6	8.3
Median value of holdings for families holding assets (thousands of 2010 dollars)	Families of color	13	1	10	50	25	50.6	8.3
	White families	20	1	25	91	54	75.3	15.6

SOURCE: Jesse Bricker, Arthur B. Kennickell, Kevin B. Moore, and John Sabelhaus, "Changes in U.S. Family Finances from 2007 to 2010: Evidence from the Survey of Consumer Finances." Federal Reserve Bulletin, vol. 98, no 2, (February 2012), pp. 1-80. http://www.federalreserve.gov/econresdata/scf/scf_2010.htm

Women and Wealth

Virtually all data on asset ownership are gathered by household. The data do not distinguish among people living in the household, which makes it difficult to uncover the real wealth gap between men and women. But the research shows a dramatic gap between the net worth of households headed by single females and those headed by single males. Never-married men had a median wealth of $9,100 in 2010, while never-married women's median wealth stood at just $101. Married women are considered to share equally in the wealth of their household, and they generally retain some of that wealth after becoming divorced or widowed.

GENDER DIFFERENCES IN MEDIAN WEALTH IN 2010 FOR NEVER-MARRIED, DIVORCED, AND WIDOWED PERSONS, AGES 18-64

SOURCE: Mariko Lin Chang (2012), "Gender Differences in Median Wealth for Never-Married, Divorced, and Widowed Persons, Ages 18-64, 2010." Available at: www.mariko-chang.com/wealthdata.html. Data derived from the 2010 Survey of Consumer Finances.

2010 MEDIAN WEALTH OF SINGLE MEN, SINGLE WOMEN, AND COUPLES (MARRIED AND COHABITATING), BY RACE/ETHNICITY, AGES 18-64

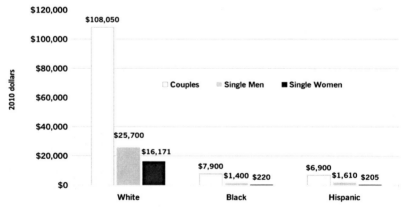

SOURCE: Mariko Lin Chang (2012), "Median Wealth of Single Men, Single Women, and Couples (Married and CohabitaEng), by Race/Ethnicity, Ages 18-64, 2010." Available at: www.mariko-chang.com/wealthdata. html

Data derived from the 2010 Survey of Consumer Finances.

By disaggregating the data by both sex and ethnicity, we can see how the gender and racial wealth gaps work together. White couples (whether married or cohabitating) have much greater wealth than Black or Hispanic couples. Even single white women, whose median wealth is much lower than white couples or single white men, have more than twice as much wealth as Black or Hispanic couples.

World Wide Wealth

Data on wealth and its distribution remain scarce compared to data on income. This is particularly true on an international scale. Many countries do not systematically collect information on individual or household wealth holdings, but some multinational entities do compile global wealth data.

SHARE OF ADULT POPULATION AND SHARE OF GLOBAL WEALTH IN 2012, BY WEALTH CATEGORY

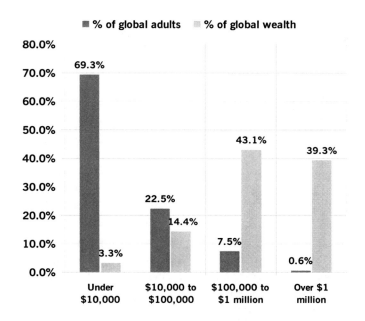

SOURCE: Credit Suisse Global Wealth Report 2012

About 70% of the world's adult population currently holds 3.3% of its wealth, while 0.6% of adults control 39.3% of global wealth. Across the world today, 3.2 billion people hold less than $10,000 in wealth. At the other end of the wealth spectrum, there are 29 million millionaires.

CHANGES IN HOUSEHOLD WEALTH
IN 2011–2012 BY REGION

Region	Total net wealth 2012 (US$ billion)	Share of total global wealth (%)	Change in total net wealth, 2011-12 (% change)
Africa	2,393	1.07%	-5
Asia-Pacific	50,724	22.77%	-2.5
China	20,190	9.07%	2.9
Europe	69,351	31.14%	-13.6
India	3,193	1.43%	-18
Latin America	8,696	3.90%	-8
North America	68,173	30.61%	1.3
Total, World	222,719	100.00%	-5.2

SOURCE: James Davies, Rodrigo Lluberas and Anthony Shorrocks, Credit Suisse Global Wealth Databook 2012

Europe and North America combined have more than 60% of the world's wealth, even though Europe's total net wealth dropped by 13.6% from 2011-2012. The four countries with the biggest increases in household wealth during this year were the United States, where total wealth increased by US $1.3 trillion, China ($560 billion), Japan ($370 billion), and Colombia ($100 billion). The four countries with the biggest losses of household wealth during this year were all eurozone members: France ($2.2 trillion), Italy ($2.1 trillion), Germany ($1.9 trillion) and Spain ($870 billion).

Nations that endured colonialist occupations in the 19th and 20th centuries are among the poorest in the world today. During the epoch of classic colonialism, the natural and human resources of the occupied countries were extracted and exploited to enrich the occupiers. Since the end of colonialism, the former imperialist powers have been able to continue extracting resources from most of the former colonies. The latter, lacking the wealth to develop their own resources, turn to multinational corporations based in the former colonial powers to help them turn resources into wealth. While some of that wealth stays in its country of origin, much of it continues to be extracted and exported to the already wealthy nations. This longstanding cycle has proven difficult to break. ❏

THE CAUSES OF INEQUALITY

Arthur MacEwan analyzes the long-term economic changes that led to the Great Recession. Since the 1970s, the United States has experienced a power shift in favor of corporations and the very rich, and MacEwan argues that a solution requires a major shift in the opposite direction.

INEQUALITY, POWER, AND IDEOLOGY

Understanding the Causes of the Current Economic Crisis

BY ARTHUR MACEWAN

March/April 2009; revised November 2012*

It is hard to solve a problem without an understanding of what caused it. For example, in medicine, until we gained an understanding of the way bacteria and viruses cause various infectious diseases, it was virtually impossible to develop effective cures. Of course, dealing with many diseases is complicated by the fact that germs, genes, diet, and the environment establish a nexus of causes.

The same is true in economics. Without an understanding of the causes of the current crisis, we are unlikely to develop a solution; certainly we are not going to get a solution that has a lasting impact. And determining the causes is complicated because several intertwined factors have been involved.

The current economic crisis was brought about by a nexus of factors that involved: a growing concentration of political and social power in the hands of the wealthy; the ascendance of a perverse leave-it-to-the-market ideology which was an instrument of that power; and rising income inequality, which both resulted from and enhanced that power. These various factors formed a vicious circle, reinforcing one another and together shaping the economic conditions that led us to the present situation. Several other factors were also involved—the growing role of credit, the puffing up of the housing bubble, and the increasing deregulation of financial markets have been very important. However, these are best understood as transmitters of our economic problems, arising from the nexus that formed the vicious circle.

What does this tell us about a solution? Economic stimulus, repair of the housing market, and new regulation are all well and good, but they do not deal with the underlying causes of the crisis. Instead, progressive groups need to work to shift each of the factors I have noted—power, ideology, and income distribution—in the other direction. In doing so, we can create a *virtuous* circle, with each change reinforcing the other changes. If successful, we not only establish a more stable economy, but we lay the foundation for a more democratic, equitable, and sustainable economic order.

---

* Date first published and date revised. All articles were originally published in *Dollars & Sense* magazine, unless otherwise noted.

A crisis by its very nature creates opportunities for change. One good place to begin change and intervene in this "circle"—and transform it from vicious to virtuous —is through pushing for the expansion and reform of social programs, programs that directly serve social needs of the great majority of the population (for example: single-payer health care, education programs, and environmental protection and repair). By establishing changes in social programs, we will have impacts on income distribution and ideology, and, perhaps most important, we set in motion *a power shift* that improves our position for preserving the changes. While I emphasize social programs as a means to initiate social and economic change, there are other ways to intervene in the circle. Efforts to re-strengthen unions would be especially important; and there are other options as well.

Causes of the Crisis: A Long Time Coming

Sometime around the early 1970s, there were some dramatic changes in the U.S. economy. The 25 years following World War II had been an era of relatively stable economic growth; the benefits of growth had been widely shared, with wages rising along with productivity gains, and income distribution became slightly less unequal (a good deal less unequal as compared to the pre-Great Depression era). There were severe economic problems in the United States, not the least of which were the continued exclusion of African Americans, large gender inequalities, and the woeful inadequacy of social welfare programs. Nonetheless, relatively stable growth, rising wages, and then the advent of the civil rights movement and the War on Poverty gave some important, positive social and economic character to the era—especially in hindsight!

In part, this comparatively favorable experience for the United States had depended on the very dominant position that U.S. firms held in the world economy, a position in which they were relatively unchallenged by international competition. The firms and their owners were not the only beneficiaries of this situation. With less competitive pressure on them from foreign companies, many U.S. firms accepted unionization and did not find it worthwhile to focus on keeping wages down and obstructing the implementation of social supports for the low-income population. Also, having had the recent experience of the Great Depression, many wealthy people and business executives were probably not so averse to a substantial role for government in regulating the economy.

A Power Grab

By about 1970, the situation was changing. Firms in Europe and Japan had long recovered from World War II, OPEC was taking shape, and weaknesses were emerging in the U.S. economy. The weaknesses were in part a consequence of heavy spending for the Vietnam War combined with the government's reluctance to tax for the war because of its unpopularity. The pressures on U.S. firms arising from these changes had two sets of consequences: slower growth and greater instability; and concerted efforts—a power grab, if you will—by firms and the wealthy to shift the costs of economic deterioration onto U.S. workers and the low-income population.

These "concerted efforts" took many forms: greater resistance to unions and unionization, battles to reduce taxes, stronger opposition to social welfare programs, and, above all, a push to reduce or eliminate government regulation of economic activity through a powerful political campaign to gain control of the various branches and levels of government. The 1980s, with Reagan and Bush Sr. in the White House, were the years in which all these efforts were solidified. Unions were greatly weakened, a phenomenon both demonstrated and exacerbated by Reagan's firing of the air traffic controllers in response to their strike in 1981. The tax cuts of the period were also important markers of the change. But the change had begun earlier; the 1978 passage of the tax-cutting Proposition 13 in California was perhaps the first major success of the movement. And the changes continued well after the 1980s, with welfare reform and deregulation of finance during the Clinton era, to say nothing of the tax cuts and other actions during Bush Jr.

Ideology Shift

The changes that began in the 1970s, however, were not simply these sorts of concrete alterations in the structure of power affecting the economy and, especially, government's role in the economy. There was a major shift in ideology, the dominant set of ideas that organize an understanding of our social relations and both guide and rationalize policy decisions.

Following the Great Depression and World War II, there was a wide acceptance of the idea that government had a major role to play in economic life. Less than in many other countries but nonetheless to a substantial degree, at all levels of society, it was generally believed that there should be a substantial government safety net and that government should both regulate the economy in various ways and, through fiscal as well as monetary policy, should maintain aggregate demand. This large economic role for government came to be called Keynesianism, after the British economist John Maynard Keynes, who had set out the arguments for an active fiscal policy in time of economic weakness. In the early 1970s, as economic troubles developed, even Richard Nixon declared: "I am now a Keynesian in economics."

The election of Ronald Reagan, however, marked a sharp change in ideology, at least at the top. Actions of the government were blamed for all economic ills: government spending, Keynesianism, was alleged to be the cause of the inflation of the 1970s; government regulation was supposedly crippling industry; high taxes were, it was argued, undermining incentives for workers to work and for businesses to invest; social welfare spending was blamed for making people dependent on the government and was charged with fraud and corruption (the "welfare queens"); and so on and so on.

On economic matters, Reagan championed supply-side economics, the principal idea of which was that tax cuts yield an increase in government revenue because the cuts lead to more rapid economic growth through encouraging more work and more investment. Thus, so the argument went, tax cuts would reduce the government deficit. Reagan, with the cooperation of Democrats, got the tax cuts—and, as the loss of revenue combined with a large increase in military spending, the federal budget deficit grew by leaps and bounds, almost doubling as a share of GDP over the course of the 1980s. It was all summed up in the idea of keeping the government out of the economy; let the free market work its magic.

Growing Inequality

The shifts of power and ideology were very much bound up with a major redistribution upwards of income and wealth. The weakening of unions, the increasing access of firms to low-wage foreign (and immigrant) labor, the refusal of government to maintain the buying power of the minimum wage, favorable tax treatment of the wealthy and their corporations, deregulation in a wide range of industries and lack of enforcement of existing regulation (e.g., the authorities turning a blind eye to off-shore tax shelters) all contributed to these shifts.

Many economists, however, explain the rising income inequality as a result of technological change that favored more highly skilled workers; and changing technology has probably been a factor. Yet the most dramatic aspect of the rising inequality has been the rapidly rising share of income obtained by those at the very top (see figures below), who get their incomes from the ownership and control of business, not from their skilled labor. For these people the role of new technologies was most important through its impact on providing more options (e.g., international options) for the managers of firms, more thorough means to control labor, and more effective

Alan Greenspan, Symbol of an Era

One significant symbol of the full rise of the conservative ideology that became so dominant in the latter part of the 20th century was Alan Greenspan, who served from 1974 through 1976 as chairman of the President's Council of Economic Advisers under Gerald Ford and in 1987 became chairman of the Federal Reserve Board, a position he held until 2006. While his predecessors had hardly been critics of U.S. capitalism, Greenspan was a close associate of the philosopher Ayn Rand and an adherent of her extreme ideas supporting individualism and *laissez-faire* (keep-the-government-out) capitalism.

While chairman of the Fed, Greenspan was widely credited with maintaining an era of stable economic growth. As things fell apart in 2008, however, Greenspan was seen as having a large share of responsibility for the non-regulation and excessively easy credit that led into the crisis.

Called before Congress in October 2008, Greenspan was chastised by Rep. Henry Waxman (D-Calif.), who asked him: "Do you feel that your ideology pushed you to make decisions that you wish you had not made?" To which Greenspan replied: "Yes, I've found a flaw. I don't know how significant or permanent it is. But I've been very distressed by that fact."

And Greenspan told Congress: "Those of us who have looked to the self-interest of lending institutions to protect shareholders' equity, myself included, are in a state of shocked disbelief."

Greenspan's "shock" was reminiscent of the scene in the film "Casablanca," where Captain Renault (Claude Rains) declares: "I'm shocked, shocked to find that gambling is going on in here!" At which point, a croupier hands Renault a pile of money and says, "Your winnings, sir." Renault replies, *sotto voce*, "Thank you very much."

ways—in the absence of regulation—to manipulate finance. All of these gains that might be associated with new technology were also gains brought by the way the government handled, or didn't handle (failed to regulate), economic affairs.

Several sets of data demonstrate the sharp changes in the distribution of income that have taken place in the last several decades. Most striking is the changing position of the very highest income segment of the population. In the mid-1920s, the share of all pre-tax income going to the top 1% of households peaked at 23.9%. This elite group's share of income fell dramatically during the Great Depression and World War II to about 12% at the end of the war and then slowly fell further during the next thirty years, reaching a low of 8.9% in the mid-1970s. Since then, the top 1% has regained its exalted position of the earlier era, with 21.8% of income in 2005. Since 1993, more than one-half of all income gains have accrued to this highest 1% of the population.

Figures 1 and 2 show the gains (or losses) of various groups in the 1947 to 1979 period and in the 1979 to 2005 period. The difference is dramatic. For example, in the earlier era, the bottom 20% saw its income in real (inflation-adjusted) terms rise by 116%, and real income of the top 5% grew by only 86%. But in the latter era, the bottom 20% saw a 1% decline in its income, while the top 5% obtained a 81% increase. Figure 3 on the next page shows what happened to the incomes of the different groups after 2005.

The Emergence of Crisis

These changes, especially these dramatic shifts in the distribution of income, set the stage for the increasingly large reliance on credit, especially consumer and mortgage credit, that played a major role in the emergence of the current economic crisis. Other factors were involved, but rising inequality was especially important in effecting the increase in both the demand and supply of credit.

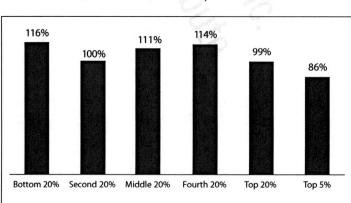

FIGURE 1: PERCENTAGE CHANGE IN REAL FAMILY INCOME BY QUINTILE AND TOP 5%, 1949–1979

Source: Analysis of U.S. Census Bureau data in Economic Policy Institute, The State of Working America 1994–95 (1994) p. 37.

FIGURE 2: PERCENTAGE CHANGE IN REAL FAMILY INCOME BY QUINTILE AND TOP 5%, 1979–2005

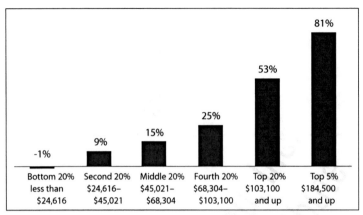

Source: U.S. Census Bureau, Historical Income Tables, Table F-3.

Credit Expansion

On the demand side, rising inequality translated into a growing gap between the incomes of most members of society and their needs. For the 2000 to 2007 period, average weekly earnings in the private sector were 12% below their average for the 1970s (in inflation-adjusted terms). From 1980 to 2005 the share of income going to the bottom 60% of families fell from 35% to 29%. Under these circumstances, more and more people relied more and more heavily on credit to meet their needs—everything from food to fuel, from education to entertainment, and especially housing.

While the increasing reliance of consumers on credit has been going on for a long time, it has been especially marked in recent decades. Consumer debt as a share of after-tax personal income averaged 20% in the 1990s, and then jumped up to an average of 25% in the first seven years of the new millennium. But the debt expansion was most marked in housing, where mortgage debt as a percent of after-tax personal income rose from 89% to 94% over the 1990s, and then ballooned to 140% by 2006 as housing prices skyrocketed.

On the supply side, especially in the last few years, the government seems to have relied on making credit readily available as a means to bolster aggregate demand and maintain at least a modicum of economic growth. During the 1990s, the federal funds interest rate averaged 5.1%, but fell to an average of 3.4% in the 2000 to 2007 period—and averaged only 1.4% in 2002 to 2004 period. (The federal funds interest rate is the rate that banks charge one another for overnight loans and is a rate directly affected by the Federal Reserve.) Corresponding to the low interest rates, the money supply grew twice as fast in the new millennium as it had in the 1990s.

The increasing reliance of U.S. consumers on credit has often been presented as a moral weakness, as an infatuation with consumerism, and as a failure to look beyond the present. Whatever moral judgments one may make, however, the expansion of the credit economy has been a response to real economic forces—inequality and government policies, in particular.

FIGURE 3: PERCENTAGE CHANGE IN REAL FAMILY INCOME BY QUINTILE AND TOP 5%*, 2005–2011

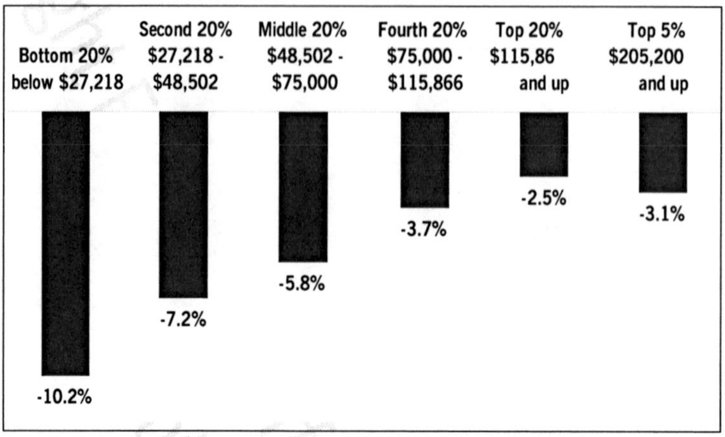

Bottom 20% below $27,218	Second 20% $27,218 - $48,502	Middle 20% $48,502 - $75,000	Fourth 20% $75,000 - $115,866	Top 20% $115,86 and up	Top 5% $205,200 and up
-10.2%	-7.2%	-5.8%	-3.7%	-2.5%	-3.1%

*Income ranges of quintiles in 2011 dollars

Source: U.S. Census Bureau, Historical Income Tables, Table F-3.

The Failure to Regulate

The credit expansion by itself, however, did not precipitate the current crisis. Deregulation—or, more generally, the failure to regulate—is also an important part of the story. The government's role in regulation of financial markets has been a central feature in the development of this crisis, but the situation in financial markets has been part of a more general process—affecting airlines and trucking, telecommunications, food processing, broadcasting, and of course international trade and investment. The process has been driven by a combination of power (of large firms and wealthy individuals) and ideology (leave it to the market, get the government out).

The failure to regulate financial markets that transformed the credit expansion into a financial crisis shows up well in three examples:

The 1999 repeal of the Glass-Steagall Act. Glass-Steagall had been enacted in the midst of the Great Depression, as a response to the financial implosion following the stock market crash of 1929. Among other things, it required that different kinds of financial firms—commercial banks, investment banks, insurance companies—be separate. This separation both limited the spread of financial problems and reduced conflicts of interest that could arise were the different functions of these firms combined into a single firm. As perhaps the most important legislation regulating the financial sector, the repeal of Glass-Steagall was not only a substantive change but was an important symbol of the whole process of deregulation.

The failure to regulate mortgage lending. Existing laws and regulations require lending institutions to follow prudent practices in making loans, assuring that borrowers have the capacity to be able to pay back the loans. And of course fraud—lying about the provisions of loans—is prohibited. Yet in an atmosphere where regulation was "out," regulators were simply not doing their jobs. The consequences are illustrated in a December 28, 2008, *New York Times* story on the failed Washington Mutual Bank. The article describes a supervisor at a mortgage processing center as having been "accustomed to seeing baby sitters claiming salaries worthy of college presidents, and schoolteachers with incomes rivaling stockbrokers'. He rarely questioned them. A real estate frenzy was under way and WaMu, as his bank was known, was all about saying yes."

One may wonder why banks—or other lending institutions, mortgage firms, in particular—would make loans to people who were unlikely to be able to pay them back. The reason is that the lending institutions quickly combined such loans into packages (i.e., a security made up of several borrowers' obligations to pay) and sold them to other investors in a practice called "securitization."

Credit-default swaps. Perhaps the most egregious failure to regulate in recent years has been the emergence of credit-default swaps, which are connected to securitization. Because they were made up of obligations by a diverse set of borrowers, the packages of loans were supposedly low-risk investments. Yet those who purchased them still sought insurance against default. Insurance sellers, however, are regulated—required, for example, to keep a certain amount of capital on hand to cover possible claims. So the sellers of these insurance policies on packages of loans called the policies "credit-default swaps" and thus were allowed to avoid regulation. Further, these credit-default swaps, these insurance policies, themselves were bought and sold again and again in unregulated markets in a continuing process of speculation.

The credit-default swaps are a form of derivative, a financial asset the value of which is derived from some other asset—in this case the value of packages of mortgages on which they were the insurance policies. When the housing bubble began to collapse and people started to default on their mortgages, the value of credit-default swaps plummeted and their future value was impossible to determine. No one would buy them, and several banks that had speculated in these derivatives were left holding huge amounts of these "toxic assets."

Bubble and Bust

The combination of easy credit and the failure to regulate together fueled the housing bubble. People could buy expensive houses but make relatively low monthly payments. Without effective regulation of mortgage lending, they could get the loans even when they were unlikely to be able to make payments over the long run. Moreover, as these pressures pushed up housing prices, many people bought houses simply to resell them quickly at a higher price, in a process called "flipping." And such speculation pushed the prices up further. Between 2000 and 2006, housing prices rose by 90% (as consumer prices generally rose by only 17%).

While the housing boom was in full swing, both successful housing speculators and lots of people involved in the shenanigans of credit markets made a lot of money. However, as the housing bubble burst—as all bubbles do—things fell apart. The packages of loans lost value, and the insurance policies on them, the credit-default swaps, lost value. These then became "toxic" assets for those who held them, assets not only with reduced value but with unknown value. Not only did large financial firms—for example, Lehman Brothers and AIG—have billions of dollars in losses, but no one knew the worth of their remaining assets. The assets were called "toxic" because they poisoned the operations of the financial system. Under these circumstances, financial institutions stopped lending to one another—that is, the credit markets "froze up." The financial crisis was here.

The financial crisis, not surprisingly, very quickly shifted to a general economic crisis. Firms in the "real" economy rely heavily on a well-functioning financial system to supply them with the funds they need for their regular operations—loans to car buyers, loans to finance inventory, loans for construction of new facilities, loans for new equipment, and, of course, mortgage loans. Without those loans (or with the loans much more difficult to obtain), there has been a general cutback in economic activity, what is becoming a serious and probably prolonged recession.

What Is to Be Done?

So here we are. The shifts in power, ideology, and income distribution have placed us in a rather nasty situation. There are some steps that will be taken that have a reasonable probability of yielding short-run improvement. In particular, a large increase in government spending—deficit spending—will probably reduce the depth and shorten the length of the recession. And the actions of the Federal Reserve and Treasury to inject funds into the financial system are likely, along with the deficit spending, to "un-freeze" credit markets (the mismanagement and, it seems, outright corruption of the bailout notwithstanding). Also, there is likely to be some re-regulation of the financial industry. These steps, however, at best will restore things to where they were before the crisis. They do not treat the underlying causes of the crisis—the vicious circle of power, ideology, and inequality.

Opportunity for Change

Fortunately, the crisis itself has weakened some aspects of this circle. The cry of "leave it to the market" is still heard, but is now more a basis for derision than a guide to policy. The ideology and, to a degree, the power behind the ideology, have been severely weakened as the role of "keeping the government out" has shown to be a major cause of the financial mess and our current hardships. There is now widespread support among the general populace and some support in Washington for greater regulation of the financial industry.

Whether or not the coming period will see this support translated into effective policy is of course an open question. Also an open question is how much the turn away from "leaving it to the market" can be extended to other sectors of the economy. With regard to the environment, there is already general acceptance of the principle that the government (indeed, many governments) must take an active role in regulating economic activity. Similar principles need to be recognized with regard to health care, education, housing, child care, and other support programs for low-income families.

The discrediting of "keep the government out" ideology provides an opening to develop new programs in these areas and to expand old programs. Furthermore, as the federal government revs up its "stimulus" program in the coming months, opportunities will exist for expanding support for these sorts of programs. This support is important, first of all, because these programs serve real, pressing needs—needs that have long existed and are becoming acute and more extensive in the current crisis.

Breaking the Circle

Support for these social programs, however, may also serve to break into the vicious power-ideology-inequality circle and begin transforming it into a virtuous circle. Social programs are inherently equalizing in two ways: they provide their benefits to low-income people and they provide some options for those people in their efforts to demand better work and higher pay. Also, the further these programs develop, the more they establish the legitimacy of a larger role for social control of—government involvement in—the economy; they tend to bring about an ideological shift. By affecting a positive distributional shift and by shifting ideology, the emergence of stronger social programs can have a wider impact on power. In other words, efforts to promote social programs are one place to start, an entry point to shift the vicious circle to a virtuous circle.

There are other entry points. Perhaps the most obvious ones are actions to strengthen the role of unions. It will be helpful to establish a more union-friendly Department of Labor and National Labor Relations Board. Raising the minimum wage—ideally indexing it to inflation—would also be highly desirable. While conditions have changed since the heyday of unions in the middle of the 20th century, and we cannot expect to restore the conditions of that era, a greater role for unions would seem essential in righting the structural conditions at the foundation of the current crisis.

Shifting Class Power

None of this is assured, of course. Simply starting social programs will not necessarily mean that they have the wider impacts that I am suggesting are possible. No one should think that by setting up some new programs and strengthening some existing ones we will be on a smooth road to economic and social change. Likewise, rebuilding the strength of unions will involve extensive struggle and will not be accomplished by a few legislative or executive actions.

Also, all efforts to involve the government in economic activity—whether in finance or environmental affairs, in health care or education, in work support or job training programs—will be met with the worn-out claims that government involvement generates bureaucracy, stifles initiative, and places an excessive burden on private firms and individuals. We are already hearing warnings that in dealing with the financial crisis the government must avoid "over-regulation." Likewise, efforts to strengthen unions will suffer the traditional attacks, as unions are portrayed as corrupt and their members privileged. The response to the auto firms' troubles demonstrated the attack, as conservatives blamed the United Auto Workers for the industry's woes and demanded extensive concessions by the union.

Certainly not all regulation is good regulation. Aside from excessive bureaucratic controls, there is the phenomenon by which regulating agencies are often captives of the industries that they are supposed to regulate. And there are corrupt unions. These are real issues, but they should not be allowed to derail change.

The current economic crisis emerged in large part as a shift in the balance of class power in the United States, a shift that began in the early 1970s and continued into the new millennium. Perhaps the present moment offers an opportunity to shift things back in the other direction. Recognition of the complex nexus of causes of the current economic crisis provides some guidance where people might start. Rebuilding and extending social programs, strengthening unions, and other actions that contribute to a more egalitarian power shift will not solve all the problems of U.S. capitalism. They can, however, begin to move us in the right direction.

AFTERWORD

November 2012

When this article was written in early 2009, the U.S. economy was in a severe recession, which came to be called the Great Recession. The economic downturn—defined in terms of a drop-off in total output, or gross domestic product (GDP)—had begun at the end of 2007. Although the recession came to a formal end by June 2009, when GDP started to grow again, economic conditions continued to be very poor. With slow economic growth, unemployment remained high, falling below 8% only in late 2012, and many people simply gave up looking for work and were not even counted among the unemployed.

Several factors contribute to an explanation of the weak recovery from the Great Recession. When economic downturns are brought about by financial crises, they tend to be more lasting because the machinery of the credit system and the confidence of lenders have been so severely damaged. Also, while the Great Recession developed in the United States, it spread to much of the rest of the world. Conditions in Europe, especially, have hampered full recovery in the United States.

The continuing economic malaise, however, also has its bases in the political conditions of Washington, in the weakness of the federal government's response to the Great Recession. While it is possible to debate the extent to which the weak response has been the responsibility of the recalcitrant role of Republicans in Congress versus the limited actions of President Obama, there is no doubt regarding the several aspects of that weak response:

- The fiscal stimulus implemented at the beginning of 2009, the American Recovery and Reinvestment Act (ARRA), was too small. This action did stem the decline of the economy, probably preventing things from getting much worse. But given the severity of the downturn, the ARRA was insufficient to reestablish growth that would have moved the United States strongly back toward full employment.
- Programs to relieve the dreadful damage done to millions of homeowners have been minimal, leaving families in dire straits and leaving the housing market in the doldrums.

- The Wall Street Reform and Consumer Protection Act, the Dodd-Frank bill, was enacted in 2010. Yet it was a weak bill, failing to deal with the most serious problems in the financial sector—for example, leaving several banks "too big to fail." Also, many of its provisions were sufficiently vague to allow the Wall Street firms to use their influence to blunt its impact.

- The huge bailout of the financial sector, the Troubled Asset Relief Program (TARP) and other actions of the Federal Reserve, probably did make an important contribution to preventing an even worse financial crisis. But TARP was a tremendous boon to the bankers who had been instrumental actors in bringing about the crisis. There were other actions that could have been taken. Moreover, the continuing weak response of the economy to the Fed's continued efforts to stimulate economic growth demonstrated the insufficiency of monetary policy to deal with a severe economic downturn.

Even if the government's actions had been more forceful, the underlying causes of the crisis remain unaddressed—economic inequality, power, and ideology remain largely as they were as the crisis emerged. Figure 3 shows that from 2005 through 2011, all groups have seen their incomes decline. However, with those at the bottom suffering the most severe decline, income inequality has increased. Also, there is no indication that the power of the elite has been curtailed. Indeed, with the evisceration of campaign finance regulations (the Citizens United Supreme Court decision in particular), money and power are increasingly tied firmly together.

What of ideology? The outcome of the 2012 election suggests that a majority of the electorate rejects the leave-it-to-the-market ideology that has supported inequality and the concentration of political power and that led into the crisis. Whatever the limits of the Obama administration, it portrayed itself with rhetoric of social responsibility and promised some regulation of markets. Regardless of the limited extent to which reality in the subsequent years will match this rhetoric, the actions of a majority of the electorate suggest that there are some possibilities for positive change. Moreover, when the Occupy Wall Street (OWS) movement appeared in late 2011, it forced a discussion of basic issues of inequality, power, and ideology onto the public agenda. Whatever happens to OWS, it is likely that these issues will continue to be well recognized.

The sorts of changes advocated in this article, changes that would affect the underlying causes of the economic crisis, continue to be necessary. They also continue to be possible. ❏

An elaboration of the points in this afterword is contained in a book that grew out of the original article: Economic Collapse and Economic Change: Getting to the Roots of the Crisis, *by Arthur MacEwan and John A. Miller, M.E. Sharpe Publisher, 2011.*

Did the rich "do it alone," or did they rely on theories and technologies developed by many people over a long period of time? Gar Alperovitz and Lew Daly consider how our common heritage of knowledge could be shared more broadly to benefit more members of society.

THE UNDESERVING RICH

Collectively produced knowledge and the (re)distribution of wealth.

BY GAR ALPEROVITZ AND LEW DALY
March/April 2010

Warren Buffett, one of the wealthiest men in the nation, is worth nearly $50 billion. Does he "deserve" all this money? Why? Did he work so much harder than everyone else? Did he create something so extraordinary that no one else could have created it? Ask Buffett himself and he will tell you that he thinks "society is responsible for a very significant percentage of what I've earned." But if that's true, doesn't society deserve a very significant share of what he has earned?

When asked why he is so successful, Buffett commonly replies that this is the wrong question. The more important question, he stresses, is why he has *so much to work with* compared to other people in the world, or compared to previous generations of Americans. How much money would I have "if I were born in Bangladesh," or "if I was born here in 1700," he asks.

Buffett may or may not deserve something more than another person working with what a given historical or collective context provides. As he observes, however, it is simply not possible to argue in any serious way that he deserves *all* of the benefits that are clearly attributable to living in a highly developed society.

Buffett has put his finger on one of the most explosive issues developing just beneath the surface of public awareness. Over the last several decades, economic research has done a great deal of solid work pinpointing— much more precisely than in the past—what share of what we call "wealth" is created by society, versus what share any individual can be said to have earned and thus deserved. This research raises profound moral—and ultimately political—questions.

Recent estimates suggest that U.S. economic output per capita has increased more than twenty-fold since 1800. Output per hour worked has increased an estimated fifteen-fold since 1870 alone. Yet the average modern person likely works with no greater commitment, risk, or intelligence than his or her counterpart from the past. What is the primary cause of such vast gains if individuals do not really "improve"? Clearly, it is largely that the scientific, technical, and cultural knowledge available to us, and the efficiency of our means of storing and retrieving this knowledge, have grown at a scale and pace that far outstrip any other factor in the nation's economic development.

A half century ago, in 1957, economist Robert Solow calculated that nearly 90% of productivity growth in the first half of the 20th century (from 1909 to

1949) could only be attributed to "technical change in the broadest sense." The supply of labor and capital—what workers and employers contribute—appeared almost incidental to this massive technological "residual." Subsequent research inspired by Solow and others continued to point to "advances in knowledge" as the main source of growth. Economist William Baumol calculates that "nearly 90 percent . . . of current GDP was contributed by innovation carried out since 1870." Baumol judges that his estimate, in fact, understates the cumulative influence of past advances: Even "the steam engine, the railroad, and many other inventions of an earlier era, still add to today's GDP."

Related research on the sources of invention bolsters the new view, posing a powerful challenge to conventional, heroic views of technology that characterize progress as a sequence of extraordinary contributions by "Great Men" (occasionally "Great Women") and their "Great Inventions." In contrast to this popular view, historians of technology have carefully delineated the incremental and cumulative way most technologies actually develop. In general, a specific field of knowledge builds up slowly through diverse contributions over time until—at a particular moment when enough has been established—the next so-called "breakthrough" becomes all but inevitable.

Often many people reach the same point at virtually the same time, for the simple reason that they all are working from the same developing information and research base. The next step commonly becomes obvious (or if not obvious, very likely to be taken within a few months or years). We tend to give credit to the person who gets there first—or rather, who gets the first public attention, since often the real originator is not as good at public relations as the one who jumps to the front of the line and claims credit. Thus, we remember Alexander Graham Bell as the inventor of the telephone even though, among others, Elisha Gray and Antonio Meucci got there at the same time or even before him. Newton and Leibniz hit upon the calculus at roughly the same time in the 1670s; Darwin and Alfred Russel Wallace produced essentially the same theory of evolution at roughly the same time in the late 1850s.

Less important than who gets the credit is the simple fact that most breakthroughs occur not so much thanks to one "genius," but because of the longer historical unfolding of knowledge. All of this knowledge—the overwhelming source of all modern wealth—comes to us today *through no effort of our own*. It is the generous and unearned gift of the past. In the words of Northwestern University economist Joel Mokyr, it is a "free lunch."

Collective knowledge is often created by formal public efforts as well, a point progressives often stress. Many of the advances which propelled our high-tech economy in the early 1990s grew directly out of research programs and technical systems financed and often collaboratively developed by the federal government. The Internet, to take the most obvious example, began as a government defense project, the ARPANET, in the early 1960s. Up through the 1980s there was little private investment or interest in developing computer networks. Today's vast software industry also rests on a foundation of computer language and operating hardware developed in large part with public support. The Bill Gateses of the world—the heroes of the "New Economy"—might still be working with vacuum tubes and punch cards were it not for critical research and technology programs created or financed by the federal government after World War II. Other illustrations range from jet airplanes and radar to the basic life science research undergirding many pharmaceutical industry advances. Yet the truth is that the role of collectively inherited knowledge is far, far greater than just the contributions made by direct public support, important as they are.

Individual vs. Social Wealth

A straightforward but rarely confronted question arises from these facts: If most of what we have today is attributable to advances we inherit in common, then why should this gift of our collective history not more generously benefit all members of society?

The top 1% of U.S. households now receives more income than the bottom 120 million Americans combined. The richest 1% of households owns nearly half of all investment assets (stocks and mutual funds, financial securities, business equity, trusts, non-home real estate). The bottom 90% of the population owns less than 15%; the bottom half—150 million Americans—owns less than 1%. If America's vast wealth is mainly a gift of our common past, what justifies such disparities?

Robert Dahl, one of America's leading political scientists—and one of the few to have confronted these facts—put it this way after reading economist Edward Denison's pioneering work on growth accounting: "It is immediately obvious that little growth in the American economy can be attributed to the actions of particular individuals." He concluded straightforwardly that, accordingly, "the control and ownership of the economy rightfully belongs to 'society.'"

Contrast Dahl's view with that of Joe the Plumber, who famously inserted himself into the 2008 presidential campaign with his repeated claim that he has "earned" everything he gets and so any attempt to tax his earnings is totally unjustified. Likewise, "we didn't rely on somebody else to build what we built," banking titan Sanford Weill tells us in a *New York Times* front-page story on the "New Gilded Age." "I think there are people," another executive tells the *Times*, "who because of their uniqueness warrant whatever the market will bear."

A direct confrontation with the role of knowledge—and especially inherited knowledge—goes to the root of a profound challenge to such arguments. One way to think about all this is by focusing on the concept of "earned" versus "unearned" income. Today this distinction can be found in conservative attacks on welfare "cheats" who refuse to work to earn their keep, as well as in calls even by some Republican senators to tax the windfall oil-company profits occasioned by the Iraq war and Hurricane Katrina.

The concept of unearned income first came into clear focus during the era of rapidly rising land values caused by grain shortages in early 19th-century England. Wealth derived *simply* from owning land whose price was escalating appeared illegitimate because no individual truly "earned" such wealth. Land values—and especially explosively high values—were largely the product of factors such as fertility, location, and population pressures. The huge profits (unearned "rents," in the technical language of economics) landowners reaped when there were food shortages were viewed as particularly egregious. David Ricardo's influential theory of "differential rent"—i.e., that land values are determined by differences in fertility and location between different plots of land—along with religious perspectives reaching back to the Book of Genesis played a central role in sharpening this critical moral distinction.

John Stuart Mill, among others, developed the distinction between "earned" and "unearned" in the middle decades of the 19th century and applied it to other forms of "external wealth," or what he called "wealth created by circumstances." Mill's approach fed into a growing sense of the importance of societal inputs which produce economic gains beyond what can be ascribed to one person working alone in nature without benefit of civilization's many contributions. Here a second element of what appears, historically, as a slowly evolving understanding also becomes clear: If contribution is important in determining rewards, then, Mill and others urged, since society at large makes major contributions to economic achievement, it too has "earned" and deserves a share of what has been created. Mill believed strongly in personal contribution and individual reward, but he held that in principle wealth "created by circumstances" should be reclaimed for social purposes. Karl Marx, of course, tapped the distinction between earned and unearned in his much broader attack on capitalism and its exploitation of workers' labor.

The American republican writer Thomas Paine was among the first to articulate a societal theory of wealth based directly on the earned\unearned distinction. Paine argued that everything "beyond what a man's own hands produce" was a gift which came to him simply by living in society, and hence "he owes on every principle of justice, of gratitude, and of civilization, a part of that accumulation back again to society from whence the whole came." A later American reformer, Henry George, focused on urban land rather than the agricultural land at the heart of Ricardo's concern. George challenged what he called "the unearned increment" which is created when population growth and other societal factors increase land values. In Britain, J. A. Hobson argued that the unearned value created by the industrial system in general was much larger than just the part which accrued to landowners, and that it should be treated in a similar (if not more radical and comprehensive) fashion. In a similar vein, Hobson's early 20th-century contemporary Leonard Trelawny Hobhouse declared that the "prosperous business man" should consider "what single step he could have taken" without the "sum of intelligence which civilization has placed at his disposal." More recently, the famed American social scientist Herbert Simon judged that if "we are very generous with ourselves, I suppose we might claim that we 'earned' as much as one fifth of [our income]."

The distinction between earned and unearned gains is central to most of these thinkers, as is the notion that societal contributions—including everything an industrial economy requires, from the creation of laws, police, and courts to the development of schools, trade restrictions, and patents—must be recognized and rewarded. The understanding that such societal contributions are both contemporary and have made a huge and cumulative contribution over all of history is also widely accepted. Much of the income they permit and confer now appears broadly analogous to the unearned rent a landlord claims. What is new and significant here is the further clarification that by far the most important element in all this is the accumulated *knowledge* which society contributes over time.

All of this, as sociologist Daniel Bell has suggested, requires a new "knowledge theory of value"—especially as we move deeper into the high-tech era through computerization, the Internet, cybernetics, and cutting-edge fields such as gene therapy and nanotechnology. One way to grasp what is at stake is the following: A person today working the same number of hours as a similar person in 1870—working just as hard but no harder—will produce perhaps 15 times as much economic output. It is clear that the contemporary person can hardly be said to have "earned" his much greater productivity.

Consider further that if we project forward the past century's rate of growth, a person working a century from now would be able to produce—and potentially receive as "income"—up to seven times today's average income. By far the greatest part of this gain will also come to this person as a free gift of the past—the gift of the new knowledge created, passed on, and inherited from our own time forward.

She and her descendents, in fact, will inevitably contribute less, relative to the huge and now expanded contribution of the past, than we do today. The obvious question, again, is simply this: to what degree is it meaningful to say that this person will have "earned" all that may come her way? These and other realities suggest that the quiet revolution in our understanding of how wealth is created has ramifications for a much more profound and far-reaching challenge to today's untenable distribution of income and wealth. ❏

Wealth inequality is neither natural nor inevitable. Progressive activists succeeded in promoting more equitable economic policies after World War II, but the rich fought back and eroded those gains since then. Sam Pizzigati recounts this hidden history, and its lessons for the future.

HAVE THE RICH WON?

BY SAM PIZZIGATI
Nov. 2009; revised Oct. 2012

Back in 1974, when *Dollars & Sense* was founded, young economic justice activists—like me—felt we had our hands full. I was working, at the time, in upstate New York, helping mobile-home owners organize against trailer-park landlord extortion. I had one friend active on a campaign to win bargaining rights for the local university's food service workers, another pushing for public housing, still another advocating for a badly needed primary health care clinic.

Everywhere we all looked, we saw people hurting, we saw unfairness, we saw economic injustice. Today, 35 years later, I've come to understand what we didn't see: the big picture.

Yes, back then in 1974, we certainly did face injustice at every turn. But we were living, thanks to years of struggle—and success—by our activist forebears, in a society where politics actually revolved around confronting those injustices and making change that could really help average working people.

And, even better, we had a realistic shot at achieving that change. The reason? Our activist forebears had sliced the single greatest obstacle to social progress—the rich and powerful—down to democratic size. In 1974 we were living——— in a society with an enfeebled wealthy, and we didn't know it.

Shame on us. By not understanding—and not appreciating—the equality our progressive predecessors had battled so hard to achieve, we failed to defend it. We let the wealthy come back. We let grand concentrations of private wealth reconstitute themselves across the American economic landscape. We let the super rich regain their power to dictate and distort America's political discourse.

How rich—and powerful—have today's rich become? Some numbers can help tell the story. In 1974, the most affluent 1% of Americans averaged, in today's dollars, $380,000 in income.

Now let's fast-forward. In 2007, the last "boom" year before the Great Recession hit, households in America's top 1% averaged $1.4 million, well over triple what top 1% households averaged back in 1974—and, remember, this tripling came *after* adjusting for inflation.

Americans in the bottom 90%, meanwhile, saw their average incomes increase a meager $47 a year between 1974 and 2007, not enough to foot the bill for a month's worth of cable TV.

The bottom line: top-1% households made 12 times more income than bottom-90% households in 1974, 42 times more in 2007.

The numbers become even more striking when we go back a bit further in time and focus not on the top 1%, but on the richest of the rich, the top 400, the living symbol of wealth and power in the United States ever since America's original Gilded Age in the late 19th century.

In 1955, our 400 highest incomes averaged $13.2 million, in 2009 dollars. But the top 400 in 1955 didn't get to enjoy all those millions. On average, after exploiting every tax loophole they could find, they actually paid over half their incomes, 51.2%, in federal income tax.

Today's super rich are doing better, fantastically better, both before *and* after taxes. In 2009, the most recent year with stats available, our top 400 averaged an astounding $202.4 million each in income. These 400 financially fortunate paid, after loopholes, just 19.9% of their incomes in federal tax.

After taxes, as a group, the top 400 of 2009 had $62.3 *billion* more in their pockets than 1955's top 400, $62.3 billion more they could put to work bankrolling politicians and right-wing think tanks and Swift Boat ad blitzes against progressive candidates and causes.

How could America's super rich have had so little, relatively speaking, back in 1955 and so much today? What changed between the mid-20th century and the first decade of the 21st? We have lost, simply put, the economic checks and balances that so significantly discouraged grand concentrations of private wealth in the years right after World War II.

Among the most important of these checks and balances: steeply graduated progressive tax rates.

Over most of the quarter-century between the early 1940s and the mid 1960s, America's richest faced at least a 91% federal tax rate on "earned" income over $400,000. By 1974, that top rate had dropped, but only to a still steep 70%. The top rate in 2012: 35%.

Tax rates on income from the sale of stocks, bonds, and other property—capital gains—have traveled the same trend line. In the postwar years, the wealthy paid a 25% tax on capital gains. The 2012 rate: just 15%.

So what should today's activists for economic justice do about all this? Hit the repeat button and re-fight the struggles of our activist forebears?

That course certainly seems reasonable. Our forebears, after all, pulled off quite a stunner. They faced, a century ago, a super rich every bit as rich and powerful as the super rich we confront today. Over the course of the next half-century, they leveled that super rich.

By the 1950s, the incomes of America's richest had been "hacked to pieces," as best-selling author Frederick Lewis Allen would marvel in a 1952 book. The grand estates of the super rich, jubilant postwar progressives would add, had become housing tracts and college campuses for the first mass middle-class nation the world had ever seen.

But this triumph would not stand the test of time. The 20th century would end as it began, with phenomenal wealth and power concentrated at America's economic summit. By century's end, the leveling institutions our progressive predecessors had fought so hard to win—progressive tax rates, a vital trade union presence, regulatory restrictions on corporate behavior—had all come unraveled.

Maybe we ought to ask why, before we rush to re-fight the struggles our fore-bears so nobly waged.

Why, for instance, did the single most potent leveling instrument of the mid-20th century, the steeply graduated rates of the progressive income tax, prove unsustainable?

These steep rates, in their time, certainly did work wonders. In the mid-20th century, with these rates in effect, the U.S. economy essentially stopped generating colossal new concentrations of wealth and power. Of the 40 richest individuals in U.S. history, not one made the bulk of his fortune during the years of this progressive tax rate heyday.

The big fortunes that did amass in these years mostly belonged to oil magnates. They enjoyed what the rest of America's rich did not: a super loophole, the oil depletion allowance, that essentially shielded them from the stiff tax rates that applied to every other deep pocket.

But steeply graduated tax rates have an Achilles' heel: the rich hate them with an incredibly intense passion. That wouldn't matter, of course, if everyone else loved these rates with equal fervor. But they don't—because high tax rates on high incomes only impact the wealthy directly. The wealthy feel the "pain." They also see no benefits—because they don't need or use the public services that high taxes on high incomes make possible.

Those who do benefit from these public services, on the other hand, don't automatically connect the availability of these services to progressive tax rates.

The end result of these political dynamics: Steeply graduated tax rates—as traditionally structured—have never been able to stand the test of time, anywhere. The rich attack these rates with far more single-minded zeal than the general public supports them.

High tax rates on high incomes typically only come into effect during periods of great social upheaval, during wars and severe economic downturns that knock the wealthy off their political stride. But after these upheavals, amid "normalcy," the wealthy's fervid and focused opposition to high rates eventually wears down the public political will to maintain these rates. The rates shrink. Wealth re-concentrates.

Today's mainstream policy makers and politicos seem to have concluded, from this history, that any attempt to tax the rich significantly makes no sense.

Obama White House policy makers, for instance, called repeatedly from 2009 through 2012 for an increase in the top federal income tax rate on the wealthy, but just to the 39.6% rate in effect before the George W. Bush tax cuts. At 39.6%, America's rich would be paying taxes at less than half the top rate they faced in the 1950s under President Dwight D. Eisenhower, a Republican.

Even worse: Merely repealing the Bush tax cuts, as former White House economist Lawrence Summers himself acknowledged in a 2007 Brookings Institution paper, would only wipe away one-sixth of the rise in income inequality the nation has experienced since 1979.

We clearly need to do more to turn back the inequality tide. But just what more do we need to be doing? How can we make steeply graduated progressive tax rates sustainable over the long term? How can we build into our tax system a lasting commitment to real progressivity?

Back in 1974, in a far more equal United States, we failed to ponder questions like these. Now we must. ❑

According to Chuck Collins, some of the richest Americans have actively used their power and privilege to change society's rules. By organizing themselves and taking advantage of their unequal influence, these "rule fixers" have been able to make the system even more unequal.

HOW THE RULES GOT RIGGED

BY CHUCK COLLINS
October 2012

The dramatic upward redistribution of wealth and income has not been a natural event but a human-created disaster. The wealthiest Americans—commonly known as the 1%—have lobbied politicians and pressed for changes in the rules, including laws governing trade, taxes, worker protections, and corporations. With the active intervention of some members of the 1%, the rules of the economy have been changed to benefit asset owners at the expense of wage earners, and to benefit global corporations at the expense of local businesses.

In one respect, the 1% is not much different from the population at large in that only a small segment is engaged in politics and actively advocating on policy matters. Some in the 1% care about the 100% and work for a fair and sustainable economy. Others are rule fixers, focused on rigging government policies in their favor to get more wealth and power. But the majority of them are unengaged and happy to watch their wealth accumulate without weighing in one way or another.

The game fixers maintain a worldview that justifies using every tool at their disposal to perpetuate and expand their wealth. Most believe they are the engines of the economic train, creating enterprises and wealth that pull everyone else along. This worldview is well captured in the introduction to the 2010 Forbes 400 survey:

> Who cares whether somebody is worth $2 billion or $6 billion? We do.
> That personal stash is a critical barometer of how well the nation—and, to a
> degree, the world—is doing. By creating wealth, the people on our list help
> share epic financial trends, as well as shifts in leadership and policy, often
> providing the spark for innovation and entrepreneurship.

They conflate extreme wealth with virtuous actions that are beneficial to the society as a whole. They believe government should step aside and not interfere with their actions—or, better yet, steer subsidies and tilt the rules in their favor. Some genuinely believe this serves the greater good. Others don't think much about the bottom 99%, and through their inaction, perpetuate the unequal status quo.

Unfortunately, three decades of rule changes in favor of the 1% have almost destroyed the economy and ecology of the planet and shattered the lives of billions around the world. The system is now wired so that, from an economic and ecological point of view, members of the 1% are acting against their long-term self-interest.

The most powerful segment of the game riggers are the organized wealthy, people who use a wide variety of tools—political contributions, charitable giving, media ownership, and control over think tanks and advocacy groups—to tip the scales in their favor. There are five primary ways that the wealthiest individuals use their power and influence.

Political Influence

Policy makers pay attention to the 1% because of their wealth, influence, and campaign contributions. Not everyone who makes a political contribution is a game rigger. But the hyper-engaged among the 1% will channel millions directly to candidates, legislative issues, political parties, and a myriad of influence channels such as political action committees (PACs) and 501(c)(4) corporations.

Political scientist Larry Bartels has studied how lawmakers give preferential treatment to richer constituents. There are several ways the top 1% directly influence politics.

Campaign Contributions. Only a tiny sliver of households give contributions of $200 or more to major-party candidates for federal office. In 2010, about one-third of 1% of the adult population gave $200, accounting for roughly two-thirds of all campaign contributions. The big donors in the 1% who max out their contributions by giving more than $2,400 are about 0.05% of the population. That's only 146,715 people out of a population of over 315 million. This is why politicians listen so carefully to the organized 1%.

Personal Relationships with Elected Officials. Most members of Congress have personal relationships with game riggers in the 1%, even if the donors live outside their districts. They have been at fund-raisers together, broken bread together, and talked on the phone. According to research, the 1% is far more likely to have contacted their member of Congress than the average person. A study examining the super-rich in the Chicago area found that half the households with a median net worth of at least $7.5 million contacted their member of Congress and other high-level government officials.

Higher Voter Turnout Among the 1%. Probably least important in terms of political influence is the fact that the 1% vote in most elections. While 64% of registered voters cast a vote in 2008 election, almost 100% of the 1% voted.

Charity Sector Influence

The majority of people in the 1% give to charity to make the world a better place. The game riggers use donations to charitable tax-exempt organizations to advance their economic interests. For example, some direct funds through private tax-exempt charitable foundations they control to fund research and policy advocacy organizations to actively lobby for their agenda.

As wealth has concentrated in fewer hands, some of that wealth, often as part of a tax avoidance strategy, flows into the creation of charitable foundations. Since 1980, when disparities in wealth began to accelerate, the number of private foundations has tripled, from 22,088 to more than 76,000 in 2010.

These private foundations, largely controlled by families in the 1%, give to a variety of issues and concerns, mostly apolitical. The largest recipients are universities, hospitals, and religious institutions—and the charity dollars are urgently needed. Only a tiny percent, however, estimated at around 3%, is given to projects that address poverty alleviation and the root causes of social problems. The largest percentage of contributions reinforces or even perpetuates the unequal status quo.

The game riggers within the 1% use charitable foundations as an extension of their advocacy power. Billionaire Steve Forbes formed a tax-exempt think tank to promote himself and his policies in advance of his run for President in 2000. George Soros gives billions through the Open Society Fund to support global development and liberal organizations in the United States.

Media Influence to Change the Conversation

The concentration of media ownership is a major factor in shaping the contours of our national debate. The ownership and actions of News Corporation, Viacom, and other major media outlets are probably more significant in shaping the economy than is money given to politicians.

The 1% own a disproportionately large share of media outlets and have an outsized ability to influence the media through public relations and communications firms. This has greatly shaped the national conversation about the existence of inequality and possible solutions. Reducing inequality will require a robust role for government action. Yet public opinion is confused about whether this is a good idea.

Over the last few decades, the 1% and Wall Street have funneled billions of dollars to think tanks, communications firms, lobbying groups, and nonprofit charitable organizations that promote the demonization of government as a solution to our common problems. So even at a time when two-thirds of the population is concerned about extreme inequality, there is abundant confusion about whether government action can solve the problem. The invisibility of inequality concerns in the media is a contributing factor to this confusion.

Organizing Others in the 1%

The most engaged rule riggers use their networks, associations, cultural institutions, and connections to other wealthy people and corporate leaders to leverage additional power and influence.

For example, some members of the 1% join with others to bundle their donations and have them come from an organized association with an agenda. In one study, 21% of the members of the 1% sampled had bundled their campaign contributions with those of other donors to increase impact. This really engages the attention of politicians.

Partnering with Wall Street Game Riggers

Individuals in the top 1% who are active game riggers are usually linked to corporations connected to Wall Street. Wall Street is the 1%'s institutional home—and the engine of activity that has fueled inequality and economic instability.

Like wealthy individuals, the mega-corporations of Wall Street fund a network of pro-free-market think tanks, research organizations, advocacy groups, and associations such as the U.S. Chamber of Commerce and the Business Roundtable that have armies of lobbyists and public relations firms.

These five uses of influence by a segment of the 1% have led to new levels of inequality—and a form of plutocracy—rule by wealthy elite that uses its power to expand its wealth and power.

Profile of a Game Rigger

Perhaps the best case study of using wealth and power to perpetuate wealth and power is the Koch brothers. David and Charles Koch, two brothers who inherited an oil business, are worth an estimated $25 billion each. They use every tool possible to advance their interests—which include blocking climate change legislation, cutting their taxes, and weakening government regulation.

In addition to active campaign and political issue contributions, they fund an infrastructure of radical libertarian and anti-government organizations, including the Tea Party movement, Americans for Prosperity, and incubators of libertarian thought such as the Mercatus Center at George Mason University.

They've donated hundreds of millions of dollars to right-wing causes over the last decade and convene semi-annual gatherings of some of the richest conservatives in the country to leverage money for issue and electoral work. They financed a gigantic database project to expand right-wing organizing and mobilize over $200 million for the 2012 elections.

What makes their use of tax-exempt charitable donations doubly offensive is that taxpayers in the bottom 99% indirectly subsidize the Koch brothers and other billionaires who fund pet political projects through tax-exempt charities. Many working-class donors don't itemize their deductions on their taxes, so they don't receive a tax break. But for the wealthy, the charitable deduction is a major incentive for giving and greatly reduces their tax obligations. For every $100 donated by the 1%, $33 in revenue is lost to the U.S. Treasury. In other words, the 99% matches a third of their donations.

Government Help for the 1%

When the rule riggers in the 1% use their substantial influence, what do they get for their efforts? What is their policy agenda and how successful has it been? Below are examples of policies widely advocated by the rule riggers within the top 1%.

Low Taxes on Income from Wealth. Capital gains taxes have been greatly reduced over the last several decades, from 39% in 1979 to 15% in 2011. The 1% receive over 80% of capital gains income, with the top 0.1% receiving over half of capital gains income.

Free Trade to Boost Investors. Free trade policies and treaties have boosted stock prices and enabled companies to pit countries against one another in a race to the bottom in wages, environmental standards, and worker protection. For several decades, free trade treaties have passed the U.S. Congress with bipartisan majorities over the objections of a majority of the population. They have benefited the top 1% of shareholders but hurt the 99% of wage earners by driving down wages.

Unlimited Inheritances. The federal estate tax is our nation's only levy on inherited wealth. Eliminating this tax, paid only by the 1%, remains a major legislative priority for many in Congress. The 1% lobbied to phase out the estate tax in 2010. We presently have a diminished estate tax on wealth over $5 million.

Weak Environmental Regulation and Enforcement. The 1% has lobbied to weaken environmental regulation and enforcement, blocking responses to the climate crisis to enable extractive industries such as oil and coal to reap short-term windfalls.

Tax Cuts for the Top. The 1% has won reductions in top income tax rates. Since 1980, top income tax rates have gone from 50% to 35%. As described earlier, the 1% has seen the percentage of its income paid in taxes decline since the 1950s.

Secret Tax Havens. Expansion of the offshore tax haven system and secrecy jurisdictions enable the 1% of companies to hide income and assets, and reduce or eliminate their taxes. Lobbying has kept Congress from cracking down.

Subsidies for the Future. Tax subsidies for 1% corporations have made it possible not just to avoid taxes but also to get money from taxpayers. General Electric received $3.3 billion in 2010.

The 1% have seen their agenda move successfully through the halls of Congress. They've also successfully fended off rule changes they opposed. Only an organized movement of the 99%—with fair-minded allies in the 1%—will reverse these trends. ❑

This article was adapted by the author from his book, 99 to 1: How Wealth Inequality is Wrecking the World and What We Can Do About It *(Berrett Koehler, 2012); www.99to1book.com.*

SOURCES: Luisa Kroll, "The Forbes 400: How Do America's Most Affluent People Make—and Enjoy—Their Riches?" *Forbes*, Oct. 11, 2010, p. 17. Larry Bartels, *Unequal Democracy: The Political Economy of the New Gilded Age* (Princeton, NJ: Princeton University Press, 2008). Center for Responsive Politics, "Donor Demographics, 2010." Benjamin Page, Fay Lomax Cook, and Rachel Moskowitz, "Wealthy Americans, Philanthropy and the Common Good," Institute for Policy Research, Northwestern University, Nov. 2011. Jordan Howard, "Wealthy More Likely to Contact Congress, Study Says," *Huffington Post*, Nov. 8, 2011. Foundation Center Statistical Information Center, "National Growth Data." Peter Dreier and Chuck Collins, "Traitors to Their Class: Social Change Philanthropy and Movements for Change," *New Labor Forum*, Winter 2012. Jeff Zeleny and Megah Thee-Brenan, "New Poll Finds a Deep Distrust of Government," *New York Times*, Oct. 25, 2011. Ed Pilkington, "Koch Brothers: Secretive Billionaires to Launch Vast Database with 2012 in Mind," *Guardian*, Nov. 7, 2011. William Randolph, "Charitable Deductions, Department of Treasury," Tax Policy Center, www.taxpolicycenter.org. Robert Lenzner, "The Top 0.1% of the Nation Earn Half of All Capital Gains," *Forbes*, Nov. 21, 2011. Stefan Karlsson, "Income Inequality: What's the Impact of Free Trade and Immigration," *Christian Science Monitor*, Oct. 27, 2010.

Not so long ago, U.S. economic growth was broadly shared by workerss at all income levels. As productivity rose, wages rose for all. In the early 1970s, however, this formula broke down. James Cypher shows how this fundamental change has hurt lower-wage workers while exacerbating inequality.

NEARLY $2 TRILLION PURLOINED FROM U.S. WORKERS IN 2009

BY JAMES M. CYPHER
July/August 2011

In 2009, stock owners, bankers, brokers, hedge-fund wizards, highly paid corporate executives, corporations, and mid-ranking managers pocketed—as either income, benefits, or perks such as corporate jets—an estimated $1.91 *trillion* that 40 years ago would have collectively gone to non-supervisory and production workers in the form of higher wages and benefits. These are the 88 million workers in the private sector who are closely tied to production processes and/or are not responsible for the supervision, planning, or direction of other workers.

From the end of World War II until the early 1970s, the benefits of economic growth were broadly shared by those in all income categories: workers received increases in compensation (wages plus benefits) that essentially matched the rise in their productivity. Neoclassical economist John Bates Clark (1847-1938) first formulated what he termed the "natural law" of income distribution which "assigns to everyone what he has specifically created." That is, if markets are not "obstructed," pay levels should be "equal [to] that part of the product of industry which is traceable to labor itself." As productivity increased, Clark argued, wages would rise *at an equal rate.*

The idea that compensation increases should equal increases in *average* labor productivity per worker as a matter of national wage policy, or a wage norm, is traceable to the President's Council of Economic Advisors under the Eisenhower and Kennedy administrations. This *macroeconomic* approach was anchored in the fact that if compensation rises in step with productivity growth, then both unit labor costs and capital's versus labor's share of national income will remain constant. This "Keynesian Consensus" never questioned the fairness of the initial capital/labor split, but it at least offered workers a share of the fruits of future economic growth.

As the figure below shows, both Clark's idea of a "natural law" of distribution and Keynesian national wage policy have ceased to function since the onset of the neoliberal/supply-side era beginning in the early 1970s. From 1972 through 2009, "usable" productivity—*that part of productivity growth that is available for raising wages and living standards*—increased by 55.5%. Meanwhile, real average hourly pay *fell* by almost 10% (excluding benefits). As a group, workers responded by increasing their labor-force participation rate. To make the calculation consistent over time, employment is adjusted to a *constant participation rate* set at the 1972 level. Had

INDEX OF WAGES, COMPENSATION, PRODUCTIVITY, AND "USABLE" PRODUCTIVITY OF U.S. NON-SUPERVISORY WORKERS, PER HOUR, 1972-2009 (1972=100)

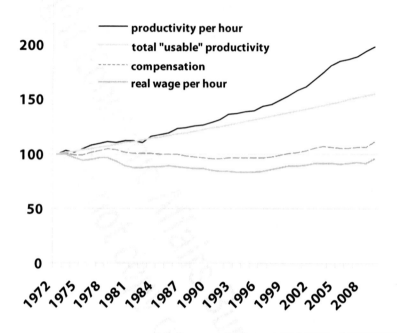

Sources and Calculations: This calculation is based on the 1972 average real hourly wage expressed in 2009 dollars, $17.88, plus $2.95 per hour in benefits, with total compensation [wages + benefits] equal to $20.83 per hour for non-supervisory workers (U.S. Department of Labor, 2010a, 2010b: 85-90; Economic Policy Institute, 2011). The growth of private productivity from 1972 to 2009 was 92.7%. Adjusting the productivity figure (downward) to account for lower economy-wide productivity, consistent deflation in both producer prices and consumer prices, and a rising rate of depreciation, the net growth of "usable" productivity was 55.5% (Baker 2007). If workers had been paid the value of their annual productivity increases (as they essentially were prior to the early 1970s) they would have received an average of $35.98 per hour in compensation in 2009 instead of the $23.14 they actually received. The differential was $12.84. Workers worked an average of 39.8 hours per week in 2009, so $511 of compensation that they would have received under conditions prior to the early 1970s instead was diverted. On an annual basis of 1,768 hours worked per year, according to the OECD, each worker lost to capital an average of $22,701. Adjusting the 88,239,000 production and non-supervisory workers employed in 2009 to the lower 1972 labor force participation rate equivalent of 84,180,000 workers, the total of purloined workers' compensation for 2009 comes to $1.91 trillion (Council of Economic Advisors, 2010: Tables B-47, B-49; U.S. Department of Labor, Bureau of Labor Statistics, 2011 Table B-6).

compensation matched "*usable*" productivity growth, the (adjusted) 84 million non-supervisory and production workers in 2009 would have received roughly $1.91 *trillion* more in wages and benefits. That is, 13.5% of the nation's Gross Domestic Product in 2009 was transferred from non-supervisory workers to capitalists (and managers) via the gap of 44.4% that had opened up between compensation and "usable" productivity since 1972.

As expected, neoclassical (or mainstream) economists offer tortured justifications for the new *status quo*. The erstwhile dauphin of neoclassical economics, Harvard economist Gregory Mankiw, agrees with Clark's formulation. But he says that even though "productivity has accelerated, workers have *become accustomed to the slow rate of wage growth since the 1970s*." Why "accustomed"? Well, believe it or not, neoclassical economists claim that today's workers suffer from "low wage aspirations." Mankiw equates the wage that workers aspire to with the wage they consider fair. So, according to this very strange formulation, workers consider that they are getting a fair shake today, even though their compensation increases lag behind their productivity increases. Yet a few decades earlier, they considered it fair (as did Clark and Mankiw) for compensation growth to keep up with productivity increases.

Some economists simply deny that any change has occurred. Noted neoclassical conjurer Martin Feldstein believes that the "productivity-compensation gap" is merely a matter of bad measurement: by dropping the Consumer Price Index as the appropriate yardstick, Feldstein alchemically transforms the way wages are adjusted for inflation. His soothing Panglossian recalibration *raises* workers' "real" income; *et voilà!*—the productivity-compensation gap all but disappears.

Leaving aside such statistical prestidigitation, a vast upward transfer of income is evident. That transfer is directly related to the rupture of the so-called "Treaty of Detroit"—an understanding between capital and labor, pounded out during the Truman administration, wherein employers accepted the idea that compensation could grow at the rate that productivity increased. In 1953 union strength was at its high point; 32.5% of the U.S. labor force was unionized. With the profit squeeze of the early 1970s and the onset of Reaganism, unionization rates began to fall—to 27% in 1979, then to 19% in 1984. By 2010 the rate was down to 11.9% (and only 6.9% in the private sector). Off-shoring, outsourcing, vigorous (and often illegal) corporate tactics to stop unionization drives, and an overall political climate of hostility to free and fair union elections have deprived workers of the countervailing power they once held. The result is that without unions struggling to divide the economic pie, non-supervisory and production workers (78% of the private-sector workforce) have been deprived of a minimal level of economic distributive justice.

The upward redistribution has remained as hidden as possible. The forms it has taken—as bonuses, bloated salaries, elephantine stock options, padded consulting fees, outsized compensation to boards of directors, sumptuous conferences, palatial offices complete with original artwork, retinues of superfluous "support" staff, hunting lodges, private corporate dining rooms, regal retirement agreements, and so on—defy exact categorization. Some would appear as profit, some as interest, some as dividends, realized capital gains, gigantic pension programs, retained earnings, or owners' income, with the remainder deeply buried as "costs of doing business."

In the final analysis, the $1.91 trillion figure is only an approximation, designed to make more concrete a concept that has lacked an important quantitative dimension. Of course, had compensation increases matched "usable" productivity increases, workers would have paid taxes on the wage portion of their compensation, leaving them with much less than the $1.91 trillion in their pockets. Meanwhile, as these funds are shifted over to capital (and management salaries), federal, state, and local taxes are paid on the portion which appears as declared income. This results in a considerable drop in the *net after-tax* transfer amount actually pocketed by capital through their appropriation of the productivity increases of non-supervisory workers. Even so, their haul remains a staggering—even astonishing—sum. ❏

Sources: Dean Baker, "The Productivity to Paycheck Gap," Center for Economic and Policy Research, 2007 (cepr.net); Lawrence Ball and Gregory Mankiw, "The NAIRU in Theory and Practice," *Journal of Economic Perspectives,* V. 16, No. 14: 115-136 (2002); Council of Economic Advisors, *Economic Report of the President, 2010,* Washington, D.C.: USGPO; Economic Policy Institute, "Wages and Compensation Stagnating," chart from *The State of Working America,* 2011 (stateofworkingamerica.org); Martin Feldstein, "Did Wages Reflect Growth in Productivity?" paper presented at the 2008 American Economics Association meetings (aeaweb.org); Steven Greenhouse, "Union Membership Fell to a 70-Year Low," *New York Times,* January 22, 2011; E.K. Hunt, *History of Economic Thought,* Belmont, Calif.: Wadsworth (1979); David Cay Johnston, "Plane Perks," *Perfectly Legal,* New York: Penguin (2005); T.C. Leonard, "A Certain Rude Honesty: John Bates Clark as a Pioneering Neoclassical Economist," *History of Political Economy* vol. 35, no. 3: 521-558 (2003); U.S. Department of Labor, Bureau of Labor Statistics, *Economic News Release: Table B-6, Employment of Production and Non-Supervisory Employees,* January 7, 2011 (bls.gov); Bureau of Labor Statistics, Table A: Employer Cost for Employee Compensation, USDL-10-1687, December 8, 2010 (bls.gov); Bureau of Labor Statistics, "Current Labor Statistics," *Monthly Labor Review,* Vol. 133, No. 7, July 2010 (bls.gov).

John Miller examines the "old story" of corporations evading taxes, but finds a new chapter: the effective corporate tax rate has been falling for decades, and recently dropped to around 1% of GDP. As the largest corporations pay less and less in federal taxes, the burden is shifted to the rest of us.

CORPORATE TAXES LEAK THROUGH LOOPHOLES

BY JOHN MILLER
May/June 2011; revised October 2012

General Electric, the third largest U.S. corporation, turned a profit of $10.3 billion in 2010, paid no corporate income taxes, and got a "tax benefit" of $1.1 billion on taxes owed on past profits, according to an April 2011 report in Forbes magazine. And from 2005 to 2009, according to its own filings, GE paid a consolidated tax rate of just 11.6%, including state, local, and foreign taxes. That's a far cry from the 35% rate nominally levied on corporate profits above $10 million.

Nor was GE alone among the top 10 U.S. corporations with no tax obligations.

Bank of America (BofA), the seventh largest U.S. corporation, racked up $4.4 billion in profits in 2010 and also paid no corporate income taxes (or in 2009 for that matter). Like GE, BofA also hauled in a whopping "tax benefit"—$1.9 billion.

For BofA, much like GE, losses incurred during the financial crisis erased its tax liabilities. BofA, of course, contributed mightily to the crisis. It was one of four banks that controlled 95% of commercial bank derivatives activity—mortgage-based securities that inflated the housing bubble and brought on the crisis.

And when the crisis hit, U.S. taxpayers bailed them out, not once but several times. All told, BofA received $45 billion of government money from the Troubled Asset Relief Program (TARP) as well as other government guarantees.

And while BofA paid no taxes on over $4 billion of profits, they managed to pay out $3.3 billion in bonuses to corporate executives.

All of that has made BofA a prime target for protests against corporate tax dodging that cost the federal government much more than the $39 billion saved by the punishing spending cuts in the 2011 budget.

These two corporate behemoths and many other major corporations paid no corporate income taxes in 2010, even though U.S. corporate profits had returned to their 2005 levels—the high levels enjoyed by corporations during the Bush expansion before the recession hit.

An Old Story

Corporations avoiding taxes on their profits is an old story. Let's take a look at the track record of major corporations paying corporate income taxes before the crisis hit, and the losses that supposedly explain their not paying taxes.

The Government Accounting Office conducted a detailed study of the burden of the corporate income tax from 1998 to 2005. The results were stunning. Over half (55%) of large U.S. corporations reported no tax liability for at least one of those eight years. And in 2005 alone, 25% of those corporations paid no corporate income taxes, even though corporate profits had more than doubled from 2001 to 2005.

In another careful study, the Treasury Department found that from 2000 to 2005, the share of corporate operating surplus that U.S. corporations paid in taxes—a proxy for the average tax rate—was 16.7%.

The same mechanisms that allowed major U.S. corporations to avoid paying taxes in the first half of the decade eliminated much of their tax burden from 2008 to 2010. In 2011, a study of 280 major corporations by the Institute on Taxation and Economic Policy (ITEP) found:

- More than one-quarter (78) of those corporations paid no federal income taxes in at least one year from 2008 to 2010. Those corporations, nonetheless, racked up $156 billion in pre-tax U.S. profits during that three-year period.
- Thirty of those corporations paid less than zero in aggregate federal income taxes from 2008 to 2010. While each of those corporations turned a profit for this three-year period, the tax subsidies they received from the federal government exceeded whatever they owed in taxes. Pepco Holdings, a group of large energy delivery companies in the Mid-Atlantic region, paid the lowest effective tax rate, -57.6% on its just under one billion dollars of pre-tax profits. General Electric, the U.S. multinational behemoth, was second, paying an effective tax of -$45.3% on its $10.5 billion of profits. And Wells Fargo, the giant U.S. financial services corporation, scored the largest tax subsidies, $18.0 billion from 2008 to 2010. Those subsidies eliminated any taxes Wells Fargo owed on its $49.4 billion of profits in that period, and left it paying an effective tax rate of -1.4%.

With so many tax loopholes at their disposal, U.S. corporations' effective rates of taxation remain well below the statutory 35% rate. The 280 major corporations in the ITEP study paid an average effective tax rate of 17.3%, about one-half the nominal rate.

Corporate income taxes are levied against reported profits, and loopholes allow corporations to inflate their reported costs and thereby reduce their taxable profits. Some of the key mechanisms are:

Accelerated Depreciation: allows corporations to write off machinery, equipment, or other assets more quickly than they actually deteriorate. Enacted in the 1980s and expanded by the Bush administration and Congress in early 2008, it dramatically lowered the effective tax rate on U.S. corporations.

Stock Options: by giving their executives the option to buy the company's stock at a favorable price, corporations can take a tax deduction for the difference between what the employees pay for the stock and what it's worth. Of the 280 corporations in the ITEP study, 185 reported "excess stock-option tax benefits" over the 2008-10 period, which lowered their taxes by a total of $12.3 billion over three years.

Debt Financing: offers a lower effective tax rate for corporate investment than equity (or stock) financing because the interest payments on debt (usually incurred by issuing bonds) get added to corporate costs and reduces reported profits. This tax advantage that the U.S. tax code grants to debt financing is unusually generous; other countries typically treat debt financing less favorably. Interest deductions accounted for 15% of the total deductions taken by corporation in the GAO study.

Overseas Investments: U.S.-based corporations don't pay U.S. corporate taxes on their foreign income until it is "repatriated," or sent back to the parent corporation from abroad. That allows multinational corporations to defer payment of U.S. corporate income taxes on their overseas profits indefinitely or repatriate their profits from foreign subsidiaries when their losses from domestic operations can offset those profits and wipe out any tax liability, as GE did in 2010.

In addition, industry-specific tax breaks, such as the loophole that allowed financial corporations not to pay taxes on foreign lending and leasing, eliminated still more of the taxes owed by some of these corporations, such as General Electric.

Overtaxed—compared to what?

Among the 34 member countries of the Organization of Economic Cooperation and Development (OECD), only Japan's statutory corporate tax rates surpassed the U.S. (average combined federal and state) rate in 2011. And the U.S. rate of 39.3% was well above the OECD average of 25.4% for that year.

But these sorts of comparisons misrepresent where U.S. corporations stand with respect to tax rates actually paid in other advanced countries. As tax analysts say, the U.S. corporate income tax has a "narrow base," or in plain English, is riddled with loopholes. As a result, U.S. effective corporate tax rates—the proportion of corporate profits actually paid out in taxes—are far lower than the nominal rate, and no higher than the effective rates of other industrialized countries.

When economist Jane Gravelle of the Congressional Research Service recently reviewed the international comparisons of effective corporate tax rates, she found study after study that placed U.S. effective corporate rates close to the average rates of other industrialized countries. One study found that U.S. effective corporate tax rates are nearly identical to the average rate of the next 14 largest countries (weighted for GDP). Another study estimated that U.S. effective corporate tax rates were one and a half percentage points lower than the weighted average of those in Canada, France, Germany, India, Japan, and the United Kingdom. A third study found the effective U.S. corporate tax rates were one percent higher than the weighted average of the other 33 industrialized countries that make up the OECD.

Current U.S. corporate tax rates are also extremely low by historical standards (see Figure 1). In 1953, government revenue from U.S. corporate income taxes was equal to 5.6% of GDP; in 1969 the figure was 4.0%. By 2000, it had dropped to 2.2% of GDP. After the financial crisis, corporate income tax revenues dropped even further, to 1% of GDP, and have hovered around that level since then.

**FIGURE 1: GOVERNMENT REVENUE FROM U.S. CORPORATE
INCOME TAXES AS PERCENT OF GDP, 1972-2011.**

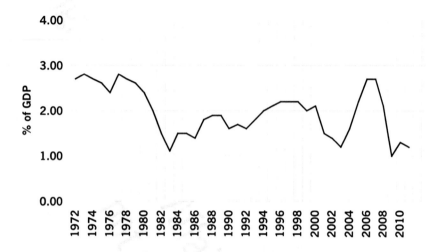

Sources: Congressional Budget Office; Office of Management and Budget.

Closing loopholes or cutting budgets

By all these measures, U.S. corporations are hardly over-taxed. And some major corporations are barely taxed, if taxed at all.

But the calls for lower taxes on corporations have only gotten louder. In the 2012 election campaign, Republican Mitt Romney proposed to cut corporate tax rates nearly in half, from 35% to 20%. President Barack Obama proposed to lower corporate rates to 25%, but close some loopholes, especially for the oil and gas industry.

A bolder proposal would be to return corporate income tax revenues to the 4.0% of GDP level of four decades ago. This would add close to $300 billion a year to government revenues. Increasing taxes to match the average OECD corporate income taxes—3.4% of GDP—would add close to $200 billion to U.S. government revenues—more than five times the $39 billion that the government raised through drastic spending cuts made in the federal budget in 2011.

The cost of not shutting down those corporate loopholes would be to let major corporations go untaxed, to rob the federal government of revenues that could, with enough political will, reverse devastating budget cuts, and to leave the rest of us to pay more and more of the taxes necessary to support a government that does less and less for us. ❑

SOURCES : Christopher Helman, "What the Top U.S. Companies Pay in Taxes," Forbes, April 1, 2011; "Corporate Tax Reform: Issues for Congress," by Jane G. Gravelle and Thomas L. Hungerford, CRS Report for Congress, Oct. 31, 2007; "Treasury Conference On Business Taxation and Global Competitiveness," U.S. Department of the Treasury, Background Paper, July

23, 2007; "Six Tests for Corporate Tax Reform," by Chuck Marr and Brian Highsmith, Center on Budget and Policy Priorities, February 28, 2011; "Tax Holiday For Overseas Corporate Profits Would Increase Deficits, Fail To Boost The Economy, And Ultimately Shift More Investment And Jobs Overseas," by Chuck Marr and Brian Highsmith, Center on Budget and Policy Priorities, April 8, 2011; "Comparison of the Reported Tax Liabilities of Foreign and U.S.-Controlled Corporations, 1998-2005," Government Accounting Office, July 2008. "International Corporate Tax Rate Comparisons and Policy Implications," by Jane G. Gravelle, Congressional Research Service, R41743, March 31, 2011; "Corporate Taxpayers & Corporate Tax Dodgers, 2008-2010," by McIntyre, Gardner, Wilkins, and Phillips, Citizens for Tax Justice and the Institute on Taxation and Economic Policy, November 2011.

A society's system of property rights underlies its distribution of wealth. It sets the rules that determine how ownership is defined, what benefits accrue to those defined as owners, and what social costs will be paid by those without property.

PROPERTY
Who Has a Right to What and Why?

BY ARTHUR MACEWAN
August 2004

In 1948, siblings Joseph and Agnes Waschak purchased a home in Taylor, Pennsylvania, in the midst of coal mining country. Within a few years, hydrogen sulfide fumes and other gases from the nearby mines and mine waste turned the Waschaks' white house black and stained all the internal fixtures yellowish-brown or black. The Waschaks filed suit for damages. According to evidence presented in the subsequent court case, the Waschaks and other area residents who were forced to breathe the gases "suffered from headaches, throat irritation, inability to sleep, coughing, light-headedness, nausea and stomach ailments."

Eric Freyfogle describes the *Waschak v. Moffat* case in his book *The Land We Share: Private Property and the Common Good* as an illustration of how changing concepts of property relate to the preservation of the natural environment. Eventually, the case worked its way up to the Pennsylvania Supreme Court. *Waschak v. Moffat* was not simply an instance of citizens challenging property owners, but of one set of property owners positioned against another. On one side were the Waschaks and others who claimed that the actions of the coal companies constituted a nuisance that prevented them from fully using their property; on the other side were the coal companies who wanted to use their mines as they saw fit. The court had to decide not *whether* property rights would prevail, but *which* set of property rights had priority.

In 1954, the court ruled that a nuisance existed only when the actions involved were intentional or the result of negligence. The coal companies, the court maintained, intended no harm and were not negligent because they were following standard practices in the mining industry. The Waschaks lost.

Four decades later, concepts of property rights and priorities had changed, as illustrated by a 1998 case in Iowa, *Borman v. Board of Supervisors*, also described by Freyfogle. In this case, the landowning plaintiffs wanted to prevent another landowner from developing a "Confined Animal Feeding Operation" (CAFO) that would involve thousands of animals generating large amounts of waste, odors, and other damage to the surrounding properties. Again, the dispute was between the conflicting rights of two sets of property owners.

The Iowa Supreme Court ruled in favor of the plaintiffs, agreeing that the nuisance that would be created by the CAFO would be an illegitimate interference with their property rights. The court did not deny that its ruling limited the property rights of the CAFO planners, but it gave priority to the rights of the plaintiffs.

Moreover, the court ruled that the CAFO planners were not due any compensation by the state, even though it was preventing them from using their land as they chose and thereby reducing the value of that property.

What changed between 1954 and 1998? Many things were different, of course, including the fact that the earlier case was in one state and the later case in another. But the most important difference was that society's views on environmental issues had changed, evolving along with the development of a broad social movement to protect the environment. As a result, concepts regarding property rights changed. What had earlier been seen as legitimate action by a property owner was, by the end of century, viewed as an illegitimate degradation of the environment.

Property rights, it turns out, are not fixed. They change. They are a product of society and of social decisions. As society changes, so too do property rights. And the changes in property rights are contested, subject to political power and social struggle.

Why Do We Protect Private Property?

Although we often take property rights for granted, as though they are based on some absolute standard, in reality they are both changing and ambiguous. Moreover, many widely accepted ideas about property rights start to fall apart when we ask: Why do we protect private property?

For example, suppose a family has a deed on a particular field. Why do we as a society say that another family cannot come along, take part of that field, and sow and reap their own crops? Does it make any difference if the family with the deed has never used the field for any productive purpose, but has simply let it sit idle?

Or, for another example, suppose a pharmaceutical company develops a new antibiotic. Why do we allow that company the right to take out a patent and then prevent other firms or individuals from producing and selling that same antibiotic? Does it make any difference if the antibiotic is one that would save the lives of many people were it more readily available—that is, available at a lower price than the company charges?

Or, for still another example, what if a man owns a large house in the suburbs, an extensive apartment in the city, a ski lodge in the mountains, a beach house at the shore, two or three other homes at convenient sites, three yachts, a jet plane, and seven cars? Why do we prevent a poor man who has nothing—no home, no car, and certainly no yacht or jet plane—from occupying one of these many homes?

Perhaps the most common argument in favor of our protection of private property is the claim: We protect private property because it works to do so. That is, secure property rights are viewed as a basis for a stable and prosperous society. If people do not know that their accumulated wealth—held in the form of cash, land, houses, or factories—will be protected by society, they will see little point in trying to accumulate. According to the argument, if the pharmaceutical company cannot be assured of the profit from its patent, it will have no incentive to finance the research that leads to the drug's development. And if the state did not protect people's wealth, society could be in a continual state of instability and conflict.

As a defense of private property rights, however, this it-works-to-do-so argument is incomplete, as the *Waschak* and *Borman* cases illustrate, because it does not tell us what to do when property rights come into conflict with one another. This defense of property rights is also flawed because it is too vague, failing to provide a sufficiently clear statement of what things can legitimately be held as private property. Can air or water or people be held as private property? Can a patent be held forever?

What's more, the argument puts defenders of property rights in a precarious position because it implicitly concedes that private property rights exist in order to serve the larger good of society. If we determine that the larger good of society dictates a change in property rights—new restrictions on the use of property, for example—then the it-works-to-do-so argument provides no defense.

In many instances, property owners have claimed that environmental regulations infringe on their property rights. Property owners who are prevented from establishing a CAFO as in the Borman case, from filling wetlands, from building along fragile coast lines, or from destroying the habitat of an endangered species argue that government regulation is, in effect, taking away their property because it is reducing the value of that property. And they demand payment for this "taking." Such a claim loses its ideological and legal force, however, in a world where property rights change, where they are a creation of society, and where the larger good of society is the ultimate justification for protecting private property.

While questions about property rights are surrounded by ideology, legal com-plications, and arguments about the larger good of society, at the core of these questions lie fundamental disputes about the distribution of wealth. Who gets to use a field, the extent of a pharmaceutical company's patent rights, the preservation of a rich man's houses—each of these examples illustrates a conflict over the distribution of wealth as much as it illustrates a complication of how we define and protect property rights. Property rights are the rules of the game by which society's wealth gets divided up, and how we shape those rules is very much connected to how we define the larger good of society.

Patents versus Life

The relationship between property rights and the larger good of society has come to a head in recent years in the dispute over patent rights and AIDS drugs. It has become increasingly apparent that, when it comes to protecting the property rights of the pharmaceutical companies that hold patents on these life-saving drugs, it-*doesn't*-work-to-do-so.

In low-income countries, multinational pharmaceutical companies have attempted to enforce their patents on life-saving AIDS drugs and prevent the provision of these drugs at affordable prices. The matter has been especially important in several African countries where governments, ignoring the companies' patents, have taken steps to allow local production or importation of low-cost generic forms of the drugs. Large pharmaceutical corporations such as Glaxo, Merck, and Roche have fought back, and their resistance has received extensive support from the U.S. government. In 1998, for example, the South African government of Nelson Mandela passed a law allowing local firms to produce low-cost versions of the AIDS drugs on which U.S. pharmaceutical firms hold patents. The Clinton administration responded on behalf of the firms, accusing the South Africans of "unfair trade practices" and threatening the country with trade sanctions if it implemented the law.

The drug companies have since backed off, seeking compromises that would allow access to the drugs in particular cases but that would avoid precedents undermining their property rights in the patents.

The conflict between patent rights and the availability of AIDS drugs, however, has continued and spread. In Thailand, for example, the Government Pharmaceutical Organization (GPO) sought permission from the country's Commerce Department to produce a drug, didanosine, for which Bristol-Myers Squibb holds the patent. In spite of the fact that the locally produced drug would allow treatment of close to a million HIV-positive people in Thailand who would otherwise be unable to afford the didanosine, the permission was rejected because the Thai Commerce Department feared trade retaliation from the United States. Instead, the GPO was only allowed to produce a form of the drug that has greater side effects. Early in 2004, however, Bristol-Myers Squibb ceded the issue. Fearing public outcry and damaging precedents in the courts, the company surrendered in Thailand its exclusive patent rights to manufacture and sell the drug.

These conflicts have not been confined to the particular case of AIDS drugs, but have also been major issues in World Trade Organization (WTO) negotiations on the international extension of patent rights in general. Popular pressure and government actions in several low-income regions of the world have forced compromises from the companies and at the WTO.

But the dispute is far from over, and it is not just about formal issues of property rights and patents. At its core, it is a dispute over whether medical advances will be directed toward the larger good of society or toward greater profits for the pharmaceutical companies and their shareholders. It is a dispute over the distribution of wealth and income.

"Free the Mouse!"

Patents and, similarly, copyrights are a form of property (known as "intellectual property") that is quite clearly a creation of society, and the way society handles patents and copyrights does a great deal to shape the distribution of wealth and income. Acting through the state (the Department of Commerce in the United States), society gives the creator of a new product exclusive rights—in effect, monopoly control —to make, use, or sell the item, based on the general rationale that doing so will encourage the creation of more products (machines, books, music, pharmaceuticals, etc.).

The general rationale for these property rights, however, does not tell us very much about their nature. How long should patents and copyrights last? What can and what cannot be patented? What, exactly, constitutes an infringement of the copyright holder's property rights? And what if the rationale is wrong in the first place? What if patent and copyright protections are not necessary to promote creative activity? The answer to each of these questions is contested terrain, changing time and again as a consequence of larger political and social changes.

Beyond the issue of AIDS drugs, there are several other patent or copyright-related conflicts that illustrate how these rights change through conflict and the exercise of political power. One case is the Napster phenomenon, where people have shared music files over the Internet and generated outcry and lawsuits from music companies. This battle over property rights, inconceivable a generation ago, is now the subject of intense conflict in the courts.

An especially interesting case where rights have been altered by the effective use of political power has been the Mickey Mouse matter. In 1998, Congress passed the Sonny Bono Copyright Term Extension Act, extending copyright protection 20 years beyond what existing regulations provided for. One of the prime beneficiaries of—and one of the strongest lobbyists for—this act was the Disney company; the act assures Disney's control over Mickey Mouse until 2023—and Pluto, Goofy, and Donald Duck until 2025, 2027, and 2029, respectively.

Not surprisingly, the Copyright Extension Act aroused opposition, campaigning under the banner "Free the Mouse!" Along with popular efforts, the act was challenged in the courts. While the challenge had particular legal nuances, it was based on the seemingly reasonable argument that the Copyright Extension Act, which protects creative activity retroactively, could have no impact now on the efforts of authors and composers who created their works in the first half of the 20th century. The Supreme Court, apparently deciding that its view of the law trumped this reasonable argument, upheld the act. Congress and the Court provided a valuable handout to Disney and other firms, but it is hard to see how a 20-year extension of copyright protection will have any significant impact on creative efforts now or in the future.

"Could You Patent the Sun?"

Indeed, in a recent paper issued by the Federal Reserve Bank of Minneapolis, economists Michele Boldrin and David K. Levine suggest that the government's granting of protection through patents and copyrights may not be necessary to encourage innovation. When government does grant these protections, it is granting a form of monopoly. Boldrin and Levine argue that when "new ideas are built on old ideas," the monopoly position embodied in patents and copyrights may stifle rather than encourage creativity. Microsoft, a firm that has prospered by building new ideas on old ideas and then protecting itself with patents and copyrights, provides a good example, for it is also a firm that has attempted to control new innovations and limit the options of competitors who might bring further advances. (Microsoft, dependent as it is on microprocessors developed in federal research programs and on the government-sponsored emergence of the Internet, is also a good example of the way property is often brought into being by public, government actions and then appropriated by private interests. But that is another story.)

Boldrin and Levine also point out that historically there have been many periods of thriving innovation in the absence of patents and copyrights. The economic historian David Landes relates how medieval Europe was "one of the most inventive societies that history has known." Landes describes, as examples, the development of the water wheel (by the early 11th century), eyeglasses (by the early 14th century), and the mechanical clock (by the late 13th century). Also, first invented by the Chinese in the ninth century, printing rapidly developed in Europe by the middle of the 15th century with the important addition of movable type. Yet the first patent statute was not enacted until 1474, in Venice, and the system of patents spread widely only with the rise of the Industrial Revolution. (There had been earlier ad hoc patents granted by state authorities, but these had limited force.)

Even in the current era, experience calls into question the necessity of patents and copyrights to spur innovations. The tremendous expansion of creativity on the Internet and the associated advances of open-access software, in spite of Microsoft's best efforts to limit potential competitors, illustrate the point.

The most famous inventor in U.S. history, Benjamin Franklin, declined to obtain patents for his various devices, offering the following principle in his autobiography: "That as we enjoy great Advantages from the Inventions of Others, we should be glad of an Opportunity to serve others by any Invention of ours, and this we should do freely and generously." Probably the most outstanding example of successful research and scientific advance without the motivation of patents and consequent financial rewards is the development of the polio vaccine. Jonas Salk, the principal creator of the polio vaccine, like Franklin, did not seek patents for his invention, one that has saved and improved countless lives around the world. Salk was once asked who would control the new drug. He replied: "Well, the people, I would say. There is no patent. Could you patent the sun?"

It turns out, then, that there is no simple answer to the question: "Why do we protect private property?" because the meaning of private property rights is not fixed but is a continually changing product of social transformation, social conflict, and political power. The courts are often the venue in which property rights are defined, but, as illustrated by the Pennsylvania and Iowa cases, the definitions provided by the courts change along with society.

The scourge of AIDS combined with the advent of the current wave of globalization have established a new arena for conflict over patent laws governing pharmaceuticals, and an international social movement has arisen to contest property laws in this area. The advances of information technology have likewise generated a new round of legal changes, and the interests, demands, and actions of a vast array of music listeners will be a major factor affecting those changes. With the emergence of the environmental movement and widespread concern for the protection of the natural environment, traditional views of how owners can use their land are coming into question. When society begins to question property rights, it is also questioning the distribution of wealth and income, and it is questioning the distribution of power.

Few realms of property rights can be taken for granted for very long. Whether we are talking about property in the most tangible form as land or property in the intangible form of patents and copyrights, the substance of property rights—who has a right to what and why—is continually changing. ❏

SOURCES: Eric Freyfogle, *The Land We Share: Private Property and the Common Good*, Island Press, 2003; Michele Boldrin and David K. Levine, *Perfectly Competitive Innovation*, Centre for Economic Policy Research working paper series, *March 2002*.

Writing just before the subprime mortgage crash of 2007, Howard Karger warned us of the policies and myths that championed home ownership, even as the system was rewarding the financial industry for taking advantage of poor and working-class borrowers. In this updated version of his article, Karger describes the results of the subprime debacle for those families who have borne the brunt of the crash.

THE HOMEOWNERSHIP MYTH

BY HOWARD KARGER
September/October 2007; revised October 2012

Anyone who has given the headlines even a passing glance recently knows the subprime mortgage industry is in deep trouble. Since 2008, more than 100 mortgage lenders (most offered subprime loans) have quit the business or gone bankrupt. In 2008, Bank of America purchased the bankrupt Countrywide Financial for the fire sale price of $4.1 billion. Two years before that, Countrywide was worth more than $20 billion and financed 20% of all U.S. mortgages, amounting to 3.5% of the nation's GDP. In 2010, Bank of America agreed to pay $108 million to about 200,000 homeowners who were charged improper late fees by Countrywide.

Despite the subprime crash of 2007, by 2012 a Federal Reserve survey of senior loan officers found that six out of sixty lenders (10%) said they still make high-cost subprime loans to high-risk home buyers. That number has been going up as the U.S. housing market has been showing more signs of life and investors have been looking for higher yields, which in subprime mortgages can top 7.5%. While mortgage foreclosures resulting from the subprime crisis had eased somewhat by 2012, still one in eight mortgages were delinquent or in foreclosure. Specifically, in late 2012, 7.6% of mortgages were delinquent and 4.3% were in foreclosure.

What's conspicuously absent from the news reports is the effect of the subprime lending debacle on poor and working-class families who bought into the dream of homeownership, regardless of the price. Sold a false bill of goods, many of these families face foreclosure and the loss of the small savings they invested in their homes. It's critical to examine the housing crisis not only from the perspective of the banks and the stock market, but also from the perspective of the families whose homes are on the line. It is also critical to uncover the systemic reasons for the burst of housing-market insanity that saw thousands upon thousands of families signing up for mortgage loans that were likely to end in failure and foreclosure.

Like most Americans, I grew up believing that buying a home represents a rite of passage. Americans typically view homeownership as the best choice for everyone, everywhere and at all times. The more people who own their own homes, the common wisdom goes, the more robust the economy, the stronger the community, and the greater the collective and individual benefits. Homeownership is the ticket to the middle class through asset accumulation, stability, and civic participation.

For the most part, this is an accurate picture. Homeowners get a foothold in a housing market which, until 2008, seemed to have an almost infinite price ceiling. They enjoy important tax benefits. Moreover, owning a home in 2012 was 45% cheaper than renting. Most importantly, homeownership builds equity and accrues assets for the next generation by promoting forced savings. These savings are reflected in the data showing that, according to the National Housing Institute's Winton Picoff, the median wealth of low-income homeowners is 12 times higher than that of renters with similar incomes. Plus, owning a home is a status symbol: homeowners are seen as winners compared to renters.

Homeownership may have positive effects on family life. Ohio University's Robert Dietz found that owning a home contributes to household stability, social involvement, environmental awareness, local political participation and activism, good health, low crime, and beneficial community characteristics. Homeowners are better citizens, are healthier both physically and mentally, and have children who achieve more and are better behaved than those of renters.

Johns Hopkins University researchers Joe Harkness and Sandra Newman looked at whether homeownership benefits kids even in distressed neighborhoods. Their study concluded that "[h]omeownership in almost any neighborhood is found to benefit children. ... Children of most low-income renters would be better served by programs that help their families become homeowners in their current neighborhoods instead of helping them move to better neighborhoods while remaining renters." (Harkness and Newman also found, however, that the positive effects of homeownership on children are weaker in unstable low-income neighborhoods. Moreover, the study cannot distinguish whether homeownership leads to positive behaviors or whether owners were already predisposed to these behaviors.)

Faith in the benefits of homeownership—along with low interest rates and a range of governmental incentives—have produced a surge in the number of low-income homeowners. In 1994, President Bill Clinton set—and ultimately surpassed—a goal to raise the nation's overall homeownership rate to 67.5% by 2000. Much of that gain was earmarked for low-income families. By 2012, 65.4% of families owned their homes, down from the peak of 69.2% in 2004. By 2003, 48% of black households were homeowners, up from 34.5% in 1950. However, by 2012 black homeownership rates had fallen to 44.8 percent. By comparison, the homeownership rate for white Americans was 74.1%.

Government efforts to increase homeownership for low-income families include both demand-side enticements (e.g., homeowner tax credits and housing cost assistance programs) and supply-side strategies (e.g., developer incentives). Federal housing programs insure millions of loans a year to help low-income homebuyers. Fannie Mae and Freddie Mac—now under federal conservatorship—buy mortgages from lenders, guarantee the notes, and then resell them to investors. By the 1990s, they had increasingly turned their attention to low-income homebuyers as the upper-income housing market became more saturated. Banking industry regulations such as the Community Reinvestment Act and the Home Mortgage Disclosure Act encouraged homeownership by reducing lending discrimination in underserved markets.

The Department of Housing and Urban Development (HUD) adapted some of its programs to help renters focus on homeownership. For instance, cities and towns could use the federal dollars they received through HOME (the Home Investment Partnerships Act) and Community Development Block Grants to provide housing grants, down payment loans, and closing cost assistance. The American Dream Downpayment Initiative, passed by Congress in 2003, authorized up to $200 million a year for down payment assistance to low-income families. Private foundations followed suit. The Ford Foundation focused its housing-related grants on homeownership rather than rental housing because it viewed homeownership as an important form of asset-building and the best option for low-income people.

The Downsides of Homeownership

Despite some undeniable benefits, homeownership is not the best option for everyone. For many low-income families, buying a home imposes burdens that end up outweighing the benefits. For example, from 2006 to 2009, national housing prices fell by almost 30%, and in some areas, by as much as 50% or more. As a result, 23% of all mortgages were "underwater" (i.e., the mortgage was higher than the cost of the home).

It is time to reassess the emphasis on homeownership, which has been driven both by an honest belief in the advantages of owning a home, but also by a wide-ranging coalition of business interests that gain when a new cohort of buyers is brought into the housing market.

Low-income families can run into numerous pitfalls when they buy a home. Some of these problems stem from the kinds of houses the poor can afford to buy (i.e., in poor condition with high maintenance costs), in affordable yet economically distressed neighborhoods, based on dodgy financing that includes high interest rates, high fees, and risky gimmicks. The often unstable employment prospects of the poor make homeownership even riskier. Taken together, these factors make a home purchase a far riskier proposition for low-income families than for middle- and upper-income households.

Most low-income families only have the financial resources to buy rundown houses in distressed neighborhoods marked by few jobs, high crime rates, a dearth of services, and poor schools. Few middle-class homebuyers would hitch themselves to 30-year mortgages in these kinds of communities. Like their wealthier counterparts, poor families also have an interest in buying a home in safe neighborhoods with good schools.

Homeownership is no automatic hedge against rising housing costs. On the contrary: lower-end affordable housing stock is typically old, in need of repair, and expensive to maintain. These are some of the first houses that take the hit in a downward housing market. Low-income families often end up paying inflated prices for homes that are beset with major structural or mechanical problems masked by cosmetic repairs. A University of North Carolina study sponsored by the national nonprofit organization NeighborWorks found that almost half of low-income homebuyers experienced major unexpected costs due to the age and condition of their homes. If you rent, you can call the landlord; but a homeowner can't take herself to court because the roof leaks, the plumbing is bad, or the furnace or hot water heater quits working.

Besides maintenance and repairs, the expenses of home ownership also include cost of property taxes and homeowners insurance, both of which have skyrocketed. Between 1997 and 2002, property tax rates rose nationally by more than 19%. Ten states (including giants Texas and California) saw their property tax rates rise by 30% or more during that period. In the suburbs of New York City, property tax rates grew two to three times faster than personal income from 2000 to 2004.

Nationally, the average homeowner's annual insurance premiums rose a whopping 62% from 1995 to 2005—twice as fast as inflation. Low-income homeowners in distressed neighborhoods are hit especially hard by high insurance costs. According to a Conning and Co. study, 92% of large insurance companies run credit checks on potential customers. These credit checks translate into insurance scores that are used to determine whether the carrier will insure an applicant at all, and if so, what they will cover and how much they will charge. Those with poor or no credit are denied coverage, while those with limited credit pay high premiums. Needless to say, many low-income homeowners lack stellar credit scores. Credit scoring may also partly explain why, according to HUD, "Recent studies have shown that, compared to homeowners in predominantly white-occupied neighborhoods, homeowners in minority neighborhoods are less likely to have private home insurance, more likely to have policies that provide less coverage in case of a loss, and are likely to pay more for similar policies."

With few cash reserves, low-income families are a heartbeat away from financial disaster if their wages decline (or if they become unemployed), property taxes or insurance rates rise, or expensive repairs are needed. With most or all of their savings in their homes, these families often have no cushion for emergencies. HUD data show that between 1999 and 2001, low- and moderate-income homeowners were the only group whose housing conditions worsened—meaning, by HUD's definition, the only group in which a larger share of households spent over 30% of gross household income on housing in 2001 than in 1999. The National Housing Conference reports that 51% of working families with critical housing needs (i.e., those spending more than 50% of gross household income on housing) are homeowners.

Most people who buy a home imagine they will live there for a long time, benefitting from a secure and stable housing situation. For many low-income families, this is not the case. According to a 2005 study by Carolina Katz Reid of the University of Washington, nationwide data from 1976 to 1993 revealed that 36% of low-income homeowners gave up or lost their homes within two years and 53% exited within five years. Reid found that very few low-income families ever bought another house after returning to renting. A 2004 HUD research study by Donald Haurin and Stuart Rosenthal reached similar conclusions. Following a national sample of African Americans from youth (ages 14 to 21) in 1979 to middle age in 2000, the researchers found that 63% of the sample owned a home at some point, but only 34% still did in 2000.

Low-income homeowners, often employed in unstable jobs with stagnant incomes, few health care benefits, limited or no sick days, and little vacation time, may find it almost impossible to keep their homes if they experience a temporary job loss or a change in family circumstances. Homeownership can also limit financial opportunities. A 1999 study by economists Richard Green (University of Wisconsin) and Patric Hendershott (Ohio State University) found that states with the highest homeownership rates also had the highest unemployment rates. Their report concluded that homeownership may constrain labor mobility since the high costs of selling a house make unemployed homeowners reluctant to relocate to find work.

Special tax breaks have been a key selling point of homeownership. If mortgage interest and other qualifying expenses come to less than the standard deduction ($11,900 for married couples filing a joint return in 2012), there is no tax advantage to homeownership. That is one reason why only 34% of taxpayers itemize their mortgage interest, local property taxes, and other deductions. Even in families who itemize, the effective tax saving is usually only from 10 to 35 cents for every dollar paid in mortgage interest. In other words, the mortgage deduction benefits primarily those in high income brackets who need to shelter their income; it means little to low-income homeowners.

Finally, homeownership promises growing wealth as home prices rise. But the homes of low-income, especially minority, homeowners generally do not appreciate (and since 2007 have depreciated) as much as middle-class housing. Low-income households typically purchase homes in distressed neighborhoods where significant appreciation is unlikely. Among other reasons, if financially-stressed property owners can't afford to maintain their homes, nearby property values fall. Reid's longitudinal study surveyed low-income minority homeowners from 1976 to 1994 and found that they realized a 30% increase in the value of their homes after owning for 10 years, while middle- and upper-income white homeowners enjoyed a 60% jump.

"Funny Money" Mortgages and Other Travesties

Buying a home and taking on a mortgage are scary, and people often leave the closing in a stupor, unsure of what they signed or why. My partner and I bought a house a few years ago and, like many buyers, we didn't retain an attorney. The title company had set aside one hour for the closing. In that hour, more than 125 single-spaced pages (much in small print) were put in front of us. More than 60 required our signature or initials. It would have been difficult for us to digest these documents in 24 hours, much less one hour. When we asked to slow down the process, we were met with impatience. After the closing, Anna asked, "What did we sign?" I was clueless.

Yet buying a home is the largest purchase most families will make in their lifetimes, the largest expenditure in a family budget, and the single largest asset for two-thirds of homeowners. It's also the most fraught with danger.

For low-income families in particular, homeownership can turn out to be more a crushing debt than an asset-building opportunity. The primary reason for this is the growing chasm between home prices and the stagnant or declining incomes of millions of working-class Americans. From 1996 to 2006, the average home price rose from $107,000 to $192,000, an 80% increase. Even though the average home price fell to $142,000 in 2008, it was still $35,000 higher than in 1996. At the same time, yearly median household income in 2010 reached its lowest level since 1996, slipping to $49,445 from $50,599. Hence, the affordability barrier continues to remain high, especially for low income earners with stagnant or declining incomes.

Current incomes simply do not support even lower home prices. For example, even with lower housing prices, only 50% of Californians can afford to purchase

A Glossary of 'Creative' Home Loans

The home loan products marketed widely to low- and moderate-income families were generally adjustable-rate mortgages (ARMs) with some kind of twist. Here are a few of those "creative" (read: confusing and risky) mortgage options.

Option ARMs: With this loan, borrowers chose which of three or four different—and fluctuating—payments to make:

• full (principal+interest) payment based on a 30-year or 15-year repayment schedule.

• interest-only payment—did not reduce the loan principal or build homeowner equity. Borrowers paid only interest for a period of time, then faced a big jump in the size of monthly payments. Many were forced to refinance at higher interest rates and more onerous terms.

• minimum payment—often lower than one month's interest. The shortfall was added to the loan balance. The result was "negative amortization": over time, the loan principal went up, not down. Eventually the borrower had an "upside down" mortgage whereby the debt was greater than the market value of the home.

Even borrowers who paid more than the monthly minimums faced payment shocks. Option ARMs often started with a temporary super-low teaser interest rate (and correspondingly low monthly payments) that allowed borrowers to qualify for "more house." The catch? Because the low initial monthly payment (based on interest rates as low as 1.25%) was not enough to cover the real interest rate, the borrower eventually faced a sudden increase in monthly payments.

Balloon Loan: This loan was written for a short 5- to 7-year term during which the borrower paid either interest and principal each month or, in a more predatory form, interest only. At the end of the loan term, the borrower had to pay off the entire loan in a lump sum—the "balloon payment." At that point, buyers either refinanced or lost their homes. Balloon loans are known to real estate pros as "bullet loans," because if the loan comes due—forcing the owner to refinance—during a period of high interest rates, it's like getting a bullet in the heart. According to ACORN, the former housing-rights organization, about 10% of all subprime loans in 2006 were balloons.

Balloon loans were sometimes structured with monthly payments that failed to cover the interest, much less pay down the principal. Although the borrower made regular payments, her loan balance increased each month (negative amortization). Many borrowers were unaware that they had a negative amortization loan until they had to refinance.

Shared Appreciation Mortgage (SAM): These were fixed-rate loans for up to 30 years that had easier credit qualifications and lower monthly payments than conventional mortgages. In exchange for a lower interest rate, the borrower relinquished part of the future value of the home to the lender. Interest rate reductions were based on how much appreciation the borrower was willing to give up. SAMs discouraged "sweat equity" since the homeowner received only some fraction of the appreciation resulting from any improvements. These loans were likened to sharecropping.

Stated-Income Loan: Aimed at borrowers who do not draw regular wages from an employer but live on tips, casual jobs that pay under the table, commissions, or investments, this loan does not require W-2 forms or other standard wage documentation. The trade-off is higher interest rates.

No-Ratio Loan: The debt-income ratio (the borrower's monthly payments on debt, including the planned mortgage, divided by monthly income) is a standard benchmark that lenders use to determine how large a mortgage they will write. In return for a higher interest rate, the no-ratio loan abandoned this benchmark and was aimed at borrowers with complex financial lives or those who were experiencing divorce, the death of a spouse, or a career change.

—Amy Gluckman

a home. The fall in mortgage interest rates is partly neutralized by higher property taxes, insurance premiums, and utility costs.

Nevertheless, Americans owed $13 trillion in mortgage debt in 2012, $10 trillion of which was for residential property.

By the mid-1990s, the mortgage finance industry had developed creative schemes to squeeze potential homebuyers, albeit often temporarily, into houses they could not afford. It was a sleight of hand that required imaginative and risky financing for both buyers and financial institutions. Most of the "creative" new mortgage products were subprime mortgages, or loans offered to borrowers with problematic credit scores or other factors that dropped them into a lower lending category. Subprime mortgages carry interest rates ranging from a few points to 10 points or more above the prime or market rate, plus onerous loan terms. The subprime mortgage industry grew like wildfire in the 1990s and early 2000s and lenders originated $173 billion in subprime loans in 2005, up from only $25 billion in 1993. By 2006 the subprime market was valued at $600 billion, one-fifth of the $3 trillion U.S. mortgage market.

Subprime lending was risky. In the 37 years since the Mortgage Bankers Association (MBA) began conducting its annual national mortgage delinquency survey, 2006 saw the highest share of home loans entering foreclosure. In early 2007, according to the MBA, 13.5% of subprime mortgages were delinquent (compared to 4.95% of prime-rate mortgages) and 4.5% were in foreclosure. These numbers proved to be only the tip of the iceberg.

Before the 2007 mortgage industry collapse, the rate of return for subprime lenders was spectacular. Forbes claimed that subprime lenders could realize returns up to six times greater than the best-run banks. Traditionally, there were two main kinds of home loans: fixed-rate and adjustable-rate mortgages (ARMs). In a fixed-rate mortgage, the interest rate stays the same throughout the 15- to 30-year loan term. In a typical ARM, the interest rate varies over the course of the loan, although there is usually a cap. Both kinds of loans traditionally required borrowers to provide thorough documentation of their finances and a down payment of at least 10% (often 20%) of the purchase price.

ARMs can be complicated, and a Federal Reserve study found that 25% of homeowners with these kinds of mortgages were confused about their loan terms. Nonetheless, ARMs were—and still are—attractive because in the short run they promise an artificially low interest rate and affordable payments.

Even ARMs proved inadequate to the tasks of ushering more low-income families into the housing market and keeping home sales up in the face of skyrocketing prices. To meet the challenge, the mortgage industry created a whole range of "affordability" products with names like "no-ratio loans," "option ARMs," and "balloon loans" that it doled out like candy to people who were never fully apprised of the intricacies of these complicated loans. (See sidebar for a glossary of alternative mortgage products.) These mortgage options opened the door for almost anyone to secure a mortgage, whether or not their circumstances augured well for repayment. They also raised both the costs and risks of buying a home—sometimes steeply—for the low- and moderate-income families to whom they were largely marketed.

Beyond the higher interest rates that characterized the "affordability" mortgages, low-income homebuyers faced other costs as well. For one, predatory and subprime lenders often required borrowers to carry credit life insurance, which paid off a mortgage if the homeowner died. This insurance was frequently sold either by the lender's subsidiary or by a company that paid the lender a commission. Despite low pay-outs, lenders frequently charged high premiums for this insurance.

As many as 80% of subprime loans included prepayment penalties if the borrower paid off or refinanced the loan early, a scam that cost low-income borrowers about $2.3 billion a year and increased the risk of foreclosure by 20%. Prepayment penalties locked borrowers into a loan by making it difficult to sell the home or refinance with a different lender. And while some borrowers faced penalties for paying off their loans ahead of schedule, others discovered that their mortgages had "call provisions" which permitted the lender to accelerate the loan term even if payments were current.

And then there are all of the costs outside of the mortgage itself. Alternative mortgage products were not often sold by banks directly, but by mortgage brokers who acted as finders or "bird dogs" for lenders. According to the National Association of Mortgage Brokers, there were approximately 53,000 mortgage brokerage companies in the United States in 2007 that employed about 418,700 people. BusinessWeek noted that brokers originated up to 80% of new mortgages.

Largely unregulated, mortgage brokers live off loan fees, and their transactions are primed for conflicts of interest. For example, borrowers pay brokers a fee to help them secure a loan. Brokers may also receive kickbacks from lenders for referring a borrower, and many brokers steer clients to lenders that pay the highest kickbacks rather than those offering the lowest interest rates. Closing documents use arcane language ("yield spread premiums," "service release fees") to hide these kickbacks. In the heyday of the market, some hungry brokers fudged paperwork, arranged for inflated appraisals, or helped buyers find co-signers who had no intention of repaying the loan in the event of a default.

Whether or not a broker was involved, lenders inflated closing costs in a variety of ways: charging outrageous document preparation fees; billing for recording fees in excess of the law; and "unbundling," whereby closing costs were padded by duplicating charges already included in other categories.

All in all, housing is highly susceptible to the predations of the fringe economy. Unscrupulous brokers and lenders have considerable latitude to ply their trade, especially with vulnerable low-income borrowers.

Time to Change Course

Despite the hype, homeownership is not a cure-all for low-income families who earn less than a living wage and have poor prospects for future income growth. In fact, for some low-income families, homeownership leads to more debt and financial misery. With mortgage delinquencies and foreclosures at record levels, especially among low-income households, millions of people would be better off today if they had remained renters. Surprisingly, rents are generally more stable than housing prices. From 1995 to 2001 rents rose slightly faster than inflation, but not as rapidly as home prices. Beginning in 2004 rent increases began to slow—even in hot markets like San Francisco and Seattle—and fell below the rate of inflation.

In the mid-1980s, low- and no-down-payment mortgages led to increased foreclosures when the economy tanked. Those mortgage loans reappeared, along with a concerted effort to drive economically marginal households into homeownership and high levels of unsustainable debt. To achieve this goal, the federal government spent $100 billion a year for homeownership programs (including the $70-plus billion that the mortgage interest deduction cost the Treasury in 2007).

Instead of focusing exclusively on homeownership, a more progressive and balanced housing policy would address the diverse needs of communities for both homes and rental units, and would facilitate new forms of ownership such as community land trusts and cooperatives. A balanced policy would certainly aim to expand the stock of affordable rental units. Unfortunately, just the opposite was occurring in 2007: rental housing assistance was being starved to feed low-income homeownership programs. From 2004 to 2006, former President Bush and the Congress cut federal funding for public housing by 11%. Over the same period, more than 150,000 rental housing vouchers were cut.

The reason the United States lacks a sound housing policy is obvious if we follow the money. Overheated housing markets and rising home prices produced lots of winners. Real estate agents reaped bigger commissions. Mortgage brokers, appraisers, real estate attorneys, title companies, lenders, builders, home remodelers, and everyone else with a hand in the housing pie did well. Cities raised more in property taxes, and insurance companies enrolled more clients at higher premiums. According to the consulting firm Oxford Analytica, housing accounted for only 5% of GDP in 2006, but was responsible for up to 75% of all U.S. job growth from 2003 to 2007. Housing buffered the economy and kept the industry ticking in the short run by herding more low-income families into homes, regardless of the consequences. The only losers were renters squeezed by higher rents and the accelerated conversion of rental units into condominiums, and young middle-income families trying to buy their first home. This hardship is especially true for the thousands of low-income families for whom a home purchase became a financial nightmare. ❑

Sources: Carolina Katz Reid, "Studies in Demography and Ecology: Achieving the American Dream? A Longitudinal Analysis of the Homeownership Experiences of Low-Income Households," Univ. of Washington, CSDE Working Paper No. 04-04; Dean Baker, "The Housing Bubble: A Time Bomb in Low-Income Communities?" *Shelterforce Online*, Issue #135, May/June 2004, www.nhi.org/online/issues/135/bubble.html; Howard Karger, *Shortchanged: Life and Debt in the Fringe Economy* (Berrett-Koehler, 2005); National Multi Housing Council (www.nmhc.org). Dennis Cauchon, "Why Home Values May Take Decades to Recover," *USA Today*.

Meizhu Lui explains how government policies of discrimination and exclusion over many generations, and continuing into the present, have created different types of barriers to wealth creation for different racial groups.

PERSISTENT AND PERNICIOUS
The Racial Wealth Gap

BY MEIZHU LUI
October 2012

Race—a myth that skin color makes some people superior and some inferior—has been a tool for justifying the social and economic dominance of whites in the "most democratic country in the world." Both in times when the overall wealth gap has widened and in times when a rising tide has lifted almost all boats, a pernicious wealth gap between whites and non-white Americans has persisted.

Let's cut the cake by race. If you lined up all African-American families by the amount of assets they owned minus their debts and then looked at the family in the middle, that median family in 2009 had a net worth of $5,677. The median net worth of white families was $113,149, according to a 2011 Pew Research Center Report. That's 20 times more: for every dollar owned by white families, black families had only a nickel!

Latinos got only a teeny bit bigger crumb from the wealth cake. Their median net worth was $6,325. We do not know how much Native Americans have in individual or family assets because so little data has been collected, and because much of their assets are in collectively held land. However, their poverty and unemployment rates are the highest among racial/ethnic groups—at least one in four lives in poverty, and on some Indian reservations, unemployment is well over 50%. Asian Pacific Islander Americans (APIAs) are an extremely diverse group, with some wealthier ethnicities (well-educated people are more likely to come from China and India) and some at the bottom (for example, Cambodians and Samoans who are rural peoples). Taken as an aggregate and noting that this data masks big differences, APIAs attain close to but not the same levels of wealth as whites.

Forty years after the passage of equal opportunity legislation and four years after the election of our first black President, it is commonly assumed that we now live in a post-racial society. We all wish this feel-good story were true, but unfortunately, pesky facts get in the way.

Much attention, especially since Occupy, has been directed to the growth of the wealth gap between the richest 1% and the rest of us. But within that widening divide, the racial wealth gap has ripped open, deepening into an almost insurmountably steep and rocky canyon. In 2001, African American families had a dime to the white family's dollar, twice the ratio we see today. The Recession had something to do with this change, but the race gap was growing even before the Recession, especially between whites and blacks. According to a 2010 Research and Policy Brief by Tom Shapiro of the Institute on Assets and Social Policy at Brandeis University, over the course of one generation, from 1984 to 2007, the wealth gap between whites and African Americans increased more than four times—from $20,000 to $95,000. In 1984, high income African Americans, as one would expect, had several thousand dollars more in wealth holdings than middle-income whites. But by 2007, a white family earning around $30,000 in 1984 had accumulated $74,000, while a black family earning over $50,000 had only $18,000. If a family had $75,000 more in assets than another family, they could send a child to college, invest in a business, save their home, and survive a few rainy days, and avoid getting knocked back down the economic ladder.

For those who believe that our nation is now post-racial, the only explanation for today's racial inequalities are—you guessed it—the inherent and inherited inferiority of people without white skin. But individual choices or cultural behaviors have little to do with it. It has been documented that people of color of all non-white races were roughly three times more likely than whites to experience the "exuberance of the marketplace," as Alan Greenspan famously called it; they were steered to sub-prime high interest home loan, even when they qualified for a lower-interest prime loan. Communities of color have now disproportionately experienced the over-exuberance of the foreclosure crisis. Over the past 25 years, tax cuts on investment income and inheritances benefit the already wealthy. Other tax deductions for retirement accounts, college savings and home mortgage interest all benefit higher income families. In addition, discrimination in housing, employment, farm and business loans, and bank services is alive and well.

In fact, throughout U.S. history, deliberate government policies have transferred wealth from nonwhites to whites—essentially, affirmative action for whites. The specific mechanisms of the transfer have varied, as have the processes by which people have been put into racial categories in the first place. But a brief review of U.S. history, viewed through the lens of wealth, reveals a consistent pattern of race-based obstacles that have prevented Native Americans, African Americans, Latinos, and Asians from enjoying the economic opportunities afforded to whites. The effects of both advantage and disadvantage accumulate over generations, so that even with "equal opportunity", if two people are standing at two very different starting lines and allowed to take an equal number of steps, they will not end up at the same place.

Native Americans: In The U.S. Government We "Trust"?

When European settlers came to what would become the United States, Indian tribes in general did not consider land to be a source of individual wealth. It was a resource to be worshipped, treasured, and stewarded to protect all forms of life for seven generations out. Unfortunately for them, that concept of common ownership and the way of life they had built around it would clash mightily with the idea that parcels of land should be owned by individuals and used to generate short-term private profit.

After the American Revolution, the official position of the new U.S. government was that Indian tribes had the same status as foreign nations and that good relations with them should be maintained. However, as European immigration increased and westward expansion continued, the settlers increasingly coveted Indian land. The federal government pressured Native Americans to sign one treaty after another giving over land: In the United States' first century, over 400 Indian treaties were signed. Indians were forcibly removed, first from the south and then from the west, sometimes into reservations.

Eventually, the Indians' last large territory, the Great Plains, was taken over by whites. In one of the clearest instances of land expropriation, the 1862 Homestead Act transferred a vast amount of land from Indian tribes to white homesteaders by giving any white family 160 acres of land for free if they would farm it for five years. Of course, this massive land transfer was not accomplished without violence. General William Tecumseh Sherman, of Civil War fame, wrote: "The more [Indians] we can kill this year, the less will have to be killed the next year, for the more I see of these Indians, the more convinced I am that they all have to be killed or be maintained as a species of paupers." (Ironically, the Homestead Act is often cited as a model government program that supported asset-building.)

Out of the many treaties came the legal concept of the U.S. government's "trust responsibility" for the Native nations, similar to the relationship of a legal guardian to a child. In exchange for land, the government was to provide for the needs of the Native peoples. Money from the sale of land or natural resources was to be placed in a trust fund and managed in the best interests of the Indian tribes. The government's mismanagement of Indian assets was pervasive; yet, by law, Indian tribes could not fire the designated manager and hire a better or more honest one. One example of poor "trust" was that when oil and valuable minerals were discovered on reservation land, the Bureau of Indian Affairs allowed white-owned companies to extract those substances at great profit, with little compensation to the Indian "owners."

The Dawes Act of 1887 was designed to pressure Indians to assimilate into white culture: to adopt a sedentary life style and end their tradition of collective land ownership. The law broke up reservation land into individual plots and forced Indians to attempt to farm "western" style; "surplus" land was sold to whites. Under this scheme, millions more acres were transferred from Native Americans to whites.

After 1953, the U.S. government terminated the trust status of the tribes. While the stated purpose was to free Indians from government control, the new policy exacted a price: the loss of tribally held land that was still the basis of some tribes' existence. This blow reduced the remaining self-sufficient tribes to poverty and broke up tribal governments.

Thus, over a 200-year period, U.S. government policies transferred Native Americans' wealth—primarily land and natural resources—into the pockets of white individuals. This expropriation of vast tracts played a foundational role in the creation of the U.S. economy. The U.S. capitalist economy required the decimation of Native American peoples and the destruction of traditional Native economies. Only in recent years, through the effective use of lawsuits to resurrect tribal rights assigned under the old treaties, have some tribes succeeded in returning to tribal government and finding ways to lift their people from poverty.

African Americans: Slaves Can't Be Owners

From the earliest years of European settlement until the 1860s, African Americans were assets to be tallied in the financial record books of their owners. They could be bought and sold, they created more wealth for their owners in the form of children, they had no rights even over their own bodies, and they worked without receiving any wages. Slaves and their labor became the basis of wealth creation for plantation owners, people who owned and operated slave ships, and companies that insured them. Before the Civil War, the South was the wealthiest region; most of the wealth was held in the form of enslaved people.

At the end of the Civil War, there was an opportunity to recognize black Americans as people, not property. It was understood that to become economically free, a person needed not just to earn a wage, but to own and control land and resources. After emancipation, the Freedmen's Bureau and the occupying Union army began to distribute land to newly freed slaves: "40 acres and a mule." Not the 160 acres given to homesteaders at the same moment in history, but a modest start. But the Freedmen's Bureau was disbanded after only seven years, and the overwhelming majority of land that freed slaves had been allotted was returned to its former white owners. Unable to get a foothold as self-employed farmers, African Americans were forced to accept sharecropping arrangements. While sharecroppers kept some part of the fruits of their labor as in-kind income, the system kept them perpetually in debt and unable to accumulate any assets.

In 1883, the Supreme Court overturned the Civil Rights Act of 1875, which had given blacks the right to protect themselves and the property they managed to hold. By 1900, the Southern states had passed laws that kept African Americans separate and unequal, at the bottom of the economy. They began migrating to the North and West in search of opportunity.

Amazingly, some African-American families did prosper as farmers and businesspeople in the early 20th century. Some African-American communities thrived, even establishing their own banks to build savings and investment within the community. However, there was particular resentment against successful African Americans, and they were often targets of the vigilante violence common in this period. State and local governments helped vigilantes destroy their homes, run them out of town, and lynch those "uppity" enough to resist, and the federal government turned a blind eye. Sometimes entire black communities were targeted. For example, the African-American business district in north Tulsa, known as the "Black Wall Street" for its size and success, was torched on the night of June 21, 1921 by white rioters, who destroyed as many as 600 black-owned businesses. No one was charged; no one was compensated.

The Depression wiped out black progress, which did not resume until the New Deal period. Even then, African Americans were often barred from the new asset-building programs that benefited whites. Under Social Security, workers paid into the system and were guaranteed money in retirement. However, domestic and agricultural workers—the occupations held by most black women and men—were excluded from the program. Unemployment insurance and the minimum wage didn't apply to domestic workers or farm workers either. Other programs also left out non-whites. The Home Owners' Loan Corporation was created in 1933 to help homeowners avoid foreclosure, but not a single loan went to a black homeowner.

Following World War II, a number of new programs provided a ladder into the middle class—for whites. The GI Bill of Rights and low-interest home mortgages provided tax-funded support for higher education and for homeownership, two keys to family wealth building. The GI Bill provided little benefit to black veterans, however, because a recipient had to be accepted into a college—and many colleges accepted whites only. Likewise, housing discrimination meant that homeownership opportunities were greater for white families; subsidized mortgages were often simply denied for home purchases in black neighborhoods.

In *The Cost of Being African American*, sociologist Thomas Shapiro shows how, because of this history, even black families whose incomes are equal to whites' generally have unequal economic standing. Whites are more likely to have parents who benefited from the land grants of the Homestead Act, who have Social Security or retirement benefits, or who own their own homes. With their far greater average assets, whites can transfer advantage from parents to children in the form of college tuition payments, down payments on homes, or simply by being self-sufficient parents who do not need their children to support them in old age.

Not the waters of righteousness, but three hundred years of institutional disadvantage has come rolling down the pages of U.S. history, drowning black aspiration like the floodwaters of Katrina.

Latinos: In The United States' Back Yard

At the time of the American Revolution, Spain, not England, was the largest colonial landowner on the American continents. Unlike the English, the Spanish intermarried widely with the indigenous populations. In the 20th century, their descendants came to be identified as a distinct, nonwhite group. (In the 1800's, Mexicans were generally considered white.) Today, Latinos come from many countries with varied histories, but the relationship of Mexicans to the United States is the longest, and people of Mexican descent are still the largest Latino group in the United States (over 10% of the population and 66% of all Latinos in 2009).

Mexico won its independence from Spain in 1821. Three years later, the Monroe Doctrine promised the newly independent nations of Latin America "protection" from interference by European powers. However, this doctrine allowed the United States itself to intervene in the affairs of the entire hemisphere. Ever since, this paternalistic relationship (reminiscent of the "trust" relationship with Native tribes) has meant U.S. political and economic dominance in Mexico and Central and South America, causing the "push and pull" of the people of those countries into and out of the United States.

Mexicans and Anglos fought together to free Texas from Mexican rule, creating the Lone Star Republic of Texas, which was then annexed to the United States in 1845. Three years later, the United States went to war against Mexico to gain more territory and continue fulfilling its "manifest destiny"—"God shed his grace" on the U.S., asking it to expand "from sea to shining sea." Mexico lost the war and was forced to accept the 1848 Treaty of Guadalupe Hidalgo, which gave the United States half of Mexico's land. While individual Mexican landowners were at first assured that they would maintain ownership, the United States did not keep that promise, and the treaty ushered in a huge transfer of land from Mexicans to Anglos.

For the first time in these areas, racial categories were used to determine who could obtain land. The English language was also used to establish Anglo dominance; legal papers in English proving land ownership were required, and many Spanish speakers lost out as a result.

In the twentieth century, government policy continued to reinforce a wealth gap between Mexicans and whites. The first U.S.-Mexico border patrol was set up in 1924, and deportations of Mexicans became commonplace. Like African Americans, Latino workers were disproportionately represented in the occupations not covered by the Social Security Act. During World War II, when U.S. farms needed more agricultural workers, the federal government established the Bracero program, under which Mexican workers were brought into the United States to work for sub-minimum wages and few benefits, then kicked out when their labor was no longer needed. Even today, Mexicans continue to be used as "guest"—or really, reserve—workers to create profits for U.S. agribusiness.

The North American Free Trade Agreement which opened up Mexico to US business is another incarnation of the Monroe Doctrine. Trade and immigration policies are still being used to maintain U.S. control over its "back yard," and at the same time to deny those it is "protecting" the enjoyment of the benefits to be found in papa's "front yard." While money is free to flow across the Mexican border to the US, people are not. Without the rights of citizenship, asset ownership in the US is not possible for the many Latinos who have lived and worked here for most of their lives.

Asian Americans: Perpetual Foreigners

The first Asian immigrants, the Chinese, came to the United States at the same time and for the same reason as the Irish: to escape economic distress at home and to walk the streets of gold. Like European immigrants, the Chinese came voluntarily, paying their own passage, ready and willing to work hard in a new land. Chinese and Irish immigrants arrived in large numbers in the same decade, but their economic trajectories later diverged.

The major reason is race. The Naturalization Act of 1790, the first act of the newly formed U.S. government, limited eligibility for citizenship to "whites;" but no one was quite sure who was included in that ambiguous term. While the Irish, caricatured as apes in early cartoons, were soon recognized as white and were thus able to become citizens, Asians were a less clear case. Neither the Chinese nor anyone else knew if they were white or not— but they wanted to be! The rights and benefits of "whiteness" were obvious. Lawsuits filed first by Chinese, then by Japanese, Indian (South Asian), and Filipino immigrants all claimed that they should be granted "white" status. The outcomes were confusing; for example, South Asians, classified as Caucasian, were at first deemed white. Then, in later cases, courts decided that while they were Caucasian, they were not white. This legal history demonstrates how race was constructed from contention, one case at a time.

A series of laws limited the right of Asians to create wealth. Chinese immigrants were drawn into the Gold Rush; the Foreign Miners Tax, however, was designed to push them out of the mining industry. The tax provided 25% of California's annual state budget in the 1860s, but the government jobs and services the tax underwrote went exclusively to whites—one of the first tax-based racial transfers of wealth. And with the passage of the Chinese Exclusion Acts in 1882, the Chinese became the first nationality to be denied the right to join this immigrant nation; the numbers of Chinese-American citizens thus remained small until the 1960s.

The next wave of Asians came from Japan. Excellent farmers, the Japanese bought land and created successful businesses. White resentment led to the passage of the 1924 Alien Land Act, which prohibited non-citizens from owning land or corporations. Japanese Americans then found other ways to create wealth, inventing plant nurseries and the cut flower business. In 1941, they had in the face of all odds accumulated $140 million of business wealth.

World War II would change all that. In 1942, the Roosevelt administration forced Japanese Americans, foreign-born and citizen alike, to relocate to internment camps in the inland Western states. They had a week to dispose of their assets. Most had to sell their homes and businesses to whites at fire sale prices—an enormous transfer of wealth. In 1988, a successful suit for reparations gave the survivors of the camps $20,000 each, a mere fraction of the wealth that was lost.

Today, Asians are the group that as a whole has moved closest to economic parity with whites. While Asian immigrants have high poverty rates, American-born Asians have moved into professional positions, with incomes and assets approaching the levels of whites. However, glass ceilings and stereotypes still persist, so while Asians are highly successful small business owners, they are still rare at the higher levels of the corporate ladder.

The divergent histories of the Irish and the Chinese in the United States illustrate the powerful role of race in the long-term accumulation of wealth. Irish-Americans faced plenty of discrimination in the labor market: consider the "No Irish Need Apply" signs that were once common in Boston storefronts. But they never faced legal prohibitions on asset ownership and citizenship as Chinese immigrants did, or the expropriation of property as the Japanese did. Today, people of Irish ancestry have attained widespread material prosperity and access to political power, and some of the wealthiest and most powerful men in business and politics are of Irish descent. Meantime, the wealth and power of the Chinese are still marginal.

Persistent and Pernicious

Throughout U.S. history, federal policies have been the major factor in creating the myth of racial difference, and perpetuating the racial wealth divide. But history is about to take a qualitative change. Within the next generation, whites will no longer be in the majority. The race gap has become pernicious, not only for the growing numbers of our non-white population, but for the country as a whole as our economy faces major challenges. Can we afford to hobble our efforts at economic recovery by refusing to educate all our children, by wasting the energy and talents of people of color, by failing to feed, house and employ all our people? Do we want American Apartheid, with a minority of whites at the top and a growing majority of non-whites at the bottom?

The racial wealth divide is at the heart of these questions. The good news is that racial economic inequality is not a fact of nature. if policies created the problem, they can undo the damage. It's past time to close the gap. ❑

There is overwhelming statistical evidence that women's incomes lag men's, but what of wealth? Since wealth data is usually collected by household, it is difficult to quantify the gender wealth gap. Amy Gluckman reviews the history and contemporary facts about women and wealth ownership, in the United States and globally.

WOMEN AND WEALTH: A PRIMER

BY AMY GLUCKMAN
August 2004; revised November 2012

Put "wealth" and "women" into the same sentence, and contradictory images jump to mind: from Cleopatra, Marie Antoinette ("let them eat cake"), or Oprah, to an anonymous Asian, Latin American, or African woman lugging buckets or bales along a rugged path. Each of these images bears some truth: women's relationship with wealth is not a simple one. Women have, historically, held every possible juxtaposition with wealth and property. They have been property themselves, essentially sold in marriage, and in some instances inherited upon a husband's death by his brother or other male relative. They have almost universally faced restricted rights to own, control, and inherit property compared to men. Yet women have also been fabulously wealthy, and in not insignificant numbers—sometimes benefiting from family-owned wealth, occasionally wealthy in their own right. According to the 2012 Forbes 400 list of the wealthiest Americans, just 10% of the wealthiest Americans are women, and 87.5% of these women inherited their fortunes.

Furthermore, women's access to wealth is always conditioned by race, ethnicity, class, and all of the other parameters that shape the distribution of wealth in any society. Her gender is never the sole factor that shapes a woman's acquisition or use of property.

Marriage in particular has acted as a double-edged sword for women. On one hand, marriage typically gives a woman access to a man's income and wealth, affording her a higher standard of living than most social orders would have allowed her to achieve on her own. On the other hand, women have widely lost rights to own, control, and inherit wealth when they married. And when divorced or widowed, women have sometimes lost the access that marriage afforded them to their husbands' property without gaining any renewed rights to the property of their birth families.

Discriminatory laws and customs in many parts of the world have broken down, although it's sobering to remember how recent this change has been. In the United States, the first state to enact a comprehensive law removing restrictions on property ownership by married women was New York, in 1848. (Mississippi passed a limited statute in 1839. In a clear illustration of the complicated nexus of race, class, and gender that always shapes wealth ownership, the Mississippi law was primarily focused on giving married women the right to own slaves; the law was likely intended to offer plantation owners a way to avoid having their slaves seized to pay the husband's debts.) Other states were still passing similar laws up to 1900. Discrimination on the basis of sex and marital status in granting credit was made illegal at the federal level only in 1974. And of course, custom and economic institutions continued to discriminate against women in the ownership and control of property, access to credit in their own names, and related matters long after laws had been changed.

Around the world, many countries have only recently granted women—or married women in particular—property rights. Many countries still lack statutes giving women an expressed right to own land or other wealth in their own names.

Free But Not Equal

Even with the right to own wealth, women have not necessarily had the means to accumulate any. Some of the key factors for asset-building are income, education, and inheritance—and for each of these, women face obstacles, whether customary or legal.

In the rich countries, women today have largely the same educational attainment as men—up to, but not including, the highest levels. In the United States, for example, more girls than boys graduate from high school, and more women than men are enrolled in bachelor's degree programs. But there are still far more men than women who hold advanced degrees, especially in lucrative fields such as engineering, business, law, and medicine. Women workers remain concentrated in female-dominated occupations that continue to pay less than male-dominated occupations requiring the same degree of skill, preparation, and responsibility. This is a key reason for the persistent gender pay gap. The median annual income of U.S. men working full-time, year-round was $49,221 in 2010; the equivalent figure for women was $38,097, or only 77.4% of men's pay.

Women in the global South continue to face far larger education and income gaps, although with great variation among countries. Plenty of factors account for women's lack of wealth accumulation across the globe, but working too little is certainly not one of them. Women work longer hours every day than men in most countries, according to time-use studies assembled by the United Nations. The unequal work burden is most pronounced in rural areas, where women typically work 20% more minutes a day than men. Environmental problems in many countries have exacerbated women's work burden; a Population Reference Bureau report notes that, "Given the variety of women's daily interactions with the environment to meet household needs, they are often most keenly affected by its degradation. In the Sudan, deforestation in the last decade has led to a quadrupling of women's time spent gathering fuelwood. Because girls are often responsible for collecting water and fuelwood, water scarcity and deforestation also contribute to higher school dropout rates for girls."

Women's Wealth Holdings: What We Know

Today's wealth distribution reflects the accumulation of assets over years, even generations. So it will take time before the uneven but dramatic changes in women's status over the past few decades will show up in the wealth statistics. Given that, what is the distribution of wealth by gender today?

The first thing to note is that we really don't know what it is, for a number of reasons. First, data on personal wealth are scarce. Most countries do not systematically collect data on wealth ownership. Among the few countries that do are the United States, Sweden, Germany, and Britain.

Where data *are* regularly collected, the unit is typically the household, not the individual. Thus the assets of most married couples are assigned to both wife and husband equally in wealth surveys, obscuring any differences in the two spouses' authority to manage or benefit from those assets or to retain them if the marriage ends. This leaves gender comparisons possible only between unmarried men and unmarried women, a minority of the adult population.

In many countries, property ownership is governed by customary or informal rules rather than legal title. The term "ownership" itself is a simplification; ownership is really a bundle of rights that don't necessarily reside in the same person. In statutory systems and particularly in customary systems, women may have limited ownership rights; for example, a woman may have the right to use a piece of property but not to transfer or bequeath it. This limits the value of any simple, quantitative snapshot of wealth distribution by gender. Instead, a complex qualitative portrait is necessary.

Given all of these limitations, what *do* we know?

In the United States, the significant gap is between married and unmarried people. Married-couple households have median net worth far more than that of households headed by unmarried adults. However, there is also a gender gap between unmarried men and unmarried women. The median net worth of single men (never married, ages 18-64) in 2010 was $9,100; of single women, just $101. There is also a vast wealth gap between white women and women of color: the median net worth of households headed by single white women ages 18-64 in 2010 was $16,171; of households headed by single African-American women, $220; and of households headed by single Hispanic women, $205.

For the global South, systematic personal wealth data simply do not exist. But it's possible to assess some of the factors that are shaping the distribution of wealth by gender in poor and middle-income nations. The transition to formal systems of property ownership has had complex effects in many poor, predominantly rural countries. In theory, holding legal title to land can benefit small farmers—many of whom around the world are women. With a legal title, a farmer can use the land as collateral and thereby gain access to credit; she can also more confidently invest in improvements. However, in the process of formalizing land titles, governments have often taken land that was customarily under a woman's control and given the title to it to a man.

Likewise, land reform programs have often bypassed women. Women were "left out of the agrarian reforms of the 1960s and 1970s" in Latin America, according to a U.N. report, because household heads, to whom land titles were given, were simply assumed to be men. Women do 60% to 80% of the agricultural labor throughout the developing world, but are not nearly as likely to be actual landowners, and their average holdings are smaller than men's.

Lacking formal title to land, women have very limited access to agricultural credit. The same is true outside of agriculture: of the 300 million low-income self-employed women in the global South, hardly any have access to credit (aside from moneylenders, who typically charge exorbitant interest rates that can range up to 100% a month). Microcredit programs have sprung up in many countries and are making a dent in this problem, but just a dent.

What Is Wealth Good For?

Does it matter if women have less wealth and less capacity to acquire and control assets than men? Most adult women across the globe are married, and for most married women, these forms of gender-specific discrimination do not prevent them from enjoying a family standard of living underwritten by their husbands' income and wealth. But a woman's ability to own property in her own name turns out to be more important than it might appear. Women with property are less vulnerable to all of life's vicissitudes.

Asset ownership changes the balance of power between women and men. In a study of 500 urban and rural women in Kerala, India, Pradeep Panda of the Centre for Development Studies, Trivandrum, and Bina Agarwal of the Institute of Economic Growth, Delhi, found that women who are wealthless are considerably more vulnerable to domestic violence than women who own property. This ground-breaking study found that "49% of the women who owned neither land nor house suffered long-term physical violence, compared with 18% and 10% respectively of those who owned either land or a house, and 7% of those who owned both. The effect of property ownership on psychological violence is even more dramatic. While 84% of property-less women suffered abuse, the figure was much lower (16%) for women who owned both land and a house." The impact of property ownership on a woman's risk of violence was significant even after household economic status, woman's age, duration of marriage, childlessness, educational and employment levels, husband's alcohol consumption, childhood exposure to violence, and other key factors were controlled.

It has long been a matter of faith in the U.S. women's movement that all women can face domestic violence regardless of their economic circumstances. But owning and controlling some wealth surely offers women in rich countries the same kinds of protection the Kerala study revealed: a stronger position in the marital power dynamic, and the ability to exit. And owning some property no doubt underwrites a woman's ability to struggle against patriarchal institutions in other ways too, at least on an individual level, and to achieve her own potential. Virginia Woolf wrote, almost a century ago, that a woman who wanted to create literature needed a modest (unearned) income and a room of her own.

Woolf's vision is no less true today. But today most women around the world still don't have the modest unearned income or the room of their own—and not only because of their gender.

What then would a progressive feminist agenda around wealth look like? Of course, it would address all of the remaining customs, statutes, and institutional barriers that limit women's economic rights relative to men's. But it would also seek to reorient all economic institutions toward the provision of social forms of wealth and the diffusion of private wealth. Only a dual agenda like this can offer any hope—for achieving either gender equity *or* a decent standard of living—to a majority of the world's women. ❏

SOURCES: Survey of Consumer Finances (2010); Population Reference Bureau (2002), Women, Men, and Environmental Change: The Gender Dimensions of Environmental Policies and Programs; United for a Fair Economy (2012), "Born On Third Base: What The Forbes 400 Really Says About Economic Equality & Opportunity In America"; Institute for Women's Policy Research (2012), *The Gender Wage Gap: 2011*; Mariko Lin Chang (2012), "Median Wealth of Single Men, Single Women, and Couples (Married and Cohabitating), by Race/Ethnicity, Ages 18-64, 2010" (available at www.mariko-chang.com/wealthdata. html); Pradeep Panda and Bina Agarwal (2005), *Marital violence, human development and women's property status in India*, World Development 33(5): 823-850.

About one-third of single-mother families currently live in poverty. In the mid-1990s, the welfare system was fundamentally altered to require poor mothers to work outside their home. Randy Albelda analyzes how this new anti-poverty philosophy has been working.

DIFFERENT ANTI-POVERTY REGIME, SAME SINGLE-MOTHER POVERTY

BY RANDY ALBELDA
January/February 2012

Four years into a period of deep recession and persistent economic crisis, only now has the p-word—poverty—finally surfaced. The Census Bureau's September 13 announcement that the U.S. poverty rate had increased to 15.1% in 2010, up from 14.3% in 2009, put the issue of poverty onto page one, albeit briefly. In fact, poverty and how to address it have not been prominent items on the national agenda since the "welfare reform" debates of the 1980s and early 1990s.

"Welfare queens" may have disappeared from politicians' rhetoric, but poor people, disproportionately single mothers and their children, are still around. Single-mother families have been and continue to be particularly vulnerable to being poor. The September report showed the poverty rate for single mothers and their children rose as well: from 32.5% in 2009 to 34.2% in 2010.

It is remarkably hard to be the primary caregiver *and* garner enough income to support a family. This reality was built into the design of the first generation of federal anti-poverty programs in the United States. Developed beginning in the New Deal era, these programs were aimed at families with no able-bodied male breadwinner and hence no jobs or wages—single mothers, people with disabilities, and elders. Putting single mothers to work was thought to be undesirable. Or, white single mothers—there was much less reluctance in the case of black single mothers, who were largely excluded from the various anti-poverty programs until the 1960s.

The most important of the anti-poverty programs for single mothers was the cash assistance program, Aid to Dependent Children (later renamed Aid to Families with Dependent Children, or AFDC), established in 1935—also commonly referred to as "welfare." Other programs developed in the succeeding decades included Food Stamps, Medicaid, and housing assistance.

Then, in 1996, with the support of President Clinton, Congress abolished AFDC, replacing it with a block grant called TANF (Temporary Assistance to Needy Families), and passed a spate of other changes to related programs. The new anti-poverty regime implied a new social compact with the non-disabled, non-elder poor, supported by both conservatives and liberals: to require employment in exchange for—and ultimately be weaned off of—government support. In other words, the new mandate for poor adults, especially single mothers, was to get a job—any job.

And, in fact, in the ensuing years the number of poor families with wages from work increased. Moreover, welfare rolls dropped. And, in the first four years following welfare "reform," the official poverty rate for single-mother families fell too. (It has been increasing since 2000, although not quite back to its 1996 level.) But despite their higher wage income, many single-mother families are no better able to provide for their basic needs today than before the mid-1990s. Even the lower poverty rate may not reflect the real material well-being of many single moms and their children, given that their mix of resources has shifted to include more of the kinds of income counted by poverty measures and less of the uncounted kinds.

While TANF and the other legislative changes promote employment in theory, they did not reshape anti-poverty programs to genuinely support employment. Key programs are insufficiently funded, leaving many without access to child care and other vital work supports; income eligibility requirements and benefit levels designed for those with no earnings work poorly for low-wage earners; and the sheer amount of time it takes to apply for and keep benefits is at odds with holding down a job.

Ironically, there has been little or no talk of revisiting these policies despite the massive job losses of the Great Recession. With job creation at a standstill, in 2010 the unemployment rate for single mothers was 14.6% (more than one out of every seven). For this and other reasons, it is time to "modernize" anti-poverty programs by assuring they do what policy makers and others want them to do—encourage employment while reducing poverty. And they must also serve as an important safety net when work is not available or possible. But changes to government policies are not enough. If employment is to be the route out of poverty, then wages and employer benefits must support workers at basic minimum levels.

Ending "Welfare" and Promoting Employment

Among the changes to U.S. anti-poverty programs in the 1990s, the most sweeping and highly politicized involved AFDC, the cash assistance program for poor parents. The 1996 legislative overhaul gave states tremendous leeway over eligibility rules in the new TANF program. For the first time there was a time limit: states are not allowed to allocate federal TANF money to any adult who has received TANF for 60 months—regardless of how long it took to accrue 60 months of aid. And the new law required recipients whose youngest child is over one year old to do some form of paid or unpaid work—most forms of education and job training don't count—after 24 months of receiving benefits.

To accommodate the push for employment, Congress expanded the Earned Income Tax Credit, which provides refundable tax credits for low-income wage earners; expanded the Child Care Development Block Grant, which gives states money to help provide child care to working parents with low incomes, including parents leaving TANF; and established the State Children's Health Insurance Program (S-CHIP), in part out of a recognition that single mothers entering the workforce were losing Medicaid coverage yet often working for employers who provided unaffordable health insurance coverage or none at all. Even housing assistance programs started promoting employment: the Department of Housing and Urban Development encouraged local housing authorities to redesign housing assistance so as to induce residents to increase their earnings.

The strategy of promoting employment was remarkably successful at getting single mothers into the labor force. In 1995, 63.5% of all single mothers were employed; by 2009, 67.8% were. This rate exceeds that of married mothers, at 66.3%. So with all that employment, why are poverty rates still so high for single-mother families? The answer lies in the nature of low-wage work and the mismatch between poverty reduction policies and employment.

Single Mothers and Low-Wage Jobs Don't Mix

There are two fundamental mismatches single mothers face in this new welfare regime. The first has to do with the awkward pairing of poor mothers and low-wage jobs. In 2009 over one-third of single mothers were in jobs that are low paying (defined as below two-thirds of the median hourly wage, which was $9.06). In addition to the low pay, these jobs typically lack benefits such as paid sick or vacation days and health insurance. Many low-wage jobs that mothers find in retail and hospitality have very irregular work hours, providing the employers with lots of flexibility but workers with almost none. These features of low-wage work wreak havoc for single moms. An irregular work schedule makes child care nearly impossible to arrange. A late school bus, a sick child, or a sick child-care provider can throw a wrench in the best-laid plans for getting to and staying at work. Without paid time off, a missed day of work is a missed day of pay. And too many missed days can easily cost you your job.

Medicaid, the government health insurance program for the poor, does not make up for the lack of employer-sponsored health insurance common in low-wage jobs. Medicaid income eligibility thresholds vary state by state, but are typically so low that many low-wage workers don't qualify. Only 63% of low-wage single mothers have any health insurance coverage at all, compared to 82% of all workers. The new Patient Protection and Affordable Care Act (a/k/a Obamacare) may help, depending on the cost of purchasing insurance, but for now many low-wage mothers go without health care coverage.

Finally, there is the ultimate reality that there are only 24 hours in a day. Low wages mean working many hours to earn enough to cover basic needs. Yet working more hours means less time with kids. This can be costly in several ways. Hiring babysitters can be expensive. Relying heavily on good-natured relatives who provide care but may not engage and motivate young children also has costs, as does leaving younger children in the care of older brothers and sisters, who in turn can miss out on important after-school learning. Long work hours coupled with a tight budget might mean little time to help do homework, meet with teachers, or participate in in- and out-of-school activities that enrich children's lives.

A New Mismatch

The first generation of anti-poverty programs were designed on the assumption that recipients would not be working outside the home. Unfortunately, their successor programs such as TANF and SNAP, despite their explicit aim of encouraging employment, still do not work well for working people.

Poverty Remeasured

According to the Census Bureau, 46.2 million Americans were poor in 2010. But what exactly does "poor" mean? The academic and policy debates over how to measure poverty fill volumes. Some questions relate to the establishment of the poverty threshold. On what basis should the poverty line be drawn? Is poverty relative or absolute—in other words, if the average standard of living in a society rises, should its poverty threshold rise as well? Other questions concern measuring income. What kinds of income should be counted? Before or after taxes and government benefits? Who is included in the poverty assessment? (For example, those in institutional settings such as prisons are excluded from the official U.S. poverty measure—not a minor point when you consider that nearly 2.3 million adults were incarcerated in the United States as of the end of 2009.)

Established in 1963 by multiplying an emergency food budget by three, and adjusted solely for inflation in the years since, the official U.S. poverty thresholds are notoriously low. A family of four bringing in over $22,314—*including* any TANF cash assistance, unemployment or workers' comp, Social Security or veterans' benefits, and child support—is not officially poor. In many parts of the United States, $22K would not be enough to keep one person, let alone four people, off the street and minimally clothed and fed.

An interagency federal effort to develop a more realistic poverty level has just released its new measure, known as the Supplemental Poverty Measure. The SPM makes many adjustments to the traditional calculation:

• It counts the Earned Income Tax Credit and non-cash benefits such as food stamps and housing assistance as income.

• It subtracts from income out-of-pocket medical costs, certain work-related expenses (e.g., child care), and taxes paid.

• Its thresholds are adjusted for cost-of-living differences by region and are relative rather than absolute—basic expenses that are the building blocks of the threshold are pegged at the 33rd percentile of U.S. households.

The SPM poverty rate for 2009 was 15.7%, somewhat higher than the 14.5% official rate. More dramatic differences between the two poverty rates appeared in some subgroups, especially the elderly: 9.9% by the traditional measure versus 16.1% by the SPM, largely due to their high out-of-pocket medical expenses.

—Amy Gluckman

Sources: "Measure by Measure," *The Economist*, January 20, 2011; Ellen Frank, "Measures of Poverty," *Dollars & Sense*, January 2006; Center for Women's Welfare, Univ. of Wash. School of Social Work, "How Does the Self-Sufficiency Standard Compare to the New Supplemental Poverty Measure?"; U.S. Census Bureau, "How the Census Bureau Measures Poverty" and "Poverty Thresholds by Size of Family and Number of Children: 2010."

What does it mean that these programs are not designed for those with employment? There are two important features. First, income thresholds for eligibility tend to be very low—that is, only those with extremely low earnings qualify. For example, only two states have income thresholds above the poverty line for TANF eligibility. To get any SNAP benefits, a single mother needs to have income below 130% of the poverty line. Working full-time at $10 an hour (that's about $1,600 a month in take-home pay) would make a single mother with one child ineligible for both programs in all states. Moreover, even if you are eligible, these benefits phase out sharply. With TANF (in most states), SNAP, and housing assistance, for every additional dollar you earn, you lose about 33 cents in each form of support. This means work just does not pay.

Second, applying for and maintaining benefits under these programs often takes a great deal of time. Each program has particular eligibility requirements; each requires different sets of documents to verify eligibility. While some states have tried to move to a "one-stop" system, most require separate applications for each program and, often, one or more office visits. Recertification (i.e., maintaining eligibility) can require assembling further documentation and meeting again with caseworkers. If you have ever applied for one of these programs, maybe you have experienced how time-consuming—and frustrating—the process can be.

In short, the programs were designed for applicants and recipients with plenty of time on their hands. But with employment requirements, this is not the right assumption. Missing time at work to provide more paperwork for the welfare office is just not worth it; there is considerable evidence that many eligible people do not use TANF or SNAP for that reason. Even the benefit levels assume an unlimited amount of time. Until recently, the maximum dollar amount of monthly SNAP benefits was based on a very low-cost food budget that assumed hours of home cooking.

Unlike cash assistance or food assistance, child care subsidies are obviously aimed at "working" mothers. But this program, too, often has onerous reporting requirements. Moreover, in most states the subsidy phases out very quickly especially after recipients' earnings reach the federal poverty line. This means that a worker who gets a small raise at work can suddenly face a steep increase in her child-care bill. (Of course, this is only a problem for the lucky parents who actually receive a child-care subsidy; as mentioned earlier, the lack of funding means that most eligible parents do not.)

The Earned Income Tax Credit is a notable exception. The refundable tax credit was established explicitly to help working parents with low incomes. It is relatively easy to claim (fill out a two page tax form along with the standard income tax forms), and of all the anti-poverty programs it reaches the highest up the income ladder. It even phases out differently: the credit increases as earnings rise, flattens out, and then decreases at higher levels of earnings. Most recipients get the credit in an annual lump sum and so use it very differently from other anti-poverty supports. Families often use the "windfall" to pay off a large bill or to pay for things long put off, like a visit to the dentist or a major car repair. While helpful and relatively easy to get, then, the Earned Income Tax Credit does not typically help with day-to-day expenses as the other anti-poverty programs do.

Has Employment-Promotion "Worked"?

The most striking change in the anti-poverty picture since welfare reform was enacted is that the welfare rolls have plummeted. In 1996, the last full year under the old system, there were 4.43 million families on AFDC nationwide; in 2010, amid the worst labor market in decades, the TANF caseload was only 1.86 million. In fact, when unemployment soared in 2008, only 15 states saw their TANF caseloads increase. The rest continued to experience reductions. Plus, when the TANF rolls fell sharply in the late 1990s, so did Medicaid and Food Stamps enrollments. These programs have since seen increases in usage, especially since the recession, but it's clear that when families lose cash assistance they frequently lose access to other supports as well.

Welfare reform has worked very well, then, if receiving welfare is a bad thing. Indeed, advocates of the new regime tout the rapid and steep decline in welfare use as their main indicator of its success. In and of itself, however, fewer families using anti-poverty programs does not mean less poverty, more personal responsibility, or greater self-sufficiency. During the economic expansion of the late 1990s, the official poverty rate for single mothers and their children fell from 35.8% in 1996 to 28.5% in 2000. It has risen nearly every year since, reaching 34.2% in 2010. But if a successful anti-poverty effort is measured at all by the economic well-being of the targeted families, then that slight drop in the poverty rate is swamped by the 60% decrease in the number of families using welfare over the same period. Far fewer poor families are being served. In 1996, 45.7% of all poor children received some form of income-based cash assistance; in 2009, only 18.7% did. The Great Recession pushed 800,000 additional U.S. families into poverty between 2007 and 2009, yet the TANF rolls rose by only 110,000 over this period.

Data from federal government reports on TANF, depicted in the charts on the following page, nicely illustrate the dilemmas of the new welfare regime. The chart shows the total average amounts of earnings and the value of major government supports ("means-tested income") for the bottom 40% of single-mother families (by total income) between 1996 and 2009. It is clear that since welfare reform, these families are relying much more on earnings. But despite the additional work effort, they find themselves essentially no better off. The bottom 20% saw their package of earnings and government benefits *fall*: their average earnings have not increased much while government supports have dropped off, leaving them with fewer resources on average in 2009 than in 1996. For the second quintile, earnings increased substantially through the early 2000s, but benefits fell nearly as much, leaving this group only slightly better off over the period. And that is without taking into account the expenses associated with employment (e.g. child care, transportation, work clothes) and with the loss of public supports (such as increased co-payments for child care or health insurance). These women are working a lot more—in the second quintile about double—but are barely better off at all! So much for "making work pay."

More hours of work also means fewer hours with children. If the time a mother spends with her children is worth anything, then substituting earnings for benefits represents a loss of resources to her family.

EARNINGS AND MEANS-TESTED INCOME FOR THE BOTTOM TWO QUINTILES OF SINGLE-MOTHER FAMILIES, 1996-2005 (IN 2005 DOLLARS)

Bottom quintile of single-mother families

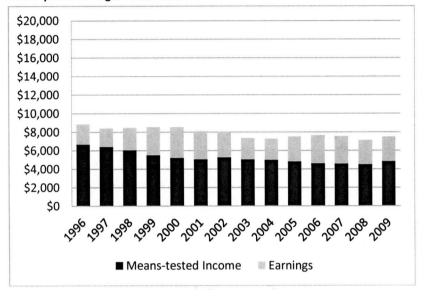

Second quintile of single-mother families

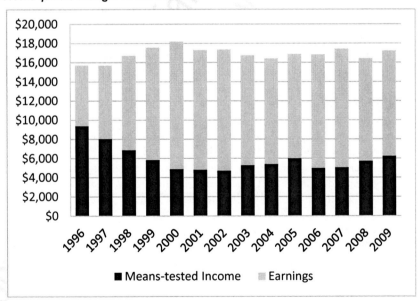

Those with negative income not included. Means-tested income is the total of Supplemental Security Income, Public Assistance, certain Veteran's Benefits, Food Stamps, School Lunch, and housing benefits.

Source: U.S. Department of Health and Human Services, The Office of Assistant Secretary for Planning and Evaluation; Table 4:3 of TANF 6th Annual Report to Congress (November 2004); Table 4:2 of TANF 8th Annual Report to Congress (June 2009); and Table 4-2 9th Annual Report to Congress (June 2012), using tabulations from the U.S. Census Bureau 1996-2009.

What Might Be Done?

Employment, even with government supports, is unlikely to provide a substantial share of single-mother families with adequate incomes. Three factors—women's lower pay, the time and money it takes to raise children, and the primary reliance on only one adult to both earn and care for children—combine to make it nearly impossible for a sizeable number of single mothers to move to stable and sufficient levels of resources.

Addressing the time- and money-squeeze that single mothers faced in the old anti-poverty regime and still face in the new one will take thoroughgoing changes in the relations among work, family, and income.

- *Make work pay by shoring up wages and employer benefits.* To ensure that the private sector does its part, raise the minimum wage. A full-time, year-round minimum wage job pays just over the poverty income threshold for a family of two. Conservatives and the small business lobby will trot out the bogeyman of job destruction, but studies on minimum-wage increases show a zero or even positive effect on employment. In addition, mandate paid sick days for all workers and require benefit parity for part-time, temporary, and subcontracted workers. This would close a loophole that a growing number of employers use to dodge fringe benefits.

- *Reform anti-poverty programs to really support employment.* To truly support low-wage employment, anti-poverty programs should increase income eligibility limits so that a worker can receive the supports even while earning and then phase out the programs more gradually so low-wage workers keep getting them until they earn enough not to need them. Also, streamline application processes and make them more user-friendly. Many states have done this for unemployment insurance, car registration, and driver's license renewal. Why not do the same for SNAP, TANF and Medicaid?

- *Support paid and unpaid care work.* A society that expects all able-bodied adults to work—regardless of the age of their children—should also be a society that shares the costs of going to work, by offering programs to care for children and others who need care. This means universal child care and afterschool programs. It also means paid parental leave and paid time off to care for an ill relative. The federal Family and Medical Leave Act gives most workers the right to take unpaid leaves, but many can't afford to. California and New Jersey have extended their temporary disability insurance benefits to cover those facing a wide range of family needs—perhaps a helpful model.

New anti-poverty regime, but same poverty problems. Most single mothers *cannot* work their way out of poverty—definitely not without the right kinds of supplemental support. There are many possible policy steps that could be taken to help them and other low-wage workers get the most out of an inhospitable labor market. But ultimately, better designed assistance to poor and low-income families, old fashioned cash assistance, and minimal employment standards must be part of the formula. ❑

Sources: Randy Albelda and Chris Tilly, *Glass Ceilings and Bottomless Pits: Women's Work, Women's Poverty*, South End Press, 1997; U.S. Census Bureau, *Historical Tables on Poverty*; Kaiser Family Foundation, "Income Eligibility Limits for Working Adults at Application as a Percent of the Federal Poverty Level by Scope of Benefit Package," statehealthfacts.org, January 2011; U.S. Dept. of Health and Human Services, *TANF 6th, 8th, and 9th Annual Report to Congress*, November 2004, July 2009, and June 2012; U.S. Dept. of Health and Human Services, *Estimates of Child Care Eligibility and Receipt for Fiscal Year 2006*, April 2010; Thomas Gabe, *Trends in Welfare, Work, and the Economic Well-being of Female Headed Families with Children: 1987-2005*, Congressional Research Service Report RL30797, 2007; Randy Albelda and Heather Boushey, *Bridging the Gaps: A Picture of How Work Supports Work in Ten States*, Center for Social Policy, Univ. of Mass. Boston and Center for Economic and Policy Research, 2007; author's calculations from the U.S. Census Bureau's Current Population Survey, various years.

Professor Richard D. Wolff traces the origins of the current economic crisis, which began in 2008, to decades of stagnating wages and rising inequality. Credit took the place of rising real wages as a way for workers to keep up with rising standards of consumption, until indebtedness reached unsustainable proportions.

CAPITALISM HITS THE FAN

BY RICHARD D. WOLFF
November/December 2008

Let me begin by saying what I think this crisis is not. It is not a *financial* crisis. It is a systemic crisis whose first serious symptom happened to be finance. But this crisis has its economic roots and its effects in manufacturing, services, and, to be sure, finance. It grows out of the relation of wages to profits across the economy. It has profound social roots in America's households and families and political roots in government policies. The current crisis did not start with finance, and it won't end with finance.

From 1820 to around 1970, 150 years, the average productivity of American workers went up each year. Average workers produced more stuff every year than they had the year before. They were trained better, they had more machines, and they had better machines. So productivity went up every year.

And, over this period of time, the wages of American workers rose every decade. Every decade, real wages—the amount of money you get in relation to the prices you pay for the things you use your money for—were higher than the decade before. Profits also went up.

The American working class enjoyed 150 years of rising consumption, so it's not surprising that it would choose to define its own self-worth, measure its own success in life, according to the standard of consumption. Americans began to think of themselves as successful if they lived in the right neighborhood, drove the right car, wore the right outfit, went on the right vacation.

But in the 1970s, the world changed for the American working class in ways that it hasn't come to terms with—at all. Real wages stopped going up. As U.S. corporations moved operations abroad to take advantage of lower wages and higher profits and as they replaced workers with machines (and especially computers), those who lost their jobs were soon willing to work even if their wages stopped rising. So real wages trended down a little bit. The real hourly wage of a worker in the 1970s was higher than what it is today. What you get for an hour of work, in goods and services, is less now that what your parents got.

Meanwhile, productivity kept going up. If what the employer gets from each worker keeps going up, but what you give to each worker does not, then the difference becomes bigger, and bigger, and bigger. Employers' profits have gone wild, and all the people who get their fingers on employers profits—the professionals who sing the songs they like to hear, the shareholders who get a piece of the action on each company's profits—have enjoyed a bonanza over the last thirty years.

The only thing more profitable than simply making the money off the worker is handling this exploding bundle of profits—packaging and repackaging it, lending it and borrowing it, and inventing new mechanisms for doing all that. That's called the finance industry, and they have stumbled all over themselves to get a hold of a piece of this immense pot of profit.

What did the working class do? What happens to a population committed to measuring people's success by the amount of consumption they could afford when the means they had always had to achieve it, rising wages, stop? They can go through a trauma right then and there: "We can't anymore—it's over." Most people didn't do that. They found other ways.

Americans undertook more work. People took a second or third job. The number of hours per year worked by the average American worker has risen by about 20% since the 1970s. By comparison, in Germany, France, and Italy, the number of hours worked per year per worker has dropped by 20%. American workers began to work to a level of exhaustion. They sent more family members—and especially women—out to work. This enlarged supply of workers meant that employers could find plenty of employees without having to offer higher pay. Yet, with more family members out working, new kinds of costs and problems hit American families. The woman who goes out to work needs new outfits. In our society, she probably needs another car. With women exhausted from jobs outside and continued work demands inside households, with families stressed by exhaustion and mounting bills, interpersonal tensions mounted and brought new costs: child care, psychotherapy, drugs. Such extra costs neutralized the extra income, so it did not solve the problem.

The American working class had to do a second thing to keep its consumption levels rising. It went on the greatest binge of borrowing in the history of any working class in any country at any time. Members of the business community began to realize that they had a fantastic double opportunity. They could get the profits from flat wages and rising productivity, and then they could turn to the working class traumatized by the inability to have rising consumption, and give them the means to consume more. So instead of paying your workers a wage, you're going to lend them the money—so they have to pay it back to you! With interest!

That solved the problem. For a while, employers could pay the workers the same or less, and instead of creating the usual problems for capitalism—workers without enough income to buy all the output their increased productivity yields—rising worker debt seemed magical. Workers could consume ever more; profits exploding in every category. Underneath the magic, however, there were workers who were completely exhausted, whose families were falling apart, and who were now ridden with anxiety because their rising debts were unsustainable. This was a system built to fail, to reach its end when the combination of physical exhaustion and emotional anxiety from the debt made people unable to continue. Those people are, by the millions, walking away from those obligations, and the house of cards comes down.

If you put together (a) the desperation of the American working class and (b) the efforts of the finance industry to scrounge out every conceivable borrower, the idea that the banks would end up lending money to people who couldn't pay it back is not a tough call. The system, however, was premised on the idea that that would not happen, and when it happened nobody was prepared.

The conservatives these days are in a tough spot. The story about how markets and private enterprise interact to produce wonderful outcomes is, even for them these days, a cause for gagging. Of course, ever resourceful, there are conservatives who will rise to the occasion, sort of like dead fish. They rattle off twenty things the government did over the last twenty years, which indeed it did, and draw a line from those things the government did to this disaster now, to reach the conclusion that the reason we have this problem now is too much government intervention. These days they get nowhere. Even the mainstream press has a hard time with this stuff.

What about the liberals and many leftists too? They seem to favor regulation. They think the problem was that the banks weren't regulated, that credit-rating companies weren't regulated, that the Federal Reserve didn't regulate better, or differently, or more, or something. Salaries should be regulated to not be so high. Greed should be regulated. I find this astonishing and depressing.

In the 1930s, the last time we had capitalism hitting the fan in this way, we produced a lot of regulation. Social Security didn't exist before then. Unemployment insurance didn't exist before then. Banks were told: you can do this, but you can't do that. Insurance companies were told: you can do that, but you can't do this. They limited what the board of directors of a corporation could do ten ways to Sunday. They taxed them. They did all sorts of things that annoyed, bothered, and troubled boards of directors because the regulations impeded the boards' efforts to grow their companies and make money for the shareholders who elected them.

You don't need to be a great genius to understand that the boards of directors encumbered by all these regulations would have a very strong incentive to evade them, to undermine them, and, if possible, to get rid of them. Indeed, the boards went to work on that project as soon as the regulations were passed. The crucial fact about the regulations imposed on business in the 1930s is that they did not take away from the boards of directors the freedom or the incentives or the opportunities to undo all the regulations and reforms. The regulations left in place an institution devoted to their undoing. But that wasn't the worst of it. They also left in place boards of directors who, as the first appropriators of all the profits, had the *resources* to undo the regulations. This peculiar system of regulation had a built-in self-destruct button.

Over the last thirty years, the boards of directors of the United States' larger corporations have used their profits to buy the president and the Congress, to buy the public media, and to wage a systematic campaign, from 1945 to 1975, to evade the regulations, and, after 1975, to get rid of them. And it worked. That's why we're here now. And if you impose another set of regulations along the lines liberals propose, not only are you going to have the same history, but you're going to have the same history faster. The right wing in America, the business community, has spent the last fifty years perfecting every technique that is known to turn the population against regulation. And they're going to go right to work to do it again, and they'll do it better, and they'll do it faster.

So what do we do? Let's regulate, by all means. Let's try to make a reasonable economic system that doesn't allow the grotesque abuses we've seen in recent decades. But let's not reproduce the self-destruct button. This time the change has to include the following: The people in every enterprise who do the work of that enterprise, will become collectively their own board of directors. For the first time in American history, the people who depend on the survival of those regulations will be in the position of receiving the profits of their own work and using them to make the regulations succeed rather than sabotaging them.

This proposal for workers to collectively become their own board of directors also democratizes the enterprise. The people who work in an enterprise, the front line of those who have to live with what it does, where it goes, how it uses its wealth, they should be the people who have influence over the decisions it makes. That's democracy.

Maybe we could even extend this argument to democracy in our political life, which leaves a little to be desired—some people call it a "formal" democracy, that isn't real. Maybe the problem all along has been that you can't have a real democracy politically if you don't have a real democracy underpinning it economically. If the workers are not in charge of their work situations, five days a week, 9 to 5, the major time of their adult lives, then how much aptitude and how much appetite are they going to have to control their political life? Maybe we need the democracy of economics, not just to prevent the regulations from being undone, but also to realize the political objectives of democracy. ❏

CONSEQUENCES OF INEQUALITY

When economic inequality increases, the rest of the economy suffers too. James Cypher explains how pro-corporate and anti-union economic policies helped accelerate inequality from the 1970s to the mid-2000s in the United States, and he explores some of the effects of the growing concentration of income and wealth.

SLICING UP AT THE LONG BARBEQUE
Who Gorges, Who Serves, and Who Gets Roasted?

BY JAMES CYPHER
January/February 2007

Economic inequality has been on the rise in the United States since the 1970s. Not since the Gilded Age of the late 19th century—during what Mark Twain referred to as "the Great Barbeque"—has the country witnessed such a rapid shift in the distribution of economic resources.

Still, most mainstream economists do not pay too much attention to the distribution of income and wealth—that is, how the value of current production (income) and past accumulated assets (wealth) is divided up among U.S. households. Some economists focus their attention on theory for theory's sake and do not work much with empirical data of any kind. Others who *are* interested in these on-the-ground data simply assume that each individual or group gets what it deserves from a capitalist economy. In their view, if the share of income going to wage earners goes up, that must mean that wage earners are more productive and thus deserve a larger slice of the nation's total income—and vice versa if that share goes down.

Heterodox economists, however, frequently look upon the distribution of income and wealth as among the most important shorthand guides to the overall state of a society and its economy. Some are interested in economic justice; others may or may not be, but nonetheless are convinced that changes in income distribution signal underlying societal trends and perhaps important points of political tension. And the general public appears to be paying increasing attention to income and wealth inequality.

Throughout the 1950s, 1960s, and 1970s, orthodox sociologists preached that the United States was an essentially "classless" society in which everyone belonged to the middle class. A new "mass market" society with an essentially affluent, economically homogeneous population, they claimed, had emerged. Exaggerated as these claims were in the 1950s, there was some reason for their popular acceptance. Union membership reached its peak share of the private-sector labor force in the early 1950s; unions were able to force corporations of the day to share the benefits of strong economic growth. The union wage created a target for non-union workers as well, pulling up all but the lowest of wages as workers sought to match the union wage and employers often granted it as a tactic for keeping unions out. Under these circumstances, millions of families entered the lower middle class and saw their standard of living rise markedly. All of this made the distribution of income more equal for decades until the late 1970s. Of course there were outliers—some millions of poor, disproportionately blacks, and the rich family here and there.

Something serious must have happened in the 1970s as the trend toward greater economic equality rapidly reversed. The share of income received by the bottom 90% of the population was a modest 67% in 1970, but by 2000 this had shrunk to a mere 52%, according to a detailed study of U.S. income distribution conducted by Thomas Piketty and Emmanuel Saez, published by the prestigious National Bureau of Economic Research in 2002. Put another way, the top 10% increased their overall share of the nation's total income by 15 percentage points from 1970 to 2000. This is a rather astonishing jump—the *gain* of the top 10% in these years was equivalent to more than the *total income received annually* by the bottom 40% of households.

To get on the bottom rung of the top 10% of households in 2000, it would have been necessary to have an adjusted gross income of $104,000 a year. The real money, though, starts on the 99th rung of the income ladder—the top 1% received an unbelievable 21.7% of all income in 2000. To get a handhold on the very bottom of this top rung took more than $384,000. The Piketty-Saez study (and subsequent updates) verified a rising *trend* in income inequality which had been widely noted by others, and a *degree* of inequality which was far beyond most current estimates.

A Brave New (Globalized) World For Workers

Why the big change from 1970 to 2000? That is too long a story to tell here in full. But briefly, we can say that beginning in the early 1970s, U.S. corporations and the wealthy individuals who largely own them had the means, the motive, and the opportunity to garner a larger share of the nation's income—and they did so.

Let's start with the motive. The 1970s saw a significant slowdown in U.S. economic growth, which made corporations and stockholders anxious to stop sharing the benefits of growth to the degree they had in the immediate postwar era.

Opportunity appeared in the form of an accelerating globalization of economic activity. Beginning in the 1970s, more and more U.S.-based corporations began to set up production operations overseas. The trend has only accelerated since, in part because international communication and transportation costs have fallen dramatically. Until the 1970s, it was very difficult—essentially unprofitable—for giants like General Electric or General Motors to operate plants offshore and then import their foreign-made products into the United States. So from the 1940s to the 1970s, U.S. workers had a geographic lever, one they have now almost entirely lost. This erosion in workers' bargaining power has undermined the middle class and decimated the unions that once managed to assure the working class a generally comfortable economic existence. And today, of course, the tendency to send jobs offshore is affecting many highly trained professionals such as engineers. So this process of gutting the middle class has not run its course.

Given the opportunity presented by globalization, companies took a two-pronged approach to strengthening their hand vis-à-vis workers: (1) a frontal assault on unions, with decertification elections and get-tough tactics during unionization attempts, and (2) a debilitating war of nerves whereby corporations threatened to move offshore unless workers scaled back their demands or agreed to givebacks of prior gains in wage and benefit levels or working conditions.

A succession of U.S. governments that pursued conservative—or pro-corporate—economic policies provided the means. Since the 1970s, both Republican and Democratic administrations have tailored their economic policies to benefit corporations and shareholders over workers. The laundry list of such policies includes:

- new trade agreements, such as NAFTA, that allow companies to cement favorable deals to move offshore to host nations such as Mexico;
- tax cuts for corporations and for the wealthiest households, along with hikes in the payroll taxes that represent the largest share of the tax burden on the working and middle classes;
- lax enforcement of labor laws that are supposed to protect the right to organize unions and bargain collectively.

Exploding Millionairism

Given these shifts in the political economy of the United States, it is not surprising that economic inequality in 2000 was higher than in 1970. But at this point, careful readers may well ask whether it is misleading to use data for the year 2000, as the studies reported above do, to demonstrate rising inequality. After all, wasn't 2000 the year the NASDAQ peaked, the year the dot-com bubble reached its maximum volume? So if the wealthiest households received an especially large slice of the nation's total income that year, doesn't that just reflect a bubble about to burst rather than an underlying trend?

To begin to answer this question, we need to look at the trends in income and wealth distribution *since* 2000. And it turns out that after a slight pause in 2000–2001, inequality has continued to rise. Look at household income, for example. According to the standard indicators, the U.S. economy saw a brief recession in 2000–2001 and has been in a recovery ever since. But the median household income has failed to recover. In 2000 the median household had an annual income of $49,133; by 2005, after adjusting for inflation, the figure stood at $46,242. This 6% drop in median household income occurred while the inflation-adjusted Gross Domestic Product *expanded* by 14.4%.

When the Census Bureau released these data, it noted that median household income had gone up slightly between 2004 and 2005. This point was seized upon by Bush administration officials to bolster their claim that times are good for American workers. A closer look at the data, however, revealed a rather astounding fact: Only 23 million households moved ahead in 2005, most headed by someone age 65 or above. In other words, subtracting out the cost-of-living increase in Social Security benefits and increases in investment income (such as profits, dividends, interest, capital gains, and rents) to the over-65 group, workers again suffered a *decline* in income in 2005.

Another bit of evidence is the number of millionaire households—those with net worth of $1 million or more excluding the value of a primary residence and any IRAs. In 1999, just before the bubbles burst, there were 7.1 million millionaire households in the United States. In 2005, there were 8.9 million, a record number. Ordinary workers may not have recovered from the 2000–2001 rough patch yet, but evidently the wealthiest households have!

Many economists pay scant attention to income distribution patterns on the assumption that those shifts merely reflect trends in the productivity of labor or the return to risk-taking. But worker productivity rose in the 2000-2005 period, by 27.1% (see Figure 1). At the same time, from 2003 to 2005 average hourly pay fell by 1.2%. (Total compensation, including all forms of benefits, rose by 7.2% between 2000 and 2005. Most of the higher compensation spending merely reflects rapid increases in the health insurance premiums that employers have to pay just to maintain the same levels of coverage. But even if benefits are counted as part of workers' pay—a common and questionable practice—productivity growth outpaced this elastic definition of "pay" by 50% between 1972 and 2005.)

And at the macro level, recent data released by the Commerce Department demonstrate that the share of the country's GDP going to wages and salaries sank to its lowest postwar level, 45.4%, in the third quarter of 2006 (see Figure 2). And this figure actually overstates how well ordinary workers are doing. The "Wage & Salary" share includes all income of this type, not just production workers' pay. Corporate executives' increasingly munificent salaries are included as well. Workers got roughly 65% of total wage and salary income in 2005, according to survey data from the U.S. Department of Labor; the other 35% went to salaried professionals—medical doctors and technicians, managers, and lawyers—who comprised only 15.6% of the sample.

Moreover, the "Wage & Salary" share shown in the National Income and Product Accounts includes bonuses, overtime, and other forms of payment not included in the Labor Department survey. If this income were factored in, the share going to nonprofessional, nonmanagerial workers would be even smaller. Bonuses and other forms of income to top employees can be many times base pay in important areas such as law and banking. Goldman Sachs's notorious 2006 bonuses are a case in point; the typical managing director on Wall Street garnered a bonus ranging between $1 and $3 million.

So, labor's share of the nation's income is falling, as Figure 2 shows, but it is actually falling much faster than these data suggest. Profits, meanwhile, are at their highest level as a share of GDP since the booming 1960s.

These numbers should come as no surprise to anyone who reads the news: story after story illustrates how corporations are continuing to squeeze workers. For instance, workers at the giant auto parts manufacturer Delphi have been told to prepare for a drop in wages from $27.50 an hour in 2006 to $16.50 an hour in 2007. In order to keep some of Caterpillar's manufacturing work in the United States, the union was cornered into accepting a contract in 2006 that limits new workers to a maximum salary of $27,000 a year—no matter how long they work there—compared to the $38,000 or more that long-time Caterpillar workers make today. More generally, for young women with a high school diploma, average entry-level pay fell to only $9.08 an hour in 2005, down by 4.9% just since 2001. For male college graduates, starter-job pay fell by 7.3% over the same period.

FIGURE 1
REAL WAGES AND PRODUCTIVITY OF
U.S. PRODUCTION WORKERS, 1972–2005

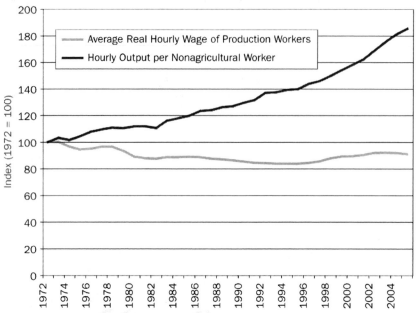

Source: *Economic Report of the President 2006*, Tables B-47 and B-49.

Aiding and Abetting

And the federal government is continuing to play its part, facilitating the transfer of an ever-larger share of the nation's income to its wealthiest households. George W. Bush once joked that his constituency was "the haves and the have-mores"—this may have been one of the few instances in which he was actually leveling with his audience. Consider aspects of the first three tax cuts for individuals that Bush implemented. The first two cut the top *nominal* tax rate from 39.6% to 35%. Then, in 2003, the third cut benefited solely those who hold wealth, reducing taxes on dividends from 39.6% to 15% and on capital gains from 20% to 15%.

So, if you made your money by the sweat of your brow and you earned $200,000 in 2003, you paid an *effective* tax rate of 21%. If you earned a bit more, say another $60,500, you paid effective tax rate of 35% on the additional income. But if, with a flick of the wrist on your laptop, you flipped some stock you had held for six months and cleared $60,500 on the transaction, you paid the IRS an effective tax rate of only 15%. What difference does it make? Well, in 2003 the 6,126 households with incomes over $10 million saw their taxes go down by an average of $521,905 from this one tax cut alone.

These tax cuts represent only one of the many Bush administration policies that abetted the ongoing shift of income away from most households and toward the wealthiest ones. And what did these top-tier households do with all

FIGURE 2
WAGES/SALARIES VS. CORPORATE PROFITS AS SHARES OF U.S. INCOME, 1972–2006

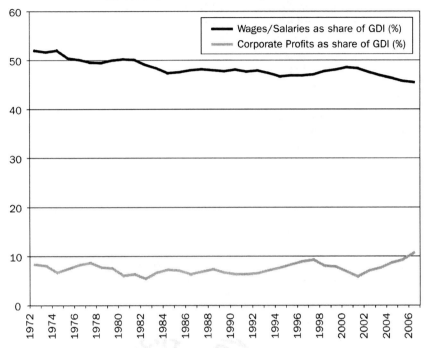

Source: U.S. Dept. of Commerce, Bureau of Economic Analysis, *National Income and Product Accounts 2006*, Table 1.10.

this newfound money? For one thing, they saved. This is in sharp contrast to most households. While the top fifth of households by income has a savings rate of 23%, the bottom 80% as a group "dissave"—in other words, they go into debt, spending more than they earn. Households headed by a person under 35 currently show a negative savings rate of 16% of income. Today, *overall* savings—the savings of the top fifth minus the dis-savings of the bottom four-fifths—are slightly negative, for the first time since the Great Depression.

Here we find the crucial link between income and wealth accumulation. Able to save nearly a quarter of their income, the rich search out financial assets (and sometimes real assets such as houses and businesses) to pour their vast funds into. In many instances, sometimes with inside information, they are able to generate considerable future income from their invested savings. Like a snowball rolling downhill, savings for the rich can have a turbo effect—more savings generates more income, which then accumulates as wealth.

Lifestyles of the Rich

Make the rich even richer and the creative forces of market capitalism will be unleashed, resulting in more savings and consequently more capital investment, raising productivity and creating abundance for all. At any rate, that's the supply-side/ neoliberal theory. However—and reminiscent of the false boom that defined the Japanese economy in the late 1980s—the big money has not gone into productive investments in the United States. Stripping out the money pumped into the residential real estate bubble, inflation-adjusted investment in machinery, equipment, technology, and structures increased only 1.4% from 1999 through 2005—an average of 0.23% per year. Essentially, productive investment has stagnated since the close of the dot-com boom.

Instead, the money has poured into high-risk hedge funds. These are vast pools of unregulated funds that are now generating 40% to 50% of the trades in the New York Stock Exchange and account for very large portions of trading in many U.S. and foreign credit and debt markets.

And where is the income from these investments going? Last fall media mogul David Geffen sold two paintings at record prices, a Jasper Johns ($80 million) and a Willem de Kooning ($63.5 million), to two of "today's crop of hedge-fund billionaires" whose cash is making the art market "red-hot," according to the *New York Times*.

Other forms of conspicuous consumption have their allure as well. Boeing and Lufthansa are expecting brisk business for the newly introduced 787 airplane. The commercial version of the new Boeing jet will seat 330, but the VIP version offered by Lufthansa Technik (for a mere $240 million) will have seating for 35 or fewer, leaving room for master bedrooms, a bar, and the transport of racehorses or Rolls Royces. And if you lose your auto assembly job? It should be easy to find work as a dog walker: High-end pet care services are booming, with sales more than doubling between 2000 and 2004. Opened in 2001, Just Dogs Gourmet expects to have 45 franchises in place by the end of 2006 selling hand-decorated doggie treats. And then there is Camp Bow Wow, which offers piped-in classical music for the dogs (oops, "guests") and a live Camper Cam for their owners. Started only three years ago, the company already has 140 franchises up and running.

According to David Butler, the manager of a premiere auto dealership outside of Detroit, sales of Bentleys, at $180,000 a pop, are brisk. But not many $300,000 Rolls Royces are selling. "It's not that they can't afford it," Butler told the *New York Times*, "it's because of the image it would give." Just what is the image problem in Detroit? Well, maybe it has something to do with those Delphi workers facing a 40% pay cut. Michigan's economy is one of the hardest-hit in the nation. GM, long a symbol of U.S. manufacturing prowess, is staggering, with rumors of possible bankruptcy rife. The best union in terms of delivering the goods for the U.S. working class, the United Auto Workers, is facing an implosion. Thousands of Michigan workers at Delphi, GM, and Ford will be out on the streets very soon. (The top three domestic car makers are determined to permanently lay off three-quarters of their U.S. assembly-line workers—nearly 200,000 hourly employees. If they do, then the number of autoworkers employed by the Big Three —Ford, Chrysler, and GM—will have shrunk by a staggering 900,000 since 1978.) So, this might not be the time to buy a Rolls. But a mere $180,000 Bentley—why not?

Had Enough of the "Haves"?

In the era Twain decried as the "great barbeque," the outrageous concentration of income and wealth eventually sparked a reaction and a vast reform movement. But it was not until the onset of the Great Depression, decades later, that massive labor/

social unrest and economic collapse forced the country's political elite to check the growing concentration of income and wealth.

Today, it does not appear that there are, as yet, any viable forces at work to put the brakes on the current runaway process of rising inequality. Nor does it appear that this era's power elite is ready to accept any new social compact. In a recent report on the "new king of Wall Street" (a co-founder of the hedge fund/private-equity buyout corporation Blackstone Group) that seemed to typify elite perspectives on today's inequality, the New York Times gushed that "a crashing wave of capital is minting new billionaires each year." Naturally, the Times was too discreet to mention is that those same "crashing waves" have flattened the middle class. And their backwash has turned the working class every-which-way while pulling it down, down, down.

But perhaps those who decry the trend can find at least symbolic hope in the new boom in yet another luxury good. Private mausoleums, in vogue during that earlier Gilded Age, are back. For $650,000, one was recently constructed at Daytona Memorial Park in Florida—with matching $4,000 Medjool date palms for shade. Another, complete with granite patio, meditation room, and doors of hand cast bronze, went up in the same cemetery. Business is booming, apparently, with 2,000 private mausoleums sold in 2005, up from a single-year peak of 65 in the 1980s. Some cost "well into the millions," according to one the nation's largest makers of cemetery monuments. Who knows: maybe the mausoleum boom portends the ultimate (dead) end for the neo-Gilded Age. ❑

Resources: Jenny Anderson, "As Lenders, Hedge Funds Draw Insider Scrutiny," *NY Times* 10/16/06; Steven Greenhouse, "Many Entry-Level Workers Feel Pinch of Rough Market," *NY Times* 9/4/06; Greenhouse and David Leonhardt, "Real Wages Fail to Match a Rise in Productivity," *NY Times* 8/28/06; Paul Krugman, "Feeling No Pain," *NY Times* 3/6/06; Krugman, "Graduates vs. Oligarchs," *NY Times* 2/27/06; David Cay Johnston, *Perfectly Legal* (Penguin Books, 2003); Johnston, "Big Gain for Rich Seen in Tax Cuts for Investments," *NY Times* 4/5/06; Johnston, "New Rise in Number of Millionaire Families," *NY Times* 3/28/06; Johnston, "'04 Income in US was Below 2000 Level," *NY Times* 11/28/06; Leonhardt, "The Economics of Henry Ford May Be Passé," *NY Times* 4/5/06; Rick Lyman, "Census Reports Slight Increase in '05 Incomes," *NY Times* 8/30/06; Micheline Maynard and Nick Bunkley, "Ford is Offering 75,000 Employees Buyout Packages," *NY Times* 9/15/06; Jeremy W. Peters, "Delphi Is Said to Offer Union a One-Time Sweetener," *NY Times* 3/28/06; Joe Sharky, "For the Super-Rich, It's Time to Upgrade the Old Jumbo Jet," *NY Times* 10/17/06; Guy Trebay, "For a Price, Final Resting Place that Tut Would Find Pleasant" *NY Times* 4/17/06.

Progressives who decry economic inequality just don't know how the economy works—or so say conservative pundits. According to those on the right, inequality fuels economic growth. But as Chris Tilly explains, exactly the opposite is true. In fact, equality boosts economic growth, while inequality puts on the brakes.

GEESE, GOLDEN EGGS, AND TRAPS
Why Inequality Is Bad for the Economy

BY CHRIS TILLY
July/August 2004

Whenever progressives propose ways to redistribute wealth from the rich to those with low and moderate incomes, conservative politicians and economists accuse them of trying to kill the goose that lays the golden egg. The advocates of unfettered capitalism proclaim that inequality is good for the economy because it promotes economic growth. Unequal incomes, they say, provide the incentives necessary to guide productive economic decisions by businesses and individuals. Try to reduce inequality, and you'll sap growth. Furthermore, the conservatives argue, growth actually promotes equality by boosting the have-nots more than the haves. So instead of fiddling with who gets how much, the best way to help those at the bottom is to pump up growth.

But these conservative prescriptions are absolutely, dangerously wrong. Instead of the goose-killer, equality turns out to be the goose. Inequality stifles growth; equality gooses it up. Moreover, economic expansion does *not* necessarily promote equality—instead, what matters most are the types of jobs and the rules of the economic game.

Inequality: Goose or Goose-Killer?

The conservative argument may be wrong, but it's straightforward. Inequality is good for the economy, conservatives say, because it provides the right incentives for innovation and economic growth. First of all, people will only have the motivation to work hard, innovate, and invest wisely if the economic system rewards them for good economic choices and penalizes bad ones. Robin Hood-style policies that collect from the wealthy and help those who are worse off violate this principle. They reduce the payoff to smart decisions and lessen the sting of dumb ones. The result: people and companies are bound to make less efficient decisions. "We must allow [individuals] to fail, as well as succeed, and we must replace the nanny state with a regime of self-reliance and self-respect," writes conservative lawyer Stephen Kinsella in *The Freeman: Ideas on Liberty* (not clear how the free woman fits in). To prove their point, conservatives point to the former state socialist countries, whose economies had become stagnant and inefficient by the time they fell at the end of the 1980s.

If you don't buy this incentive story, there's always the well-worn trickle-down theory. To grow, the economy needs productive investments: new offices, factories, computers, and machines. To finance such investments takes a pool of savings. The rich save a larger fraction of their incomes than those less well-off. So to spur growth, give more to the well-heeled (or at least take less away from them in the form of taxes), and give less to the down-and-out. The rich will save their money and then invest it, promoting growth that's good for everyone.

Unfortunately for trickle-down, the renowned economist John Maynard Keynes debunked the theory in his *General Theory of Employment, Interest, and Money* in 1936. Keynes, whose precepts guided liberal U.S. economic policy from the 1940s through the 1970s, agreed that investments must be financed out of savings. But he showed that most often it's changes in investment that drive savings, rather than the other way around. When businesses are optimistic about the future and invest in building and retooling, the economy booms, all of us make more money, and we put some of it in banks, 401(k)s, stocks, and so on. That is, saving grows to match investment. When companies are glum, the process runs in reverse, and savings shrink to equal investment. This leads to the "paradox of thrift": if people try to save too much, businesses will see less consumer spending, will invest less, and total savings will end up diminishing rather than growing as the economy spirals downward. A number of Keynes's followers added the next logical step: shifting money from the high-saving rich to the high-spending rest of us, and not the other way around, will spur investment and growth.

Of the two conservative arguments in favor of inequality, the incentive argument is a little weightier. Keynes himself agreed that people needed financial consequences to steer their actions, but questioned whether the differences in payoffs needed to be so huge. Certainly state socialist countries' attempts to replace material incentives with moral exhortation have often fallen short. In 1970, the Cuban government launched the *Gran Zafra* (Great Harvest), an attempt to reap 10 million tons of sugar cane with (strongly encouraged) volunteer labor. Originally inspired by Che Guevara's ideal of the New Socialist Man (not clear how the New Socialist Woman fit in), the effort ended with Fidel Castro tearfully apologizing to the Cuban people in a nationally broadcast speech for letting wishful thinking guide economic policy.

But before conceding this point to the conservatives, let's look at the evidence about the connection between equality and growth. Economists William Easterly of New York University and Gary Fields of Cornell University have recently summarized this evidence:

- Countries, and regions within countries, with more equal incomes grow faster. (These growth figures do not include environmental destruction or improvement. If they knocked off points for environmental destruction and added points for environmental improvement, the correlation between equality and growth would be even stronger, since desperation drives poor people to adopt environmentally destructive practices such as rapid deforestation.)
- Countries with more equally distributed land grow faster.
- Somewhat disturbingly, more ethnically homogeneous countries and regions grow faster—presumably because there are fewer ethnically based inequalities.

In addition, more worker rights are associated with higher rates of economic growth, according to Josh Bivens and Christian Weller, economists at two Washington think tanks, the Economic Policy Institute and the Center for American Progress.

These patterns recommend a second look at the incentive question. In fact, more equality can actually *strengthen* incentives and opportunities to produce.

Equality as the Goose

Equality can boost growth in several ways. Perhaps the simplest is that study after study has shown that farmland is more productive when cultivated in small plots. So organizations promoting more equal distribution of land, like Brazil's Landless Workers' Movement, are not just helping the landless poor—they're contributing to agricultural productivity!

Another reason for the link between equality and growth is what Easterly calls "match effects," which have been highlighted in research by Stanford's Paul Roemer and others in recent years. One example of a match effect is the fact that well-educated people are most productive when working with others who have lots of schooling. Likewise, people working with computers are more productive when many others have computers (so that, for example, e-mail communication is widespread, and know-how about computer repair and software is easy to come by). In very unequal societies, highly educated, computer-using elites are surrounded by majorities with little education and no computer access, dragging down their productivity. This decreases young people's incentive to get more education and businesses' incentive to invest in computers, since the payoff will be smaller.

Match effects can even matter at the level of a metropolitan area. Urban economist Larry Ledebur looked at income and employment growth in 85 U.S. cities and their neighboring suburbs. He found that where the income gap between those in the suburbs and those in the city was largest, income and job growth was slower for everyone.

"Pressure effects" also help explain why equality sparks growth. Policies that close off the low-road strategy of exploiting poor and working people create pressure effects, driving economic elites to search for investment opportunities that pay off by boosting productivity rather than squeezing the have-nots harder. For example, where workers have more rights, they will place greater demands on businesses. Business owners will respond by trying to increase productivity, both to remain profitable even after paying higher wages, and to find ways to produce with fewer workers. The CIO union drives in U.S. mass production industries in the 1930s and 1940s provide much of the explanation for the superb productivity growth of the 1950s and 1960s. (The absence of pressure effects may help explain why many past and present state socialist countries have seen slow growth, since they tend to offer numerous protections for workers but no right to organize independent unions.) Similarly, if a government buys out large land-holdings in order to break them up, wealthy families who simply kept their fortunes tied up in land for generations will look for new, productive investments. Industrialization in Asian "tigers" South Korea and Taiwan took off in the 1950s on the wings of funds freed up in exactly this way.

Inequality, Conflict, and Growth

Inequality hinders growth in another important way: it fuels social conflict. Stark inequality in countries such as Bolivia and Haiti has led to chronic conflict that hobbles economic growth. Moreover, inequality ties up resources in unproductive uses such as paying for large numbers of police and security guards—attempts to prevent individuals from redistributing resources through theft.

Ethnic variety is connected to slower growth because, on the average, more ethnically diverse countries are also more likely to be ethnically divided. In other words, the problem isn't ethnic variety itself, but racism and ethnic conflict that can exist among diverse populations. In nations like Guatemala, Congo, and Nigeria, ethnic strife has crippled growth—a problem alien to ethnically uniform Japan and South Korea. The reasons are similar to some of the reasons that large class divides hurt growth. Where ethnic divisions (which can take tribal, language, religious, racial, or regional forms) loom large, dominant ethnic groups seek to use government power to better themselves at the expense of other groups, rather than making broad-based investments in education and infrastructure. This can involve keeping down the underdogs—slower growth in the U.S. South for much of the country's history was linked to the Southern system of white supremacy. Or it can involve seizing the surplus of ethnic groups perceived as better off—in the extreme, Nazi Germany's expropriation and genocide of the Jews, who often held professional and commercial jobs.

Of course, the solution to such divisions is not "ethnic cleansing" so that each country has only one ethnic group—in addition to being morally abhorrent, this is simply impossible in a world with 191 countries and 5,000 ethnic groups. Rather, the solution is to diminish ethnic inequalities. Once the 1964 Civil Rights Act forced the South to drop racist laws, the New South's economic growth spurt began. Easterly reports that in countries with strong rule of law, professional bureaucracies, protection of contracts, and freedom from expropriation—all rules that make it harder for one ethnic group to economically oppress another—ethnic diversity has *no* negative impact on growth.

If more equality leads to faster growth so everybody benefits, why do the rich typically resist redistribution? Looking at the ways that equity seeds growth helps us understand why. The importance of pressure effects tells us that the wealthy often don't think about more productive ways to invest or reorganize their businesses until they are forced to. But also, if a country becomes very unequal, it can get stuck in an "inequality trap." Any redistribution involves a tradeoff for the rich. They lose by giving up part of their wealth, but they gain a share in increased economic growth. The bigger the disparity between the rich and the rest, the more the rich have to lose, and the less likely that the equal share of boosted growth they'll get will make up for their loss. Once the gap goes beyond a certain point, the wealthy have a strong incentive to restrict democracy, and to block spending on education which might lead the poor to challenge economic injustice—making reform that much harder.

Does Economic Growth Reduce Inequality?

If inequality isn't actually good for the economy, what about the second part of the conservatives' argument—that growth itself promotes equality? According to the conservatives, those who care about equality should simply pursue growth and wait for equality to follow.

"A rising tide lifts all boats," President John F. Kennedy famously declared. But he said nothing about which boats will rise fastest when the economic tide comes in. Growth does typically reduce poverty, according to studies reviewed by economist Gary Fields, though some "boats"—especially families with strong barriers to participating in the labor force—stay "stuck in the mud." But inequality can increase at the same time that poverty falls, if the rich gain even faster than the poor do. True, sustained periods of low unemployment, like that in the late 1990s United States, do tend to raise wages at the bottom even faster than salaries at the top. But growth after the recessions of 1991 and 2001 began with years of "jobless recoveries"—growth with inequality.

For decades the prevailing view about growth and inequality within countries was that expressed by Simon Kuznets in his 1955 presidential address to the American Economic Association. Kuznets argued that as countries grew, inequality would first increase, then decrease. The reason is that people will gradually move from the low-income agricultural sector to higher-income industrial jobs—with inequality peaking when the workforce is equally divided between low- and high-income sectors. For mature industrial economies, Kuznets's proposition counsels focusing on growth, assuming that it will bring equity. In developing countries, it calls for enduring current inequality for the sake of future equity and prosperity.

But economic growth doesn't automatically fuel equality. In 1998, economists Klaus Deininger and Lyn Squire traced inequality and growth over time in 48 countries. Five followed the Kuznets pattern, four followed the reverse pattern (decreasing inequality followed by an increase), and the rest showed no systematic pattern. In the United States, for example:

- incomes became more equal during the 1930s through 1940s New Deal period (a time that included economic decline followed by growth);
- from the 1950s through the 1970s, income gaps lessened during booms and expanded during slumps;
- from the late 1970s forward, income inequality worsened fairly consistently, whether the economy was stagnating or growing.

The reasons are not hard to guess. The New Deal introduced widespread unionization, a minimum wage, social security, unemployment insurance, and welfare. Since the late 1970s, unions have declined, the inflation-adjusted value of the minimum wage has fallen, and the social safety net has been shredded. In the United States, as elsewhere, growth only promotes equality if policies and institutions to support equity are in place.

Trapped?

Let's revisit the idea of an inequality trap. The notion is that as the gap between the rich and everybody else grows wider, the wealthy become more willing to give up overall growth in return for the larger share they're getting for themselves. The "haves" back policies to control the "have-nots," instead of devoting social resources to educating the poor so they'll be more productive.

Sound familiar? It should. After two decades of widening inequality, the last few years have brought us massive tax cuts that primarily benefit the wealthiest, at the expense of investment in infrastructure and the education, child care, and income supports that would help raise less well-off kids to be productive adults. Federal and state governments have cranked up expenditures on prisons, police, and "homeland security," and Republican campaign organizations have devoted major resources to keeping blacks and the poor away from the polls. If the economic patterns of the past are any indication, we're going to pay for these policies in slower growth and stagnation unless we can find our way out of this inequality trap. ❑

The advertising industry is adapting to the shrinking middle class. Sam Pizzigati reports that advertisers are shifting their focus to the wealthy because they now control most of the disposal income in the U.S.

MADISON AVENUE DECLARES 'MASS AFFLUENCE' OVER

SAM PIZZIGATI
May 2011

The chain-smoking ad agency account execs of Mad Men, the hit cable TV series set in the early 1960s, all want to be rich someday. But these execs, professionally, couldn't care less about the rich. They spend their nine-to-fives marketing to average Americans, not rich ones.

Real-life admen, 50 years ago, behaved the exact same way—for an eminently common-sense reason: In mid-20th century America, the entire U.S. economy revolved around middle class households. The vast bulk of U.S. income sat in middle class pockets.

The rich back then, for ad execs, constituted an afterthought, a niche market.

Not anymore. Madison Avenue has now come full circle. The rich no longer rate as a niche. Marketing to the rich—and those about to gain that status—has become the only game that really counts.

"Mass affluence," a new white paper from Ad Age, the advertising industry's top trade journal, has declared, "is over."

The Mad Men 1960s America—where average families dominated the consumer market—has totally disappeared, this Ad Age New Wave of Affluence study details. And Madison Avenue has moved on—to where the money sits.

And that money does not sit in average American pockets. The global economic recession, Ad Age relates, has thrown "a spotlight on the yawning divide between the richest Americans and everyone else."

Taking inflation into account, Ad Age goes on to explain, the "incomes of most American workers have remained more or less static since the 1970s," while "the income of the rich (and the very rich) has grown exponentially."

The top 10% of American households, the trade journal adds, now account for nearly half of all consumer spending, and a disproportionate share of that spending comes from the top 10's upper reaches.

"Simply put," sums up Ad Age, "a small plutocracy of wealthy elites drives a larger and larger share of total consumer spending and has outsize purchasing influence—particularly in categories such as technology, financial services, travel, automotive, apparel, and personal care."

The new Ad Age white paper makes no value judgments about any of this. The ad industry's only vested interest: following the money, because that money determines who consumes.

In the future, if current trends continue, no one else but the rich will essentially matter—to Madison Avenue.

"More than ever before," Ad Age bluntly sums up, "the wealthiest households will be the households with significant disposable income to spend."

On the one hand, that makes things easy for Madison Avenue. To thrive in a top-heavy America, a marketer need only zero in on the rich. On the other hand, a real challenge remains: How can savvy Madison Avenue execs identify—and capture the consuming loyalties of—people on their way to wealth?

Before the Great Recession, the Madison Avenue conventional wisdom put great stock in the $100,000 to $200,000 income demographic, a consuming universe populated largely by men and women 35 and older. These "aspirational" households, ad men and women figured, could afford a taste of the good life. They rated as a worthwhile advertising target.

Targeting this $100,000 to $200,000 cohort, Ad Age now contends, no longer makes particularly good marketing sense. These consumers don't "feel rich" today and won't likely "graduate into affluence later on."

Only under-35s who make between $100,000 and $200,000, says Ad Age, will likely make that graduation. This under-35 "emerging" tier will have "a far greater chance of eventually crossing the golden threshold of $200,000 than those who achieve household income of $100,000 later in life."

So that's it. If you want to be a successful advertising exec in a deeply unequal America, start studying up on 20-somethings making over $100,000 a year.

And those of us who don't make $200,000 a year, and don't have much chance of ever making it, what about us? No need to worry. Who needs purchasing power? We have Mad Men reruns.

SOURCES: David Hirschman, "On the Road to Riches: Those Under 35 With $100K Household Income," Ad Age, May 22, 2011.

This article was originally published in Too Much, a weekly newsletter edited by Sam Pizzigati. Too Much is a project of the Institute for Policy Studies' Program on Inequality and the Common Good. <toomuchonline.org>

"Dr. Dollar" (Arthur MacEwan) responds to a reader's concerns about speculative bubbles in 2009, just after housing and stock market values plummeted. He explains what happened to the "lost trillions" in home equity and stock values.

TAX CUTS AND ECONOMIC GROWTH

BY ARTHUR MacEWAN
July/August 2011

Dear Dr. Dollar:

It seems to be an article of faith amongst the "serious people" that low taxes on dividends and capital gains will stimulate the economy. While most economists (I understand) pretty much agree that any reduction in taxes will have some positive effect on the economy by stimulating demand, is there any empirical evidence that these particular tax cuts help the economy by encouraging productive investment (as opposed to increasing demand)?

—*Stuart E. Baker, Tallahassee, Fla.*

In 1993, when Clinton and the Democrats in Congress increased taxes, Republicans screamed that this action would stifle economic growth. The remaining seven years of the Clinton administration saw the economy grow at the relatively high rate of 4% per year.

After the 2001 recession, the Bush tax cuts were enacted as "The Economic Growth and Tax Relief Reconciliation Act of 2001." Then, between 2001 and 2007, the economy expanded at only 2.7% per year, the slowest post-recession recovery on record. So the general experience of the last two decades is hardly a brief for the positive impact of tax cuts on economic growth.

The Clinton tax increase mainly affected society's highest income groups. The Bush tax cuts were focused on the wealthy and included specific reductions in tax rates on capital gains and dividends. So these two cases provide some empirical evidence—albeit crude empirical evidence—that tax cuts on these categories of income do not generate more productive investment and more rapid economic growth, and that tax increases on these categories of income do not curtail investment and growth. (Moreover, no one should expect much impact on demand, one way or the other, from changes in taxes on high-income groups because their expenditures are not very sensitive to changes in their incomes.)

There is also more finely focused evidence that lowering taxes on capital gains and dividends does not have much, if any, positive impact on economic growth. For example, in a 2005 "Tax Facts" piece from the Tax Policy Center, economists Troy Kravitz and Leonard Burman point out that "Capital gains [tax] rates display no contemporaneous correlation with real GDP growth during the last 50 years."

One reason that preferential tax treatment for capital gains does not have much, if any, positive impact on productive investment is that this treatment creates strong incentives for the wealthy to invest in non-productive tax shelters. Burman, who is the author of *The Labyrinth of Capital Gains Tax Policy*, comments: "…the creative energy devoted to cooking up tax shelters could otherwise be channeled into something productive."

Also, when tax reductions for the rich result in an increase in the federal deficit, as is generally the case, and thus more government borrowing, the result could be higher interest rates. And the higher interest rates would tend to negate any positive impact of the tax reduction on investment.

A useful summary of the issues, including references to relevant studies, is the November 2005 report by Joel Friedman of the Center on Budget and Policy Priorities, "Dividend and Capital Gains Tax Cuts Unlikely to Yield Touted Economic Gains."

Those who support the reduction of taxes on the wealthy, capital gains taxes, and taxes on dividends do tout studies that tend to support their position. And there is no denying the fact that people's behavior is affected by tax policy, including the investment behavior of those with high levels of income. Yet the evidence we have does not support the argument that tax adjustments on capital gains and dividends are major factors affecting the course of the economy.

Many of these issues were examined by Joel Slemrod, professor of business economics and public policy, director of the Office of Tax Policy Research at the University of Michigan, and a leading expert on tax issues, in a 2003 interview in *Challenge* magazine. Slemrod summed his view thus: "there is no evidence that links aggregate economic performance to capital gains tax rates." ❏

Sources: Troy Kravitz and Leonard Burman, "Capital Gains Tax Rates, Stock Markets, and Growth," *Tax Notes*, November 7, 2005 (taxpolicycenter.org); Leonard Burman, "Under the Sheltering Lie," Tax Policy Center, December 20, 2005 (taxpolicycenter.org); Joel Friedman, "Dividend and Capital Gains Tax Cuts Unlikely to Yield Touted Economic Gains," Center on Budget and Policy Priorities, November 2005 (cbpp.org); "The Truth about Taxes and Economic Growth: Interview with Joel Semrod," *Challenge*, vol. 46, no. 1, January/February 2003, pp. 5–14 (challengemagazine.com).

The government won't publicly reveal the incomes and tax payments of the wealthy. A little data on a wealthy enclave in Manhattan is an eye-popping view into the heart of tax inequity.

TAXES AND TRANSPARENCY: OUR OPAQUE OPULENT

SAM PIZZIGATI
February 2012

How much of their mega-million incomes did the Koch brothers—the secretive billionaire funders of much of America's right-wing political infrastructure—pay in federal taxes last year? We have simply no idea. The IRS closely guards the confidentiality of income tax returns. We have no way of knowing exactly how much or how little the Koch brothers pay in taxes.

The U.S. Census Bureau guards rich people's privacy even more zealously. The annual Census income reports, the Congressional Budget Office notes, do not even "report an individual's earnings if they exceed a certain level." The result? We know exactly how many Americans make between $50,000 and $100,000. But we have no clue how many make between $500 million and $1 billion.

The reason the Census Bureau gives for this contrast? If more specific information about how much rich Americans are making ever became public, the argument goes, someone might be able to attach some names to the numbers—and violate the privacy of our wealthiest.

We certainly wouldn't want that to happen. But why? Why not make public the incomes of the rich? As a society, after all, we show no similar privacy-protecting zeal on other personal economic fronts.

Take home values, for instance. You can go into county courthouses all across the United States and find out exactly how much our nation's richest—and everyone else—have paid for the properties where they live. So why the special treatment on income? In 1934, back in the Great Depression, lawmakers in Congress essentially asked that same exact question.

If rich people had to annually reveal both their incomes and their federal income tax, these lawmakers believed, the rich might think twice before conniving to cheat Uncle Sam—and Congress would be able to more quickly identify and plug whatever new loopholes the rich might be tunneling through the tax code.

A congressional majority would soon agree. The resulting 1934 Revenue Act would apply a disclosure mandate to all individuals subject to the federal income tax. At that time, only the nation's most affluent 7.25% faced any income tax liability.

The new Revenue Act almost immediately outraged America's most affluent. They quickly began lining up friendly lawmakers to introduce legislation that would repeal disclosure.

Observers gave this repeal campaign no chance. But the deep pockets behind the effort tied their "cause" to the sensational Lindbergh baby kidnapping trial then filling the nation's front pages. If the rich had to disclose their incomes, the argument went, kidnappers would gain targets.

This PR push would carry the day. In less than three months, historian Marjorie Kornhauser notes, the campaign to repeal income tax disclosure "went from hopeless to a complete success."

Privacy for the privileged has reigned ever since. But every once in a while an enterprising scholar will breach that privacy wall. Economist Martin Sullivan has done just that—in the trade journal Tax Notes. He has placed his sleuthing skills to work on the Helmsley Building, a 35-story Manhattan landmark now home to 130 of New York's deepest pockets.

The IRS, if you ask, won't tell you how much any of those deep pockets make. But the IRS, as Sullivan observes, does tabulate "individual tax return data by ZIP code." The Helmsley Building just happens to have its own zip code.

In 2007, Sullivan discovered, the 130 federal tax returns filed from the Helmsley zip code averaged $1.17 million in income. The Helmsley deep pockets paid only 13.7% of that income in federal income tax.

These fortunates paid another 1% of their incomes in Social Security and Medicare payroll tax. In all, their 2007 federal tax bill averaged 14.7%.

Sullivan's analysis places this 14.7% in a rather stunning context. New York janitors, Sullivan notes, averaged $33,080 in 2007. They paid 24.9% of their incomes in federal taxes. Security guards in New York made $27,640. They paid 23.8% of their incomes in federal taxes.

In other words, the residents of the Helmsley reported around 35 times more income than their janitors and 42 times more than their security guards, yet paid substantially less of their incomes in federal taxes.

SOURCES: Changes in the Distribution of Workers' Hourly Wages Between 1979 and 2009, Congressional Budget Office report, February 16, 2011; Marjorie E. Kornhauser, "Shaping Public Opinion and the Law: How a 'Common Man' Campaign Ended a Rich Man's Law," Law and Contemporary Problems, Vol. 73, No. 1, 2009; Martin A. Sullivan, "At the Helmsley Building, the Little People Pay the Taxes," tax.com, Feb. 17, 2011;

This article was originally published in Too Much, a weekly newsletter edited by Sam Pizzigati. Too Much is a project of the Institute for Policy Studies' Program on Inequality and the Common Good. <toomuchonline.org>

Despite a growing awareness that stock fluctuations don't affect most families, some commentators have been claiming that Wall Street has been "democratized." Sylvia Allegretto debunks the myth that most Americans benefit when the stock market swells.

STOCK MARKET GAINS INCONSEQUENTIAL FOR MOST AMERICANS

BY SYLVIA A. ALLEGRETTO
October 2012

The U.S. economy officially came out of recession in June 2009 and is growing again—albeit tepidly. But the modest gains from three and a half years of recovery have not reached everyone. The recovery seems to be on two tracks: one track for typical families and workers, who continue to struggle against high rates of unemployment and declining incomes; and another track for the investor/wealthy class, who have enjoyed significant improvements in their portfolios due to stock market gains and record corporate profits.

The Wall Street-Main Street divide—the disconnect between stock market performance and the underlying economy—has often marked recent economic experience, particularly over the last several years. But how can this be the case if

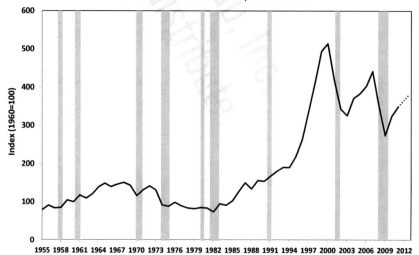

**FIGURE 1: BOOMS AND BUSTS:
THE U.S. STOCK MARKET, 1955-2011**

Note: Shaded areas denote recessions. Data are Standard and Poor's Composite Index (inflation adjusted). Dotted line represents S&P on Oct. 23, 2012 using 2.2% Blue Chip forecast for inflation for 2012.

Source: Economic Policy Institute's State of Working America (2012), Figure 6F.

FIGURE 2: SHARE OF HOUSEHOLDS OWNING STOCK

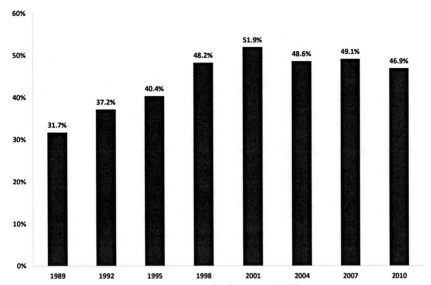

Source: Economic Policy Institute's stateofworkingamerica.com/subjects/wealth.

Survey of Consumer Finances data from Table 6.1 based on calculations by Edward N. Wolff (2012).

the stock market, as we so often hear, has been "democratized" over the last few decades?

The attention given to the minute-by-minute gyrations of the stock market—fed by dedicated news channels obsessively analyzing their performance—may give the impression that everyone in the United States is heavily invested. Further, given all the attention, one may think that the economic well-being of most Americans is directly tied to stock market performance and that the resulting benefits are broadly dispensed. This is a widely held misconception. A look at the data tells the true story.

First, let's start with how stocks have fared since the Great Recession. As Figure 1 shows, the Standard & Poor's Composite Index (adjusted for inflation) has made significant gains since it bottomed out in early 2009. The figure also includes a point for 2012 (as of Oct. 23). Another sharp rise seems to be mirroring those of the recent past—which proved to be bubbles in the making.

For context, the labor market continues its painfully slow "recovery," as incomes for typical households have declined each year from 2007 through 2011, totaling 8.1%—putting incomes back to where they were in the mid-1990s.

Has the stock market really been "democratized"? The most recent triennial data from the Survey of Consumer Finances (Figure 2) show that less than half of all households (46.9%) have any investments in the stock market.[1] This figure is down from its high of 51.9% in the boom year of 2001. A further breakdown shows that 95% of households in the top 1% of the wealth distribution own stock, versus

---

1. Stock ownership may be direct (owning shares in a particular company) or indirect (owning shares through a mutual fund or a retirement account).

FIGURE 3: DISTRIBUTION OF STOCK MARKET WEALTH, 1989–2010

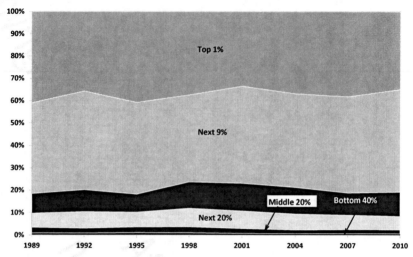

Source: Economic Policy Institute's State of Working America (2012), Figure 6G, based on Survey of Consumer Finances data and calculations by Edward N. Wolff (2012).

44.6% of those in the middle quintile, and 21.5% of those in the bottom quintile. The once increasing shares of families invested in the stock market have leveled off, leaving more than half not invested.

For those who are invested, Figure 3 illustrates who gets what—this is where the notion of a "democratized" stock market really breaks down. The distribution of stocks, by value, is highly tilted to the wealthiest Americans. Generally, the historical trend has been that the top 10% hold about four-fifths of all stock market wealth while the bottom 90% own just one-fifth. In 2010, the top 1% held over a third (35%) of all stock value, while the bottom 60% held just 2.5%. On average, the top 1% had holdings worth $3.5 million, the middle 20% had $8,900, and the bottom 40% had $1,700.

For the most part, lower-, middle-, and even upper-middle-income working-age households depend on their paychecks, not stock portfolios, to meet their everyday economic needs. Typical working families that own stock do so in retirement plans that are costly to turn into cash and deplete future retirement income. Therefore, increasing stock value does little to help most families make ends meet during times of economic hardship. Furthermore, much of the inequality that exists in the U.S. is fostered on Wall Street. ❏

SOURCES: Sylvia A. Allegretto, Berkeley Blog post "Slip slidin' away," Oct. 24, 2012, http://blogs.berkeley.edu/2012/09/12/slip-slidin-away/; Edward N. Wolff, "The Asset Price Meltdown and the Wealth of the Middle Class," Russell Sage Foundation 2010 Project, forthcoming.

"Dr. Dollar" responds to a reader's concerns about speculative bubbles in 2009, just after housing and stock market values plummeted. He explains what happened to the "lost trillions" in home equity and stock values.

WHO GETS THOSE TRILLIONS?

BY ARTHUR MacEWAN
January/February 2009

Dear Dr. Dollar,

As housing prices have fallen, it seems that people have lost a huge amount in terms of the value of their homes. We are told that, over the whole country, trillions of dollars in home equity have been lost. Who gets those trillions? And, likewise, what about the trillions lost in the stock market?
— *Carlos Rafael Alicea Negrón, Bronx, N.Y.*

Dear Carlos:

The simple answer to your question is that no one gets the lost trillions; they are simply gone. But, like all simple answers, this one doesn't explain very much.

Suppose that seven years ago, you bought your house for $200,000. Housing prices continued to rise, and at the beginning of 2007 you saw that other people in your neighborhood were selling houses similar to yours for $400,000. So you, quite reasonably, figured that your house was worth $400,000.

But now the housing bubble has burst. Similar houses in your neighborhood are selling for "only" $300,000 and thus it is now quite reasonable to figure that the value of your house has dropped by $100,000 as compared to the beginning of 2007. (Multiply this $100,000 by roughly 75 million homes across the country, and you have losses of $7.5 trillion.)

Your house, however, was not involved in any actual transaction at this lower value. So no one has gained the value you lost. If, for example, last year one of your neighbors had sold an equivalent house for $400,000 and now buys your house for $300,000 this neighbor would have gained what you lost. But most houses are not bought and sold in any given year. Their value is determined by those equivalent (or similar) houses that are actually bought and sold.

Moreover, even if someone bought your house at $300,000, that person would gain the value you lost only in the special case of the example above, where the person was lucky enough to have sold an equivalent house at $400,000. If instead that person wasa new entrant to the housing market or a person who had just sold a similar house elsewhere for $300,000, then no one would be gaining what you lost.

Thus in the great majority of cases, the $100,000 value would simply be gone, and no one would have gotten it.

The situation on the stock market is similar. The values of stocks are determined by the sales that actually take place. When we hear that today the value of Mega

Corporation's stock fell from $100 a share to $75 dollars a share, this means that the price of shares that were traded today were selling at $75 while those that were traded yesterday were selling for $100. But most shares of Mega Corporation were not actually traded either day. Their value fell—just like the value of your house fell when neighbors sold their houses—but no one gained this lost value. As in the housing market, the values of stocks have declined by trillions, but the trillions are simply gone.

Of course as with the situation in the housing market, some actual gains of value can take place when stock prices fall. If someone sold a share of Mega Corporation yesterday for $100 and bought it today for $75, this person obtained a gain. But with most of the declines in stock values, no one gets a gain.

To understand what has happened recently, it is useful to keep in mind that the high housing values of recent years were the result of a speculative bubble. The values increased not because there was some real change in the houses themselves. The houses were not providing more living services to the degree that their prices rose. The prices of housing rose because people expected them to rise more. The situation was a speculative bubble, and housing prices rose far above their historical trend.

And just as, in general, the loss of value when prices fell was not balanced by a gain, the gains that people saw when the bubbles expanded were not balanced by losses. As the bubble grew and the value of your house rose from $200,000 to $400,000, no one experienced an equivalent loss. Virtually all home buyers and owners were winners.

But speculative bubbles do not last. ❏

The Great Recession hit black families particularly hard. Economist Jeannette Wicks-Lim explains why the housing market crisis contributed to a sharp increase in the racial wealth divide.

THE GREAT RECESSION IN BLACK WEALTH

BY JEANNETTE WICKS-LIM
January/February 2012

The Great Recession produced the largest setback in racial wealth equality in the United States over the last 25 years. In 2009 the average white household's wealth was 20 times that of the average black household, nearly double that in previous years, according to a 2011 report by the Pew Research Center.

Driving this surge in inequality is a devastating drop in black wealth. The typical black household in 2009 was left with less wealth than at any time since 1984 after correcting for inflation.

It's important to remember wealth's special role—different from income—in supporting a household's economic well-being. Income pays for everyday expenses—groceries, clothes, and gas. A family's wealth, or net worth, includes all the assets they've built up over time (e.g., savings account, retirement fund, home, car) minus any money they owe (e.g., school loans, credit card debt, mortgage). Access to such wealth determines whether a layoff or medical crisis creates a bump in the road, or pushes a household off a financial cliff. Wealth can also provide families with financial stepping-stones to advance up the economic ladder—such as money for college tuition, or a down payment on a house.

Racial wealth inequality in the United States has always been severe. In 2004, for example, the typical black household had just $1 in net worth for every $11 of a typical white household. This is because families slowly accumulate wealth over their lifetime and across generations. Wealth, consequently, ties the economic fortunes of today's households to the explicitly racist economic institutions in America's past—especially those that existed during key phases of wealth redistribution. For example, the Homesteading Act of 1862 directed the large-scale transfer of government-owned land nearly exclusively to white households. Also starting in the 1930s, the Federal

MEDIAN HOUSEHOLD NET WORTH (2009 DOLLARS)

	1984	1988	1991	1993	1995	2004	2009
White	$76,951	$75,403	$68,203	$67,327	$68,520	$111,313	$92,000
Black	$6,679	$7,263	$7,071	$6,503	$9,885	$9,823	$4,900
Ratio of White to Black	12	10	10	10	7	11	19

Source: Taylor et al., *Twenty-to-One: Wealth Gaps to Rise to Record High Between Whites, Blacks and Hispanics,* Pew Research Center.

Housing Authority made a major push to subsidize home mortgages—for primarily white neighborhoods. On top of that, Jim Crow Laws—in effect until the mid-1960-s—and racial violence severely curtailed efforts by the black community to start their own businesses to generate their own wealth.

The housing market crisis and the Great Recession made racial wealth inequality yet worse for two reasons. First, the wealth of blacks is more concentrated in their homes than the wealth of their white counterparts. Homes of black families make up 59% of their net worth compared to 44% among white families. White households typically hold more of other types of assets like stocks and IRA accounts. So when the housing crisis hit, driving down the value of homes and pushing up foreclosure rates, black households lost a much greater share of their wealth than did white households.

Second, mortgage brokers and lenders marketed subprime mortgages specifically to black households. Subprime mortgages are high-interest loans that are supposed to increase access to home financing for risky borrowers—those with a shaky credit history or low income. But these high-cost loans were disproportionately peddled to black households, even to those that could qualify for conventional loans. One study estimated that in 2007 nearly double the share of upper-income black households (54%) had high-cost mortgages compared to low-income white households (28%).

Subprime mortgages drain away wealth through high fees and interest payments. Worse, predatory lending practices disguise the high-cost of these loans with initially low payments. Payments then shoot up, often leading to default and foreclosure, wiping out a family's home equity wealth. In 2006, Mike Calhoun, president of the Center for Responsible Lending, predicted that the surge of subprime lending within the black community would "…likely be the largest loss of African-American wealth that we have ever seen, wiping out a generation of home wealth building." It was a prescient prediction.

To reverse the rise in racial wealth inequality, we need policies that specifically build wealth among black households, such as the "baby bonds" program proposed by economists William Darity of Duke University and Darrick Hamilton of The New School. Baby bonds would be federally managed, interest-bearing trusts given to the newborns of asset-poor families, and could be as large as $50,000 to $60,000 for the most asset-poor. By using a wealth means-test, this program would disproportionately benefit black communities, while avoiding the controversy of a reparations policy. When recipients reach age 18, they could use the funds for a house down payment, tuition, or to start a business. This program would cost about $60 billion per year, which could easily be covered by letting the Bush-era tax cuts expire for the top 1% of income earners. ❏

Sources: Amaad Rivera, Brenda Cotto-Escalera, Anisha Desai, Jeannette Huezo, and Dedrick Muhammad, *Foreclosed: State of the Dream 2008*, United for a Fair Economy, 2008; Citizens for Tax Justice, "The Bush Tax Cuts Cost Two and a Half Times as Much as the House Democrats' Health Care Proposal," CTJ Policy Brief, September 9, 2009; Darrick Hamilton and William Darity, Jr., "Can 'Baby Bonds' Eliminate the Racial Wealth Gap in Putative Post-Racial America?" *Review of Black Political Economy*, 2010; Paul Taylor, Rakesh Kochhar, Richard Fry, Gabriel Velasco, and Seth Motel, *Twenty-to-One: Wealth Gaps to Rise to Record High Between Whites, Blacks and Hispanics*, Washington DC: Pew Research Center, 2011.

Amy Gluckman and Allison Thuotte interviewed Harvard epidemiologist Ichiro Kawachi in November 2007 about his research on social and economic factors that affect health in different societies. Kawachi explains how economic inequality can have a profound impact on our health.

INEQUALITY: BAD FOR YOUR HEALTH

AN INTERVIEW WITH ICHIRO KAWACHI
January/February 2008

How do you stay healthy? That's a no brainer, right? Eat the right foods, exercise, quit smoking, get regular medical checkups. Epidemiologist Ichiro Kawachi wants to add a new item to the list: live in a relatively egalitarian society. Kawachi, a professor of social epidemiology at the Harvard School of Public Health, has carried out a wide range of research studies on the social and economic factors that account for average health outcomes in different societies. Among the most novel conclusions of this body of research is that people in societies with high levels of economic inequality are less healthy than those living in more equal societies regardless of their absolute levels of income.

The work of Kawachi and his colleagues suggests that the public debate about health really needs to be much broader, encompassing a wide range of public policies—in many cases economic policies—that do not explicitly address health but that nonetheless condition how long and how robust our lives will be. Their work traces the multidimensional relationship between an individual's health and the qualities of her social world, many of which can shift dramatically when the gap between rich and poor widens.

Dollars & Sense: Your research looks at the relationship between economic factors and health, especially whether living in a more unequal society, in itself, has a negative effect on health outcomes—and you have found evidence that it does. But I want to start by being really clear about what this hypothesis means. There seems to be such a complicated web of possible relationships between income and health.

Ichiro Kawachi: Let's start with how your own income affects your health. Most obviously, income enables people to purchase the goods and services that promote health: purchasing good, healthy food, being able to use the income to live in a safe and healthy neighborhood, being able to purchase sports equipment. Income enables people to carry out the advice of public health experts about how to behave in ways that promote longevity.

But in addition to that, having a secure income has an important psychosocial effect. It provides people with a sense of control and mastery over their lives. And lots of psychologists now say that sense of control, along with the ability to plan for the future, is in itself a very important source of psychological health. Knowing that your future is secure, that you're not going to be too financially stressed, also provides incentives for people to invest in their health. Put another way, if my mind is taken up with having to try to make ends meet, I don't have sufficient time to listen to my doctor's advice and invest in my health in various ways.

So there are some obvious ways in which having adequate income is important for health. This is what we call the absolute income effect—that is, the effect of your own income on your own health. If only absolute income matters, then your health is determined by your income alone, and it doesn't matter what anybody else makes. But our hypothesis has been that relative income might also matter: namely, where your income stands in relation to others'. That's where the distribution of income comes in. We have looked at the idea that when the distance between your income and the incomes of the rest of society grows very large, this may pose an additional health hazard.

How could people's relative income have an impact on health, even if their incomes are adequate in absolute terms? There are a couple of possible pathways. One is this ancient theory of relative deprivation: the idea that given a particular level of income, the greater the distance between your income and the incomes of the rest of society, the more miserable you feel. People *are* sensitive to their relative position in society vis-à-vis income. You may have a standard of living above the poverty level; nonetheless, if you live in a community or a society in which everyone else is making so much more, you might feel frustrated or miserable as a result, and this might have deleterious psychological and perhaps behavioral consequences. So that's one idea.

Another hypothesis about why income distribution matters is that when the income or wealth gap between the top and bottom grows, certain things begin to happen within the realm of politics. For example, when the wealthiest segment of society pulls away from the rest of us, they literally begin to segregate themselves in terms of where they live, and they begin to purchase services like health care and education through private means. This translates into a dynamic where wealthy people see that their tax dollars are not being spent for their own benefit, which in turn leads to a reduced basis for cooperation and spending on public goods. So I think there is an entirely separate political mechanism that's distinct from the psychological mechanism involved in notions of relative deprivation.

These are some of the key ways in which income inequality is corrosive for the public's health.

D&S: When you talk about relative deprivation, are you talking primarily about poor people, or does the evidence suggest that inequality affects health outcomes up and down the income ladder? For instance, what about the middle class? I think for the public to understand the inequality effect as something different from just the absolute-income effect, they would have to see that it isn't only poor people who can be hurt by inequality.

IK: Exactly, that's my argument. If you subscribe to the theory that it's only your own income that matters for health, then obviously middle-class people would not have much to worry about—they're able to put food on the table, they have adequate clothing and shelter, they're beyond poverty. What the relative-income theory suggests is that even middle-class people might be less healthy than they would be if they lived in a more egalitarian society.

D&S: That's what I was wondering about. Say we compared a person at the median income level in the United States versus Germany, both of whom certainly have enough income to cover all of the basic building blocks of good health. Would this hypothesis lead you to expect that, other things being equal, the middle-income person in the United States will likely have worse health because economic inequality is greater here?

IK: Yes, that's exactly right. And that's borne out. Americans are much less healthy than Europeans, for example, in spite of having higher average wealth.

D&S: But, unlike most other rich countries, the United States does not have universal health care. Couldn't that explain the poorer health outcomes here?

IK: Not entirely. There was a very interesting paper that came out last year comparing the health of Americans to the health of people in England, using very comparable, nationally representative surveys. They looked at the prevalence of major conditions such as heart attack, obesity, diabetes, hypertension. On virtually every indicator, the *top* third of Americans by income—virtually all of whom had health insurance—were still sicker than the *bottom* third of people in England. The comparison was confined to white Americans and white Britons, so they even abstracted out the contribution of racial disparities.

Health insurance certainly matters—I'm not downgrading its importance—but part of the reason Americans are so sick is because we live in a really unequal society, and it begins to tell on the physiology.

D&S: Has anyone tried to compare countries that have universal health care but have differing levels of inequality?

IK: There have been comparisons across Western European countries, all of which pretty much have universal coverage. If you compare the Scandinavian countries against the U.K. and other European countries, you generally see that the Scandinavians do have a better level of health. The more egalitarian the country, the healthier its citizens tend to be. But that's about as much as we can say. I'm not aware of really careful comparative studies; I'm making a generalization based on broad patterns.

D&S: It sounds like there is still plenty of research to do.

IK: Yes.

D&S: You have already mentioned a couple of possible mechanisms by which an unequal distribution of income could affect health. Are there any other mechanisms that you would point to?

IK: I think those are the two big ones: the political mechanism, which happens at the level of society when the income distribution widens, and then the individual mechanism, which is the relative deprivation that people feel. But I should add that relative deprivation itself can affect health through a variety of mechanisms. For instance, there is evidence that a sense of relative deprivation leads people into a spending race to try to keep up with the Joneses—a pattern of conspicuous, wasteful consumption, working in order to spend, to try to keep up with the lifestyle of the people at the top. This leads to many behaviors with deleterious health consequences, among them overwork, stress, not spending enough time with loved ones, and so forth.

Very interestingly, a couple of economists recently analyzed a study of relative deprivation, which used an index based upon the gap between your income and the incomes of everybody above you within your social comparison group, namely, people with the same occupation, or people in the same age group or living in the same state. What they found was that the greater the gap between a person's own income and the average income of their comparison group, the shorter their lives, the lower their life expectancy, as well as the higher their smoking rates, the higher their utilization of mental health services, and so on. This is suggestive evidence that deprivation relative to average income may actually matter for people's health.

D&S: It's interesting—this part of your analysis almost starts to dovetail with Juliet Schor's work.

IK: Absolutely, that's right. What Juliet Schor writes about in *The Overspent American* is consumerism. It seems to me that in a society with greater income inequality, there's so much more consumerism, that the kind of pathological behavior she describes is so much more acute in unequal societies, driven by people trying to emulate the behavior of those who are pulling away from them.

D&S: Your research no doubt reflects your background as a social epidemiologist. However, it seems as though many mainstream economists view these issues completely differently: many do not accept the existence of *any* causal effect running from income to health, except possibly to the degree that your income affects how much health care you can purchase.

IK: Yes, there is a lot of pushback from economists who, as you say, are even skeptical that absolute income matters for health. What I would say to them is, try to be a little bit open-minded about the empirical evidence. It seems to me that much of the dismissal from economists is not based upon looking at the empirical data. When they do, there is a shift: some economists are now beginning to publish studies that actually agree with what we are saying. For example, the study on relative deprivation and health I mentioned was done by a couple of economists. Another example: some studies by an erstwhile critic of mine, Jeffrey Milyo, and Jennifer Mellor, who in the past have criticized our studies on income distribution and health in the United States as not being robust to different kinds of model specifications—a very technical debate. Anyway, most recently they published an interesting study based on an experiment in which they had participants play a prisoners' dilemma kind of game to see how much they cooperate as opposed to act selfishly. One of the things Mellor and Milyo found was that as they varied the distribution of the honoraria they paid to the participants, the more unequal the distribution of this "income," the more selfishly the players acted. They concluded that their results support what we have been contending, which is that income inequality leads to psychosocial effects where people become less trusting, less cohesive, and less likely to contribute to public spending.

D&S: That's fascinating.

IK: Yes, it's very interesting. Some of the recent evidence from economists themselves has begun to support what we're saying.

D&S: In other parts of the world, and especially in Africa, there are examples of societies whose economies are failing or stagnating *because of* widespread public health issues, for example HIV/AIDS. So it seems as if not only can low income cause poor health, but also that poor health can cause low income. I wonder if your research has anything to say about the complicated web between income and health that those countries are dealing with.

IK: There's no doubt that in sub-Saharan Africa, poor health is the major impediment to economic growth. You have good econometric studies suggesting that the toll of HIV, TB, and malaria alone probably slows economic growth by a measurable amount, maybe 1.5% per year. So there's no question that what those countries need is investment to improve people's health in order for them to even begin thinking about escaping the poverty trap.

The same is true in the United States, by the way. Although I've told the story in which the direction of causation runs from income to health, of course poor health is also a major cause of loss of income. When people become ill, for example, they can lose their jobs and hence their income.

What I'll say about the developing world is that in many ways, the continuing lack of improvement in health in, for example, the African subcontinent is itself an expression of the maldistribution of income in the world. As you know, the rich countries are persistently failing to meet the modest amount of funding that's being asked by the World Health Organization to solve many of these problems, like providing malaria tablets and bed nets and HIV pills for everyone in sub-Saharan Africa. If you look at inequality on a global scale, the world itself could benefit from some more redistribution. Today the top 1% of the world's population owns about a third of the world's wealth. So, although certainly the origins of the HIV epidemic are not directly related to income inequality, I think the solution lies in redistributing wealth and income through overseas development aid, from the 5% of the world who live in the rich countries to everyone else.

D&S: Leaving aside some of the countries with the most devastating public health problems, poor countries in general are often focused just on economic growth, on getting their per capita GDP up, but this often means that inequality increases as well—for example, in China. Do you view the inequality effect as significant enough that a developing country concerned about its health outcomes should aim to limit the growth of inequality even if that meant sacrificing some economic growth?

IK: It depends on the country's objectives. But I'd ask the question: what is the purpose of economic growth if not to assure people's level of well-being, which includes their health? Why do people care about economic growth? In order to lead a satisfying and long life, many people would say. If that's the case, then many people living in developing countries may feel exactly as you suggest: they would prefer policies that attend to egalitarian distribution over policies that are aimed purely at growth.

Amartya Sen has written about this; he has pointed to many countries that are poor but nonetheless enjoy a very good level of health. He cites examples like Costa Rica and the Kerala region in India, which are much, much poorer than the United States but enjoy a high level of health. It really depends on the objectives of the country's politicians. In Kerala and Costa Rica, their health record is very much a reflection of how their governments have invested their income in areas that promote health, like education and basic health services—even if doing so means causing a bit of a drag on economic growth.

China also had this record until perhaps ten years ago. Now they're in this era of maximizing growth, and we're seeing a very steep rise in inequality. Although we don't have good health statistics from China, my guess is that this is probably going to tell on its national health status. Actually, we already know that improvement in their child mortality rates for children under five has begun to slow down in the last 20 years, since the introduction of their economic reforms. In the 1950s and 1960s, the records seemed to suggest quite rapid improvements in health in China. But that's begun to slow down.

D&S: Certainly your research on the health effects of inequality could represent a real challenge in the United States in terms of health care policy. In many ways we have a very advanced health care system, but many people are not well served by it. What effect do you think your work could or should have on U.S. health policy?

IK: Regardless of whether you believe what I'm saying about income inequality, the most basic interpretation of this research is that there are many things that determine people's health besides simply access to good health services. We spend a lot of time discussing how to improve health insurance coverage in this country. In the current presidential debates, when they talk about health policy, they're mostly talking about health insurance. But it's myopic to confine discussions of health policy to what's going to be done about health insurance. There are many social determinants of health and thus many other policy options for improving Americans' health. Investing in education, reducing the disparities in income, attacking problems of poverty, improving housing for poor people, investing in neighborhood services and amenities—these are all actually health policies. The most fundamental point about this whole area of research is that there are many determinants of health besides what the politicians call health policy.

D&S: Besides doctors and medical care.

IK: Yes, that's right. I used to be a physician, and physicians do a lot of good, but much of health is also shaped by what goes on outside the health care system. That's probably the most important thing. The second thing is the implication that income certainly matters for health. So policies that affect peoples' incomes, both absolute and relative income, may have health consequences. For instance, I think the kinds of tax policies we have had in recent years—where most of the benefits have accrued to the top 1% and the resulting budget deficits have led to cutbacks of services to the rest of us, especially those in the bottom half of the income distribution—have been a net negative for public health, through the kind of political mechanism I have described.

D&S: It's almost as though there should be a line for health care in the cost-benefit analysis of any change in tax policies or other economic policies.

IK: Absolutely. There's an idea in public health called the health impact assessment. It's a technique modeled after environmental impact assessments, a set of tools that people are advocating should be used at the Cabinet level. The idea is that when, say, the treasury secretary suggests some new economic measure, then we can formally put the proposal through a modeling exercise to forecast its likely effects on health. Health certainly is very sensitive to decisions that are made elsewhere in the Cabinet besides what goes on in Health and Human Services.

D&S: What about global health policy? Are groups like the World Health Organization paying attention to the kind of research that you do?

IK: Yes, they are. Maybe seven or eight years ago, the WHO had a commission on macroeconomics and health, headed by Jeffrey Sachs. The idea was, by increasing funding to tackle big health problems in the developing world, we can also improve their economic performance and end poverty. That commission posed the direction of causality from health to income. In the last three years, the WHO has had a new commission on the social determinants of health, headed by a social epidemiologist from England, Michael Marmot. That group is looking at the other direction of causality—namely, from poverty to ill health—and considering the ways in which government policies in different areas can improve people's social environment in order to improve their health. I think they are due to report next year with some recommendations as well as case examples from different countries, mostly developing countries whose governments have tried to tackle the economic side of things in order to improve health outcomes.

D&S: Right now the United States is continuing on this path of becoming more and more economically stratified. Your work suggests that that doesn't bode well for us in terms of health. I wonder—this is very speculative—but if we stay on this path of worsening inequality, what do you predict our health as a country is likely to look like in 20 or 30 years?

IK: We're already in the bottom third of the 23 OECD countries, the rich countries, in terms of our average health status. Most people are dimly aware that we spend over half of the medical dollars expended on this planet, so they assume that we should therefore be able to purchase the highest level of health. I teach a course on social determinants of health at Harvard, and many of my students are astonished to discover that America is not number one in life expectancy.

I predict that if we continue on this course of growing income inequality, we will continue to slip further. That gains in life expectancy will continue to slow down. Life expectancy is increasing every year, probably because of medical advances, but I suspect that eventually there will be a limit to how much can be delivered through high-tech care and that our health will slip both in relative terms, compared to the rest of the OECD countries, and maybe even in absolute terms, losing some of the gains we have had over the last half century. For example, some demographers are already forecasting that life expectancy will drop in the coming century because of the obesity academic. Add that to the possible effects of income inequality, and I could easily imagine a scenario in which life expectancy might decline in absolute terms as well as in relative terms. We have not yet seen the full impact of the recent rise in inequality on health status, because it takes a while for the full health effects to become apparent in the population. ❑

Sam Pizzigati presents more evidence that inequality is bad for our health as well as our happiness, while also exploring the paradox that regions with greater equality and more happiness also have more suicides.

SWEDES, EQUALITY, AND SUICIDES

SAM PIZZIGATI
May 2011

Any analyst who compares the quality of life in more and less equal societies—and points out that people seem to lead longer and more rewarding lives in more egalitarian places—sooner or later runs into the "suicide" defense.

If greater equality does so much good, defenders of inequality will invariably and accusingly ask, then why do more equal nations like Sweden and Denmark have higher suicide rates than nations with less equality?

Egalitarians have always had trouble with this suicide defense, mainly because this defense of inequality rests on a statistical fact: The more equal nations of the developed world *do* have higher suicide rates than the less equal.

But these more equal nations, as science journalist Maia Szalavitz observes, also have fewer homicides, higher levels of trust and health, and just plain more happiness. What's going on here?

Maybe long, dark winters, some have argued, are driving Scandinavians to take their own lives. Maybe some deeply rooted cultural factors are playing out in ways we don't yet understand. Or maybe, suggests a new paper from two academic economists and two analysts with the Federal Reserve Bank of San Francisco, we really don't have to grasp at theoretical straws any more.

These four authors, tapping a treasure chest of newly available data from the 50 U.S. states and the District of Columbia, have documented—for the first time ever—that what they call the "happiness-suicide paradox" doesn't just operate in dark, cold climes. It's playing out right here in the United States.

New York, one of America's most economically unequal states, rates 45th in the nation for "life satisfaction," a researcher code phrase for happiness. Yet New York has America's lowest suicide rate. Much more equal Utah, the state ranking first in life satisfaction, has the nation's ninth highest suicide rate.

The four authors behind this new research have crunched their data to take "differences in age, gender, race, education, income, marital status, and employment status" into effect. The paradox still holds.

And that brings us back to the original question: What's going on here? How can happier, more equal populations have this greater suicidal hurting within them?

"A detailed conceptual explanation for the paradox," the authors acknowledge, will have to "await future research." But they do take a crack at an explanation.

We need first to reject the "ecological fallacy," the four note, the notion "that individual members of a group have the average characteristics of the group at large."

If you live in a society where the vast majority of people seem to be happy, in other words, that doesn't mean that you are going to be happy, too.

In a more equal, happier society, that becomes a problem—for the unhappy. They live surrounded by people doing just fine.

"Personal unhappiness may be at its worst," as the authors put it, "when surrounded by those who are relatively more content with their lives."

The four analysts note a variety of other research efforts that point in this same direction. Twenty years ago, for instance, analysts found that "suicide rates by the unemployed seem to be higher in low-unemployment regions."

"Discontented people in a happy place," the authors conclude, "may feel particularly harshly treated by life."

We have a tragedy here. What we don't have: a reason to reject the equality that helps leave societies, from Sweden to Utah, happier and healthier places. Misery loves company. We need to confront the misery, not create the company.

SOURCES: Maia Szalavitz, "Why the Happiest States Have the Highest Suicide Rates," Time.com, April 25, 2011; Mary C. Daly, Andrew J. Oswald, Daniel Wilson and Stephen Wu, "The Happiness-Suicide Paradox," Federal Reserve Bank of San Francisco Working Paper Series, February 2010, www.frbsf.org/publications/economics/papers/2010/wp10-30bk.pdf

This article was originally published in Too Much, a weekly newsletter edited by Sam Pizzigati. Too Much is a project of the Institute for Policy Studies' Program on Inequality and the Common Good. <toomuchonline.org>

STRATEGIES FOR CHANGE

Mainstream pundits say taxing the rich is a radical idea, or even a crazy idea, that no re-spectable economist or responsible political leader could support. But today's advocates of wealth taxation have plenty of intellectual and historical backing. Economist John Miller explains that some of the most influential political economists of the 19th and 20th cen-turies understood the importance of taxing wealth. So, too, did Andrew Carnegie, the 19th-century robber baron.

TAX WEALTH
Great Political Economists and Andrew Carnegie Agree

BY JOHN MILLER
ART BY NICK THORKELSON
August 2004

A few years ago, I appeared regularly on talk radio as part of a campaign to block the repeal of the estate tax. As an economist, my job was to cor-rect the distortions and outright hucksterism that the Heritage Foundation and other right-wing think tanks used to demonize the estate tax. In their hands, this modest tax on the inheritance of the richest 2% of U.S. taxpayers became a "death tax" that double-taxed assets in family estates, destroyed family farms and small businesses, and put a brake on economic growth.

After debunking these myths, I was supposed to make the affirmative case for taxing wealth. But before I got very far, whichever con-servative expert I was debating would inevitably interrupt and ask, "Isn't what you advocate straight out of Marx's *Communist Manifesto*?" After my first stammer-ing reply, I got pretty good at saying, "Perhaps, but calls for taxing wealth are also straight out of *The Gospel of Wealth* by Andrew Carnegie. Do you think he was anti-capitalist?" Then it was the conservative's turn to stammer.

In fact, Marx, the philosopher of socialism, and Carnegie, the predatory capital-ist turned philanthropist, weren't the only ones to call for heavy taxation of estates. Over the 19th and 20th centuries, they were joined by great political economists who, unlike Marx, were more concerned with saving capitalism from its excesses than replacing it. Let's take a look at what all these writers had to say.

Karl Marx

Sure enough, the manifesto of the Communist League, penned by Karl Marx and Fredrick Engels in 1848, called for the heavy taxation and even confiscation of inherited wealth. In the *Communist Manifesto*, Marx and Engels developed a transitional program intended to lead Europe away from the horrors of industrial capitalism—a system guided by "naked self interest"—and toward a socialist soci-ety. The 10-step program that Marx and Engels laid out for the most advanced countries began with these demands:

"1. Abolition of property in land and application of all rents of land to public purposes.
2. A heavy or progressive graduated income tax.
3. Abolition of all rights of inheritance."

These clauses need to be understood in context of the socialist debate of the day and Marx's other writings. The first clause did not target the capitalist who directed production on the farm or in the mine, but the landowner or rentier who collected a return merely by owning the land or mine. It was their rents, not the capitalist's profits, that Marx and Engels argued should go to the state to be used for public purposes.

A heavy or progressive graduated income tax, the second clause, hardly seems radical. The U.S. federal income tax had a top tax bracket of 90% in the early post-World War II period (prior to 1962), although effective income tax rates were far lower than that.

Abolishing rights of inheritance, on the other hand, would be a radical change. The third clause targeted large estates; despite its wording, it was not intended to apply to small holders of property. "The distinguishing feature of Communism," as Marx and Engels made clear, "is not the abolition of property generally, but the abolition of bourgeois property." Marx and Engels were concerned with the social relation of capital based on the private ownership of the means of production. They saw this as the root of capitalist class power and the basis of class antagonisms that involved "the exploitation of the many by the few." The abolition of capitalist private property was surely the backbone of the Communist Manifesto, the most influential economic pamphlet ever written.

John Stuart Mill

Writing in the middle of the 19th century as well, the far more respectable John Stuart Mill also called for limitations on inheritance. Mill was a radical, but also a member of the English parliament and the author of the Principles of Political

Economy, the undisputed bible of economists of his day. Mill regarded the laws of distribution of capitalism (who got paid what) to be a matter of social custom and quite malleable, unlike the inalterable market laws that governed production (how commodities were made). Indeed, he devoted long sections of the later editions of Principles to then-novel experiments with workers' cooperatives and utopian communities which he thought could distribute resources more equitably. Mill openly attacked the institution of inheritance and entered a plea for progressive death duties. Observing the gaping inequalities that the industrial system had produced in England, he wrote that there existed "an immense majority" who were condemned from their birth to a life of "never-ending toil" eking out a "precarious subsistence." At the same time, "a small minority" were born with "all the external advantages of life without earning them by any merit or acquiring them by an any exertion of their own."

To curtail this "unearned advantage," Mill called for the "limitation of the sum which any one person may acquire by gift or inheritance to the amount sufficient to constitute a moderate independence." He argued for a "system of legislation that favors equalityof fortunes" to allow individuals to realize "the just claim of the individual to the fruits, whether great or small, of his or her own industry." Otherwise, as he famously observed, all the mechanical inventions of the industrial revolution would only enable "a greater population to live the same life of drudgery and imprisonment and an increased number of manufacturers and others to make fortunes."

Henry George

Henry George, a journalist who taught himself economics, burst onto the American scene in 1879 with the publication of *Progress and Poverty*. This instant bestseller launched a crusade for a "single tax" on land that would put an end to the speculation that George saw as the root cause of the country's unjust distribution of wealth. Although rejected by the economics profession, *Progress and Poverty* sold more cop-

ies than all the economic texts previously published in the United States. It is easy to see why. In epic prose, George laid out the problem plaguing U.S. society at the close of the 19th century:

"The association of poverty with progress is the greatest enigma of our times. It is the central fact from which spring industrial, social, and political difficulties that perplex the world... It is the riddle which the Sphinx of Fate puts to our civilization and which not to answer is to be destroyed. So long as all the increased wealth which modern progress brings goes but to build up great fortunes, to increase luxury, and make sharper the contrast between the House of Have and the House of Want, progress is not real and cannot be permanent."

George traced the maldistribution of wealth to the institution of private property in land. To end the association of poverty with progress, he argued that "we must make land common property." But, he argued, "it is not necessary to confiscate land; it is only necessary to confiscate rent." Taxation was his means for appropriating rent, and George proposed "to abolish all taxation save that upon land values."

Henry George's single tax on land (excluding improvements) was meant to lift the burden of taxation from labor and all productive effort and place it on the rising of value of land. That rising value, he wrote, was the product of social advancement, and should be socialized. It was unjust for such gains to remain in the hands of an individual land owner—"someone whose grandfather owned a pasture on which two generations later, society saw fit to erect a skyscraper," as Robert Heilbroner, the historian of economic ideas, put it.

Progress and Poverty spawned an impressive grassroots movement dedicated to undoing the wealth gap. Georgist Land and Labor clubs sprang up across the nation, and despite a concerted counter-attack by the economics profession, Georgists exerted considerable influence on U.S. tax policy. Most recently, Alaska adopted a George-like proposition. The state created the Alaska Permanent Fund and in its constitution vested the ownership of the state's oil and natural resources in the people as a whole. The Permanent Fund distributes substantial oil revenues as citizen dividends to state residents.

John Maynard Keynes

During the Great Depression of the 1930s, John Maynard Keynes, the pre-eminent economist of the 20th century, warned that a worsening maldistribution of wealth threatened to bring capitalism to its knees. Keynes was no radical. Instead, he was concerned with rescuing capitalism from its own excesses. Keynes's analysis of the instabilities of capitalist economies, and his prescriptions for taming them, guided U.S. economic policy from the 1940s through the 1970s and are still tremendously influential today.

"The outstanding faults of the economic society in which we live," he wrote in The General Theory of Employment, Interest, and Money in 1936, "are its failure to provide for full employment and its arbitrary and inequitable distribution of wealth and incomes." Keynes argued that income inequality and financial instability made for unstable demand among consumers. Without stable demand for goods and services, corporations invested less and cut jobs. Indeed, during the worst years of the Great Depression, this chain of economic events cost more than one-quarter of U.S. workers their jobs.

By 1936, Keynes wrote, British death duties, along with other forms of direct taxation, had made "significant progress toward the removal of very great disparities of wealth and income" of the 19th century. Still, he thought that much more was needed. In the last chapter of the *General Theory*, Keynes went so far as to propose what he called the "euthanasia of the rentier." By this he meant the gradual elimination of "the functionless investor," who made money not by working but by investing accumulated wealth. Keynes imagined a capitalist economy in which public policy kept interest rates so low that they eroded the income of the functionless investor and at the same time lowered the cost of capital (or borrowing funds) so that it was abundant enough to provide jobs for everyone. This was Keynes's plan to support continuous full employment.

Neither the United States nor Britain ever instituted such a policy, but Keynes provided the theoretical bulwark for the "mixed economy" in which public and private investment complemented one another. He showed how government spending could compensate for the instability of private investment, with government investment rising when private investment fell. The mixed economy, which moderated capitalist instability during the post-war period, remains, in the words of economist

Dani Rodrik, "the most valuable heritage the 20th century bequeaths to the 21st century in the realm of economic policy."

Today, just a few years into the 21st century, a conservative movement is trying to rob us of that bequest. The repeal of the estate tax, all but accomplished in 2001, is the sharp end of the axe its adherents are using to cut government down to size. That move is sure to fuel the very excesses that Keynes worried were likely to undo capitalism during the 1930s. It will starve the public sector of revenue, compromising its ability to stabilize the private economy. By showering tax cuts on the richest of our society, it will also exacerbate inequality at a time when the richest 1% already receive their largest share of the nation's income (before taxes) since 1936, the very year that Keynes published the *General Theory*. Finally, repealing the estate tax is unlikely to improve the management of our economic affairs: as Keynes caustically wrote, "the hereditary principle in the transmission of wealth and the control of business is the reason why the leadership of the capitalist cause is weak and stupid."

Andrew Carnegie

It is not easy for me to invoke Andrew Carnegie's defense of the estate tax. For over a decade, I lived in Pittsburgh, where Andrew Carnegie is remembered as the ruthless capitalist who built his public libraries up and down the Monongahela River valley with the money he sweated out of his immigrant workforce, and only after he had busted the union in the local steel mill. Carnegie actually applauded the maldistribution of wealth that Marx, Mill, George, and even Keynes railed against. As he argued, concentrated wealth "is not to be deplored, but welcomed as highly beneficial. Much better this great irregularity than universal squalor."

But despite these apologetics, Carnegie was deeply troubled by large inheritances. "Why should men leave great fortunes to their children?" he asked in his 1889 book, *The Gospel of Wealth*. "If this is done from affection, is it not misguided affection? Observation teaches that, generally speaking, it is not well for the children that they should be so burdened."

Carnegie was also an unabashed supporter of the estate tax. "The growing disposition to tax more and more heavily large estates left at death," Carnegie declared, "is a cheering indication of the growth of a salutary change in public opinion." He added that "of all forms of taxation, this seems the wisest.... By taxing estates heavily at death, the state marks its condemnation of the selfish millionaire's unworthy life." Finally, Carnegie warned that "the more society is organized around the preservation of wealth for those who already have it, rather than building new wealth, the more impoverished we will all be."

From Here To There

Today, whether one is out to save capitalism from its excesses or to bring capitalist exploitation to a halt, taxing accumulated wealth and especially large estates is essential. On that point, Marx, Mill, George, Keynes, and even Carnegie all agreed. But to subject wealth to fair taxation, we will need to do more than resurrect the ideas of these thinkers. We will need a spate of grassroots organizing—from workers' organizations to organizations of the socially-conscious well-to-do—dedicated to the demand that those who have benefited most from our collective efforts give back the most.

This can be done. A hundred years ago, populists concerned about the concentration of wealth forced Congress to enact the original estate tax. They also pushed through a constitutional amendment allowing a progressive income tax that raised revenue for public services. These kinds of advances can happen again.

It will be no easy task. Politics at the beginning of the 21st century are far less progressive than they were at the beginning of the 20th century. But with the greatest of political economists and even a predatory capitalist on our side, perhaps we have a chance. ❑

The current battle to increase the estate tax—which applies to fewer than the wealthiest 1%—is related to the movement to reduce inequality. Chuck Collins and Dedrick Muhammad propose tying the estate tax to a bold set of asset-building initiatives in order to mobilize support for wealth taxation.

TAX WEALTH TO BROADEN WEALTH

BY CHUCK COLLINS AND DEDRICK MUHAMMAD
JAN/FEB 2004; REVISED OCTOBER 2012

For the past decade, a coalition of business lobbyists and wealthy families has waged a crusade to abolish the nation's only tax on inherited wealth. They've misled the public into believing that the estate tax falls on everyone (when it applies to fewer than the wealthiest 1%) and that it destroys small businesses and family farms (it doesn't). In 2001, their multimillion-dollar lobbying effort paid off. Congress voted to phase out the estate tax by gradually raising the exemption level from $1 million in 2002 to $3.5 million in 2009. The tax disappeared in 2010—millionaires and billionaires who died that year passed on their fortunes tax-free. The future of the estate tax has yet to be determined.

In a time of state budget crises, a skyrocketing national deficit, and continued cuts to the social safety net, this gift to the richest 1% comes at too high a price. In 2011, the estate tax added $20 billion to the U.S. Treasury and stimulated an estimated $10 billion in charitable giving. Its abolition is expected to cost the nation $1 trillion over 20 years, and will only deepen the growing wealth divide.

Progressives need to respond to this polarizing economic agenda with a bold economic agenda of their own. One proposal that has real potential to galvanize public support for preserving the tax is a plan to link it to wealth-broadening policies that would directly augment people's personal and household assets. If estate tax revenues were dedicated to a "wealth opportunity fund"—a public trust fund—and used to underwrite wealth-expanding programs, the benefits of taxing inherited fortunes would be made clear: the wealth tax would directly reduce asset disparities, including longstanding racial inequities. In the process, the proposal would reassert a positive role for redistributive government spending.

Diverging Fortunes

The concentration and polarization of wealth have reached levels that would have been unfathomable just 30 years ago. Between 1971 and 2007, the share of wealth held by the richest 1% of households grew from 19.9% to 35.6%. Within this top 1%, the largest wealth gains accrued to people with household net worth over $50 million. As New York University economist Edward N. Wolff has observed: "The 1990s also saw an explosion in the number of millionaires and multimillionaires.

The number of households worth $1,000,000 or more grew by almost 60%; the number worth $10,000,000 or more almost quadrupled."

Meanwhile, almost one in five households reported zero or negative net worth (excluding the value of their automobiles) throughout the 1990s "boom" years—and racial wealth disparities continued to widen. The median net worth of white households in 2009 was $113,149, which was more than 20 times the median net worth of African American households ($5,677) and 18 times that of Hispanic households ($6,325). The racial wealth gap widened between 2007 and 2010, as households of color lost trillions in home equity in the aftermath of the subprime mortgage crisis.

British commentator Will Hutton observed that "U.S. society is polarizing and its social arteries hardening. The sumptuousness and bleakness of the respective life-styles of rich and poor represent a scale of difference in opportunity and wealth that is almost medieval."

Shrink, Shift, and Shaft

The drive to abolish the estate tax is just one part of a much broader attack on the progressive tax system. Neo-conservatives are pushing their "shrink, shift, and shaft" fiscal agenda: Shrink the regulatory and welfare states (while enlarging the "warfare" and the "watchtower" states); shift the tax burden from progressive taxes (like the estate tax) to regressive payroll and sales taxes; and shaft the overwhelming majority of the population that depends on government programs and services like public schools, libraries, and roads.

In contrast to the period after World War II, when the federal government carried out massive public investment in wealth-broadening initiatives like the GI Bill, the last three years have seen the Bush administration and Congress institute historic federal tax cuts that disproportionately benefit the very wealthy. In five decades, we've gone from a system of progressive taxation that funded America's biggest middle-class expansion to an increasingly regressive tax system inadequate to fund the most basic of social services.

Democrats have been loath to support anything that looks like a tax hike. Many actually voted for the estate tax phase-out. But taxing wealth is good policy, and in the context of a major wealth-building program, it would make good politics.

Consider how such a program would work: By simply freezing the estate tax at its 2009 level (taxing inherited fortunes in excess of $3.5 million at a rate of 45%), the tax could initially generate $20-$25 billion a year for a wealth opportunity fund. But in the coming decades, an enormous intergenerational transfer of wealth will occur and estate tax revenue will grow to between $157 billion and $750 billion a year, depending on which estimated annual growth rate one uses. (The lower projection assumes 2% real growth in wealth. The higher figure assumes a 4% growth rate. See <www.bc.edu/research/swri> for more information about these assumptions.)

If the estate tax were made more progressive, with a top rate returning to 70% on fortunes over $100 million, it would generate enough revenue for a wealth-broadening program similar to the size of the GI Bill.

Asset Building Solutions

How could these revenues be spent? Good proposals and pilot projects already exist to broaden assets and reduce wealth disparities. Taken together, these ideas form the modest beginning of a policy agenda for greater wealth equality.

One example is a wealth-broadening initiative in England. In 2003, the British Parliament established what have become known as "baby bonds"—small government-financed trust funds for each newborn in the country. Small sums are deposited and invested for each newborn infant, and available for withdrawal at age 18.

In 1998, then-U.S. Senator Robert Kerrey introduced similar legislation to create what he called "KidSave" accounts. The KidSave initiative would guarantee every child $1,000 at birth, plus $500 a year for children ages one to five, to be invested until retirement. Through compound returns over time, the accounts would grow substantially, provide a significant supplement to Social Security and other retirement funds, and enable many more Americans to leave inheritances to their children.

Another important program is the national Individual Development Account (IDA) demonstration project. This project gives low-income people matching funds for their savings. While the number of households that benefit from IDAs has been small to date, and the amounts that low-income people have managed to save have been modest, the idea is to ramp up this concept, through expanded public funding, to assist many more households.

Nationwide, many community-based organizations are working to expand homeownership opportunities using a patchwork of development subsidies, low-interest mortgages, and down-payment assistance programs.

A challenge for all of these wealth-broadening programs, including the British baby bonds, is that they don't have an adequate or dedicated source of revenue to bring the efforts to a meaningful scale. Here is where some interesting theoretical proposals are emerging as to how to pay for asset programs.

Yale professors Bruce Ackerman and Anne Alstott put forward an "equality of opportunity" proposal in their book, *The Stakeholder Society*. They advocate imposing an annual 2% tax on wealth, to be paid by the wealthiest 41% of the country. The wealth tax would fund an $80,000 "stake" given to every American at age 21, conditioned on graduating from high school. This notion of "stakeholding," or providing people a piece of the nation's wealth as they come of age, has a long history. In 1797, Tom Paine argued that all new democratic republics, including France and the United States, should guarantee every 21-year-old citizen a wealth stake. And in the United States, land grants and subsidized housing loans have been among the ways that the government has helped individuals build personal property.

Sources other than a wealth tax could provide an additional stream of revenue for wealth building—one interesting example is a proposed "cap and dividend" initiative that would put a price on carbon and generate revenue. Recognizing that the environmental "commons" is being destroyed, Peter Barnes, in *Who Owns the Sky*, proposes a trust capitalized by pollution credits. Polluting companies would purchase carbon and sulfur permits and the permit revenue would be paid into the trust. Barnes compares the idea to the Alaska Permanent Fund, which pays annual dividends to Alaska residents from the state's oil wealth.

By directly contradicting the thrust of the right-wing fiscal agenda, which aims to reduce taxation on the wealthiest and dismantle the ladder of economic opportunity for the rest, a wealth-broadening initiative could move progressive constituencies and candidates from their current defensive posture to a positive new agenda.

Such an initiative would recapture the possibility of affirmative, activist government, reconnecting the people with the potential for productive government spending—as the GI Bill and homeownership expansion programs did for the postwar generation—and dramatize the limitations of the Republican Party's "want another tax cut?" social policy.

At the same time, this emerging movement must defend existing safety nets and investments in opportunity as a foundation for moving forward. Broadening individual wealth alone has its limitations and is not a substitute for a robust social safety net and adequately funded Social Security program.

The Wealth-Broadening Movement

From a constituency mobilization perspective, the proposal solves a problem: From the outset, there has been a fundamental imbalance in the estate tax debate. The wealthy individuals and business interests that pay the tax are highly motivated to abolish it. On the other side, the constituencies that would benefit from retaining it are immobilized.

Eliminating the estate tax will lead to budget cuts and a shifting of the tax burden onto those less able to pay—but this has been hard for the public to see. Because the revenues go into the general treasury, the benefits appear remote.

Linking estate tax revenue to a public "trust fund" would help secure support from the vast majority of Americans who are on the wrong side of today's wealth divide by addressing fundamental aspirations of the middle class and the poor alike: the desire for a degree of economic security, a foothold of opportunity, and the means to pass along assets to the next generation.

On the ground, a nascent "wealth-broadening movement" already exists, made up of community-development corporations and agencies that promote affordable housing and homeownership, credit unions, and Individual Development Accounts, as well as savings and investment clubs within religious congregations. These groups aspire to broaden their programs through state and federal legislation, but are hampered by the absence of sizable funding streams. They could provide organizational infrastructure and resources for the effort.

The cumulative impact of a program to broaden wealth by taxing wealth would be to dramatically reduce, over a generation, the disparities of wealth in the United States. This agenda is particularly important for people of color who were themselves excluded, or whose parents or ancestors were excluded, from previous government-led wealth-building opportunities (see "Last Century's Wealth Broadening Program").

Wealth is a great equalizing force. Cutting across racial lines, families with equal wealth have similar educational results, economic practices, and health conditions. Asset assistance will be all the more meaningful to those who possess few or no assets—disproportionately people of color. In the aftermath of the 2008 Great Recession, Black and Latino households are nearly twice as likely as whites to have zero or negative net worth. A total of 18.6% of white households, 33.9% of black

Last Century's Wealth Broadening Program

In the two decades after World War II, federal education and housing programs moved millions of families onto the multigenerational wealth-building train. Between 1945 and 1968, the percentage of American families living in owner-occupied dwellings rose from 44% to 63%, thanks in large part to a massive public commitment to subsidized and insured mortgages from the Federal Housing Authority (FHA), the Veterans Administration (VA), and the Farmers Home Administration (FmHA).

Prior to the 1940s, mortgages averaged only 58% of property value, excluding all but those with substantial savings from owning homes. The FHA and other mortgage subsidies enabled lenders to lengthen the terms of mortgages and dramatically lower down payments to less than 10%. Government guarantees alone enabled interest rates to fall by two or three points.

Between World War II and 1972, 11 million families bought homes and another 22 million improved their properties, according to Kenneth T. Jackson's history of the FHA, Crabgrass Frontier: The Suburbanization of the United States. The FHA also insured 1.8 million dwellings in multifamily projects. The biggest beneficiary was white suburbia, where half of all housing could claim FHA or VA financing in the 1950s and 1960s. All these housing-subsidy programs helped finance private wealth in the form of homeownership for 35 million families between 1933 and 1978. The home mortgage interest deduction also benefited suburban homeowners, and interstate highway construction served as an indirect subsidy, as it opened up inexpensive land for suburban commuters.

Unfortunately, for a host of reasons—including racial discrimination in mortgage lending practices, housing settlement patterns, income inequality, and unequal educational opportunities—many nonwhite and Latino families were left standing at the wealth-building train station.

Today, racial wealth disparities persist, and are far more extreme even than disparities in income. Homeownership rates for blacks and Latinos are currently stalled at the level where whites were at the end of World War II. While over 73% of non-Latino whites owned their own homes in 2011, homeownership rates for blacks and Latinos combined averaged just 46%.

The post-World War II investment in middle-class wealth expansion was paid for by a system of progressive taxation. The top income-tax rate coming out of the war was 91% (it's 35% today)—and the estate tax included a provision to tax fortunes over $50 million at a 70% rate. In turn, many of the widely shared benefits of post-war spending meant that the progressivity of the tax system enjoyed widespread political support.

households, and 35.8% of Latino households have no wealth, or have liabilities exceeding their assets.

In a sense, this agenda would fulfill the next phase of the American civil rights movement. The movement was able to push through legislation that outlawed the most extreme white supremacist practices, but the reforms never adequately addressed the economic dimension of white supremacy. Efforts such as Dr. Martin Luther King's Poor People's Campaign and the War on Poverty were never fully institutionalized. The implementation of asset-building policies that are racially and ethnically inclusive will strengthen the social fabric for future generations.

Obviously, questions about how to design a program to tax wealth in order to broaden wealth remain. Should wealth-broadening go beyond these notions of individual wealth ownership to include community wealth? For instance, public or community-owned housing units with low monthly fees may not represent private wealth for an individual, but are a tremendous source of economic stability and security. Should the wealth-creation vehicles have strings attached, with funds restricted to education, homeownership, and retirement? How should we recognize, in some financial way, the legacy of racial discrimination in wealth-building? How do we protect these ideas from being co-opted by neo-conservatives and avoid risking greater erosion of the welfare state? And what are the politically winnable forms of wealth taxation?

Wealth-building efforts need a revenue stream in order to have a real impact. Organizations working at the state and national levels to defend the estate tax, and progressive taxes more generally, need a positive, galvanizing policy agenda. In sum, wealth taxation and asset development need one another. Taxing concentrated wealth and linking the revenues to programs that will spread wealth in the next generation is the political heart of a winning strategy to expand wealth ownership and build a more equitable society. ❑

Amid the debate over the U.S. stimulus package, Ryan Dodd urges a more direct attack upon unemployment—a program in which the government guarantees the right to work by offering a minimum-wage job to anyone who may need one. Dodd argues that the costs of unemployment in the capitalist system more than justify government expenditures on such a program.

A NEW WPA?

BY RYAN A. DODD
March/April 2008; revised October 2012

In March 2008, the U.S. economy witnessed the opening salvo of a financial crisis that would eventually bring the global economy to the brink of collapse. After many months of reeling from significant losses at two of its hedge fund units, the investment giant Bear Sterns was forced to sell itself for pennies on the dollar to rival JP Morgan Chase, subsequently followed by an almost endless stream of similar events throughout the summer. It would be another six months until the failure of Lehman Brothers brought on the onset of a truly global panic, exacerbating the recession that had begun in the U.S. in December 2007.

The stock market boom and then the housing boom came to an end, along with the fountains of cheap credit that were their mainspring. Unemployment exploded to 10% of the labor force, workers' wages stagnated, and their work hours increased. Health insurance became less and less affordable for the typical family. And as U.S. military spending escalated, government spending on essential services was drastically reduced. Public infrastructure continued crumbling.

All of these facts serve to remind us that capitalist economies are inherently unstable and structurally incapable of creating full employment at decent wages and benefits. While tax rebates and debt relief may provide some minor protection from economic storms, these measures are temporary—and inadequate—responses to a perpetual problem.

The crisis could have helped initiate a much-needed discussion of the problem of involuntary unemployment as a structural feature of advanced capitalist economies, one that requires a persistent and not merely a temporary policy response. Alas, such a discussion hasn't materialized. While President Obama's 2009 American Recovery and Reinvestment Act included some public investment projects, the emphasis over the past few years has increasingly shifted towards the status quo ante—an uncritical attachment to monetary policy as the only legitimate means of directing the macroeconomy, coupled with an obsessive drive to balance the federal budget.

As an alternative to these ad hoc policies, or to the free-market fundamentalism still widely preached in Washington, some economists and policymakers in the United States and abroad are touting a policy that seeks to end unemployment via a government promise to provide a job to anyone ready, willing, and able to work.

Argentina's Experiment in Direct Job Creation

In early December 2001, following nearly two decades of neoliberal restructuring, the Argentine economy collapsed. Apparently, two decades of privatization, liberalization, and government austerity, ushered in by Argentina's brutal military junta (in power from 1976 to 1983), were not enough to sate the appetites of global financial capital: earlier that year the International Monetary Fund had withheld $1.3 billion in loans the country needed to service its $142 billion external debt. In response to the IMF's action, the government froze all bank accounts (although many wealthy Argentines managed to relocate their funds abroad before the freeze) and drastically cut government spending. As a consequence, the economy experienced a severe depression as incomes and expenditures fell through the floor. The unemployment rate shot up to a record 21.5% by May 2002, with over 50% of the population living in poverty.

The popular response to the crisis was massive. Protests and demonstrations erupted throughout the country. The government went through five presidents in the course of a month. Workers eventually reclaimed dozens of abandoned factories and created democratically run cooperative enterprises, many of which are still in operation today and are part of a growing co-op movement.

Reclaiming factories was a lengthy and difficult process, however, and the immediate problem of unemployment remained. In response, in April 2002 the Argentine government put into place a direct job creation program known as Plan Jefes de Hogar ("Heads-of-Household Plan"), which promised a job to all heads of households satisfying certain requirements. In order to qualify, a household had to include a child under the age of 18, a person with a disability, or a pregnant woman; the household head had to be unemployed; and each household was generally limited to only one participant in the program. The program provided households with 150 pesos a month for four hours of work a day, five days a week. Program participants mainly engaged in the provision of community services and/or participated in worker training programs administered by local nonprofits.

While limited in scope and viewed by many in the government as an emergency measure, the program was incredibly successful and popular with its workers. It provided jobs and incomes to roughly two million workers, or 13% of Argentina's labor force, as well as bringing desperately needed goods and services—from community gardens to small construction projects—to severely depressed neighborhoods. The entry of many women into the program, while their husbands continued to look for jobs in the private sector, had a liberating effect on traditional family structures. And by some accounts, the program helped facilitate the cooperative movement that subsequently emerged with the takeover of abandoned factories. Not surprisingly, as Argentina's economy has recovered from the depths of the crisis, the government has recently made moves to discontinue this critical experiment in direct job creation.

"Employer of Last Resort"

The Argentine experience with direct job creation represents a real-world example of what is often referred to as the employer of last resort (ELR) proposal by a number of left academics and public policy advocates. Developed over the course of the past two decades, the ELR proposal is based on a rather simple idea. In a capitalist economy, with most people dependent on private employment for their livelihoods, the government has a unique responsibility to guarantee full employment. This responsibility has been affirmed in the U.N. Universal Declaration of Human Rights, which includes a right to employment. A commitment to full employment is also official U.S. government policy as codified in the Employment Act of 1946 and the Humphrey-Hawkins Act of 1976.

Although many versions of the ELR proposal have been put forward, they all revolve around the idea that national governments could guarantee full employment by providing a job to anyone ready, willing, and able to work. The various proposals differ mainly on the wage and benefit packages they would provide to participants. The most common proposal calls for paying all participants a universal basic wage and benefit package, regardless of skills, work experience, or prior earnings. This wage and benefit package would then form the effective minimum for both the public and private sectors of the economy. After fixing a wage and benefit package, the government would allow the quantity of workers in the program to float, rising and falling in response to cyclical fluctuations in private-sector employment.

As with Argentina's program, ELR proposals typically call for participants to work in projects to improve their local communities—everything from basic infrastructure projects to a Green Jobs Corps. Most ELR proponents also advocate a decentralized approach similar to Argentina's, with local public or nonprofit institutions planning and administering the projects, though it is essential that the program be funded at the national level.

This raises an important question: How will governments pay for such a large-scale program? Wouldn't an ELR program require significantly raising taxes or else result in exploding budget deficits? Can governments really afford to employ everyone who wants a job but cannot find one in the private economy? Advocates of ELR address the issue of affordability in different ways, but all agree that the benefits to society vastly outweigh the expense. Many ELR advocates go even further, arguing that any talk of "costs" to society misrepresents the nature of the problem of unemployment. The existence of unemployed workers represents a net cost to society, in terms of lost income and production as well as the psychological and social stresses that result from long spells of unemployment. Employing them represents a net benefit, in terms of increased incomes and enhanced individual and social wellbeing. The real burden of an ELR program, from the perspective of society, is thus effectively zero.

Most estimates of the direct cost of an ELR program are in the range of less than 1% of GDP per year. For the United States, this was less than $132 billion in 2006, or about 5% of the federal budget. (By way of comparison, in 2006 the U.S. government spent over $120 billion on the wars in Iraq and Afghanistan—and that figure does not include the cost of lives lost or ruined or the future costs incurred, for example, for veterans' health care.) Furthermore, an ELR program provides benefits to society in the form of worker retraining, enhanced public infrastructure, and increased social output (e.g., cleaner parks and cities, free child care, public performances, etc.). By increasing the productivity of those participants who attend education or training programs, an ELR program would also decrease real costs throughout the economy. Estimates of program costs take into account a reduction in other forms of social assistance such as food stamps, cash assistance, and unemployment insurance, which would instead be provided to ELR participants in the form of a wage and benefit package. Of course, those who cannot work would still be eligible for these and other forms of assistance.

Today, the ELR idea is mostly confined to academic journals and conferences. Still, proponents can point to a number of little known real-world examples their discussions have helped to shape. For example, the Argentine government explicitly based its Jefes de Hogar program on the work of economists associated with the Center for Full Employment and Price Stability (CFEPS) at the University of Missouri-Kansas City. Daniel Kostzer, an economist at the Argentine Ministry of Labor and one of the main architects of the program, had become familiar with the CFEPS proposal and was attempting to create such a program in Argentina a few years before the collapse provided him with the necessary political support. Similar experiments are being considered or are currently underway in India, France, and Bolivia. Advocates of ELR proposals can also be found at the Levy Economics Institute (U.S.), the Center for Full Employment and Equity (Australia), and the National Jobs for All Coalition (U.S.).

The Case for Direct Job Creation

Involuntary unemployment is a fundamental and inherent feature of a capitalist economy left to its own devices. In a society where most people depend on employment in the private sector for their livelihood, the inability of a capitalist economy to consistently create enough jobs for all who seek work is deeply troubling, pointing to the need for intervention from outside of the private sector. ELR advocates view national governments—with their unique spending abilities, and with their role as, in principle, democratically accountable social institutions—as the most logical institutions for collective action to bring about full employment. In addition, government job creation is viewed as the simplest and most direct means for overcoming the problem of involuntary unemployment in a capitalist economy.

The standard mainstream response to the problem of unemployment is to blame the victims of capitalism for lacking the necessary talents, skills, and effort to get and keep a job. Hence, the mainstream prescription is to promote policies aimed at enhancing the "human capital" of workers in order to make them more "competitive" in a rapidly globalizing economy. The response of ELR advocates is that such policies, if they accomplish anything at all, simply redistribute unemployment and poverty more equitably. For example, according to the Bureau of Labor Statistics, the number of unemployed workers (including so-called "discouraged" and "underemployed" workers) in August 2007 was 16.4 million, while the number of job vacancies was 4.1 million. No amount of investment in human capital is going to change the fact that there simply aren't enough jobs to go around.

Advocates of ELR also consistently reject the Keynesian rubric, with its focus on demand-management strategies—that is, policies aimed at increasing aggregate demand for the output of the economy. This approach has been pursued either directly, through government spending on goods and services (including transfer payments to households), or indirectly, largely through policies intended to increase private investment. Such an approach exacerbates inequality by biasing policy in favor of the already well-to-do, through tax cuts and investment credits to wealthy individuals and powerful corporations. These policies also tend to privilege the more highly skilled and better-paid workers found in the industries that generally benefit from the government's largesse (often arms manufacturers and other military-related companies). For example, much of the increase in government spending during the Cold War era went into the high-tech, capital-intensive, and oligopolized sectors of the economy. Capital-intensive industries require relatively small amounts of labor, and, thus, produce little employment growth per dollar of government expenditure. Under this policy approach, the most that lower-paid or unemployed workers could hope for would be to snatch a few crumbs from the great corporate feast as the economy expanded over time.

In contrast to both the human-capital and demand-management approaches, ELR provides a means for rapidly achieving zero involuntary unemployment. By definition, anyone who is unemployed and chooses not to accept the ELR offer would be considered voluntarily unemployed. Many individuals with sufficient savings and decent job prospects may forgo the opportunity to participate in the ELR program, but ELR always provides them with a backup option.

In addition to the immediate effects of ELR on employment, the program acts as an "automatic stabilizer" in the face of cyclical fluctuations in the private sector of the economy. During a recession, the number of participants in the program can be expected to grow as people are laid off and/or find it increasingly difficult to find private-sector employment. The opposite happens during the recovery phase of the business cycle, as people find it easier to find private-sector employment at wages above the ELR minimum. As a result, ELR advocates argue, the existence of such a program would dampen fluctuations in private-sector activity by setting a floor to the decline in incomes and employment.

A final and less discussed benefit of the program is its socializing effect. The example of Argentina is instructive in this respect. The nature of employment in the Jefes program, oriented as it was toward community rather than market imperatives, created a sense of public involvement and responsibility. Participants reported increases in morale and often continued to work beyond the four hours a day for which they were getting paid; they appreciated the cooperative nature of most of the enterprises and their focus on meeting essential community needs as opposed to quarterly profit targets. By expanding the public sphere, the Jefes program created a spirit of democratic participation in the affairs of the community, unmediated by the impersonal relations of market exchange. These are the kinds of experiences that are essential if capitalist societies are to move beyond the tyranny of the market and toward more cooperative and democratic forms of social organization.

Some economists and advocates have pressed for a similar proposal, the basic income guarantee (BIG). Instead of guaranteeing jobs, under this proposal the government would guarantee a minimum income to everyone by simply giving cash assistance to anyone earning below that level, in an amount equal to the gap between his or her actual income and the established basic income. (Hence this proposal is sometimes referred to as a "negative income tax.") BIG is an important idea deserving wider discussion than it has so far received. But ELR advocates have a number of concerns. One is that a BIG program is inherently inflationary: by providing income without putting people to work, it creates an additional claim on output without directly increasing the production of that output. Another is that BIG programs are less politically palatable—and hence less sustainable—than ELR schemes, which benefit society at large through the provision of public works and other social goods, and which avoid the stigma attached to "welfare" programs. Finally, a job offers social and psychological benefits that an income payment alone does not: maintaining and enhancing work skills, keeping in contact with others, and having the satisfaction of contributing to society. When, for instance, participants in Argentina's Jefes program were offered an income in place of a job, most refused; they preferred to work. Consequently, ELR programs meet the same objectives as basic income guarantee schemes and more, without the negative side effects of inflation and stigmatization. Nonetheless, a BIG program may be appropriate for those who should not be expected to work.

Learning from the Past

The idea that the government in a capitalist economy should provide jobs for the unemployed is not new. In the United States, the various New Deal agencies created during the Great Depression of the 1930s offer a well-known example. Organizations such as the Works Progress Administration and the Civilian Conservation Corps were designed to deal with the massive unemployment of that period. Unemployment peaked at almost 25% of the civilian labor force in 1933 and averaged over 17% for the entire decade. These programs were woefully inadequate, largely due to their limited scale. It ultimately took the massive increases in government expenditure precipitated by the Second World War to pull the U.S. economy out of depression.

The onset of the postwar "Golden Age" and the dominance of Keynesian economics sounded the death knell of direct job creation as a solution to unemployment. The interwar public employment strategy was replaced with a "demand-management" strategy—essentially a sort of trickle-down economics in which various tax incentives and government expenditure programs, mainly military spending, were used to stimulate private investment. Policymakers believed that this would spur economic growth. The twin problems of poverty and unemployment would then be eliminated since, according to President Kennedy's famous aphorism, "a rising tide lifts all boats."

In the mid-1960s, the civil rights movement revived the idea of direct job creation as a solution to the problems of poverty and unemployment. Although the Kennedy and Johnson administrations had declared a so-called War on Poverty, the movement's call for direct job creation fell on deaf ears as the Johnson administration, at the behest of its Council of Economic Advisers, pursued a more conservative approach based on the standard combination of supply-side incentives to increase private investment and assorted strategies to "improve" workers' "human capital" so as to make them more attractive to private employers.

The rise to dominance of neoliberalism since the mid-1970s has resulted in a full-scale retreat from even the mildly social democratic policies of the early postwar period. While a commitment to full employment remains official U.S. policy, the concerns of central bankers and financial capitalists now rule the roost in government circles. This translates into a single-minded obsession with fighting inflation at the expense of all other economic and social objectives. Not only is fighting inflation seemingly the only concern of economic policy, it is seen to be in direct conflict with the goal of full employment (witness the widespread acceptance among economists and policymakers of the NAIRU, or "non-accelerating inflation rate of unemployment" theory, which posits that the economy has a set-point for unemployment, well above zero, below which rapidly rising inflation must occur). Whenever falling unemployment leads to concerns about "excessive" wage growth, central banks are expected to raise interest rates in an attempt to force slack on the economy and thereby decrease inflationary pressures. The resulting unemployment acts as a kind of discipline, tempering the demands of working-class people for higher wages or better working conditions in favor of the interests of large commercial and financial institutions. The postwar commitment to full employment has finally been sacrificed on the altar of price stability.

Different Paths Toward Justice

As demonstrated by the history of public employment programs in the United States and the example of Argentina, direct job-creation programs do not happen absent significant political pressure from below. This is the case whether or not those calling for change explicitly demand an ELR program. Given the hegemonic position of neoliberal ideology, there are many powerful forces today that would be hostile to the idea of governments directly creating jobs for the unemployed. These forces represent a critical barrier to the implementation of an ELR program. In fact, these forces represent a critical barrier to virtually any project for greater social and economic justice. The purpose of initiating a wider discussion of ELR proposals is to build them into more comprehensive programs for social and economic justice. As is always the case, this requires the building of mass-based social movements advocating for these and other progressive policies.

A significant objection to the ELR proposal remains: it's capitalism, stupid. If you don't like unemployment, poverty, and inequality—not to mention war, environmental destruction, and alienating and exploitative work—then you don't like capitalism, and you should seek alternatives instead of reformist employment policies. ELR advocates would not disagree. In the face of the overlapping and myriad problems afflicting a capitalist economy, the achievements of even a full-scale ELR program would be limited. The political difficulties involved in establishing an ELR program in the first place, in the face of opposition from powerful elements of society, would be immense. And certainly, the many experiments in non-capitalist forms of economic and social organization currently being carried out, for example, in the factories of Argentina and elsewhere, should be championed. But it is fair to ask: shouldn't we also champion living wage laws, a stronger social safety net for those who cannot or should not be expected to work, and universal health care—as well as an end to imperialist wars of aggression, environmentally unsustainable practices, and the degradation of work? In sum, shouldn't we seek to alleviate all of the symptoms of capitalism, even as we work toward a better economic system?

One thing remains certain: the problem of involuntary unemployment is not going away anytime soon and the unwillingness to deal with the more specific problems of the past decade in a fundamental way will surely lead to new crises in the future. Perhaps, then, a policy proposal that seeks to "end unemployment as we know it," via a government promise to provide a job to anyone ready, willing, and able to work, will get the hearing it so urgently deserves. ❏

Sources: Joseph Halevi, "The Argentine Crisis," Monthly Review, (April 2002); Pavlina Tcherneva, "Macroeconomic Stabilization Policy in Argentina: A Case Study of the 2002 Currency Collapse and Crisis Resolution through Job Creation," (Bard College Working Paper, 2007); L. Randall Wray, *Understanding Modern Money: The Key to Full Employment and Price Stability* (Edward Elgar, 1998); Congressional Research Service, "The Cost of Iraq, Afghanistan and Other Global War on Terror Operations Since 9/11" (www.fas.org/sgp/crs/natsec/RL33110.pdf, update 7/07); National Jobs for All Coalition, "September 2007 Unemployment Data," www.njfac.org/jobnews.html); Nancy Rose, "Historicizing Government Work Programs: A Spectrum from Workfare to Fair Work" (Center for Full Employment and Price Stability, Seminar Paper No. 2, March 2000); Judith Russell, Economics, Bureaucracy and Race: How Keynesians Misguided the War on Poverty (Columbia Univ. Press, 2004); Fadhel Kaboub, "Employment Guarantee Programs: A Survey of Theories and Policy Experiences" (Levy Economics Institute, Working Paper No. 498, May 2007).

The Great Recession highlighted the vulnerability of the poor. One step to fight poverty is to raise wages for the lowest-paid workers. Jeannette Wicks-Lim debunks the claim that raising the minimum wage would increase unemployment and hurt the poor.

HOW HIGH COULD THE MINIMUM WAGE GO?

A 70% boost would help millions of workers, without killing jobs.

BY JEANNETTE WICKS-LIM
July/August 2012

The minimum wage needs a jolt—not just the usual fine-tuning—if it's ever going to serve as a living wage. Annual full-time earnings at today's $7.25 federal minimum wage are about $15,000 per year. This doesn't come anywhere near providing a decent living standard by any reasonable definition, for any household, least of all households with children. But among the 17 states that either have active campaigns to raise their minimum wage or have raised them already this year, none have suggested raising the wage floor by more than 20%.

How high can the minimum wage go? As it turns out, a lot higher. Economists typically examine whether current minimum-wage laws hike pay rates up too high and cause employers to shed workers from their payrolls in response. But the current stockpile of economic research on minimum wages suggests that past increases have not caused any notable job losses. In other words, minimum wages in the United States have yet to be set too high. In fact, if we use past experience as a guide, businesses should be able to adjust to a jump in the minimum wage as great as 70%. That would push the federal minimum wage up to $12.30. In states with average living costs, full-time earnings at $12.30 per hour can cover the basic needs of the typical low-income working household (assuming both adults in two-adult households are employed).

Why is such a large increase possible? It's because minimum-wage hikes—particularly those in the 20-to-30% range adopted in the United States—impose very modest cost increases on businesses. This is true even for the low-wage, labor-intensive restaurant industry. And because these cost increases are so modest, affected businesses have a variety of options for adjusting to their higher labor costs that are less drastic than laying off workers.

Take, for example, the 31% rise in Arizona's state minimum wage in 2006, from $5.15 to $6.75. My colleague Robert Pollin and I have estimated that the average restaurant in Arizona could expect to see its costs rise between 1% and 2% of their sales revenue. What kind of adjustment would this restaurant need to make? A price hike of 1% or 2% would completely cover this cost increase. This would amount to raising the price of a $10.00 meal to $10.20.

To figure out what is the largest increase businesses can adjust to without laying off workers, we can take stock of what we know about how businesses have adjusted in the past and then figure out how much businesses can adjust along those lines.

Let's stick with the example of restaurants, since these businesses tend to experience the largest rise in costs. And let's start with a big increase in the minimum wage: 50%. If we add together all the raises mandated by such an increase in the minimum wage (assuming the same number of workers and hours worked), the raises employers would need to give workers earning wages above the minimum wage to maintain a stable wage hierarchy, and their higher payroll taxes, the total cost increase of a 50% minimum-wage hike would be 3.2% of restaurant sales.

The cost increase that these restaurants need to absorb, however, will actually be even smaller than 3.2% of their sales revenue. That's because when workers' wages rise, workers stay at their jobs for longer periods of time, saving businesses the money they would otherwise have spent on recruiting and training new workers. These savings range between 10% and 25% of the costs from raising the minimum wage. If the higher wage motivates workers to work harder, businesses would experience even more cost savings.

So what would happen if restaurants raised their prices to cover their minimum wage cost increases? One answer is that people may react to the higher prices by eating out less often and restaurant owners would lose business. With a large enough falloff in business, restaurants would have to cut back on their workforce. But it's unlikely that a price increase as small as 3% would stop people from eating out. Think about it: if a family is already willing to pay $40.00 to eat dinner out, it hardly seems likely that a price increase as small as $1.20 would to cause them to forgo all the benefits of eating out like getting together with family or friends and saving time in meal preparation, clean up, and grocery shopping.

Still, let's assume that a 3% price hike actually does influence people to eat out less. The key questions now are how much less and can restaurant owners make up their lost business activity? Economists have found that restaurant patrons do not react strongly to changes in menu prices (economists call this an "inelastic" demand). Estimates from industry research suggest that a price increase of 3% may reduce consumer demand by about 2%.

However, if these small price increases take place within a growing economy—even a slow-growing economy—restaurant owners will probably see little change in their sales, because people eat out more when the economy expands and their incomes rise. In an economy growing at a rate of 3% annually, which is slower than average for the U.S. economy, consumer demand for restaurant meals will typically rise by about 2.4%. This would boost sales more than enough to make up for any loss that restaurants may experience from a 3% price increase. In other words, consumers would still eat out more often even after a 50% minimum-wage hike.

After taking account of the ways that restaurants can adjust to the higher labor costs from a minimum wage hike, it turns out that the biggest minimum wage increase that restaurants can absorb while maintaining at least the same level of business activity is 70%. In 2004, Santa Fe, New Mexico, came close to this. Its citywide living-wage ordinance raised the wage floor by 65%—from $5.15 to $8.50. A city-commissioned report after it was put into effect found that "overall employment levels have been unaffected by the living wage ordinance."

However, even if the federal minimum rate were 70% higher, or $12.30, it would still fall short for two major groups of workers. First, one-worker families raising young children need generous income supports in addition to minimum wage earnings to help cover the high cost of raising children. Second, minimum-wage workers who live in expensive areas, such as New York City and Washington, D.C., require affordable housing programs.

A 70% minimum-wage hike is the biggest one-time increase that U.S. businesses can absorb without cutting jobs, but it's not the end of the story. In the future, the minimum wage can inch further upward. For example, it could rise in step with the expanding productive capacity of the U.S. economy, as it did in the 1950s and 1960s. A $12.30 minimum wage today rising each year with worker productivity would reach $17.00 in just over ten years (in 2011 dollars). This wage would be high enough so that a single parent with one child could support a minimally decent living standard. We would finally begin transforming the minimum wage into a living wage for all workers.

Policy discussions around the minimum wage need to move past the debate of whether or not it causes job loss. The evidence is clear: minimum wages, in the range of what's been adopted in the past, do not produce any significant job losses. Now it is time to focus on how we can use minimum wages to maximally support low-wage workers. Can we raise the minimum wage rate to a level we can call a living wage? By my reckoning, we can. ❑

Sources: Jeannette Wicks-Lim and Jeffrey Thompson, "Combining the Minimum Wage and Earned Income Tax Credit Policies to Guarantee a Decent Living Standard to All U.S. Workers" (Political Economy Research Institute, October 2010).

The idea of capping income is not new, but it's rarely been discussed in the United States since the Great Depression. Sam Pizzigati considers this bold idea to reduce wealth inequality.

A BOLD NEW LABOR CALL FOR A 'MAXIMUM WAGE'

SAM PIZZIGATI
August 2012

Americans working at the federal minimum wage are now taking home just $7.25 an hour.

On paper, minimum wage workers are making exactly what they made in July 2009, the last time the minimum wage bumped up. In reality, minimum wage workers are making less today than they made last year—and the year before that—since inflation has eaten away at their incomes.

And if we go back a few decades, today's raw deal on the minimum wage gets even rawer. Back in 1968, minimum wage workers took home $1.60 an hour. To make that much today, adjusting for inflation, a minimum wage worker would have to be earning $10.55 an hour.

In effect, minimum wage workers today are taking home almost $7,000 less over the course of a year than minimum wage workers took home in 1968.

Figures like these don't particularly discomfort our nation's most powerful. We live in tough times, their argument goes. The small businesses that drive our economy, we're informed, can't possibly afford to pay their help any more than they already do.

But the vast majority of our nation's minimum wage workers don't labor for Main Street mom-and-pops. They labor for businesses that no average American would ever call small. Two-thirds of America's low-wage workers, the National Employment Law Project documents, work for companies with over 100 employees on their payrolls.

The 50 largest of these low-wage employers are doing just fine, even with the Great Recession. Over the last five years, these 50 corporations—outfits that range from Wal-Mart to Office Depot—have together returned $175 billion to shareholders in dividends or share buybacks.

And the CEOs at these companies in 2011 averaged $9.4 million in personal compensation. A minimum wage worker would have to labor 623 years bring in that kind of pay.

So what can we do to bring some semblance of fairness back into our workplaces? For starters, we obviously need to raise the minimum wage. But some close observers of America's economic landscape believe we need to do more. A great deal more.

Count Larry Hanley among these more ambitious change agents. Hanley, the president of the Amalgamated Transit Union, sits on the AFL-CIO executive council, the American labor movement's top decision-making body. Hanley has called for a "maximum wage," a cap on the compensation that goes to the corporate execs who profit so hugely off low-wage labor.

This maximum, if Hanley had his way, would be defined as a multiple of the pay that goes to a company's lowest-paid worker. If we had a "maximum wage" set at 100 times that lowest wage, the CEO at a company that paid workers as little as $15,080—the annual take-home for a minimum wage worker—could waltz off with annual pay no higher than just over $1.5 million.

During World War II, Amalgamated Transit Union President Hanley points out, President Franklin D. Roosevelt called for what amounted to a maximum wage. FDR urged Congress to place a 100% tax on income over $25,000 a year, a sum now equal, after inflation, to just over $350,000.

Congress didn't go along. But FDR did end up winning a 94% top tax rate on income over $200,000, a move that would help usher in the greatest years of middle-class prosperity the United States has ever known.

Throughout World War II, FDR enjoyed broad support from within the labor movement—and the general public—for his pay cap notion. Now's the time, Hanley believes, to put that notion back on the political table. We need, he says, "to start a national discussion about creating a maximum wage law."

SOURCES: Bureau of Labor Statistics' Consumer Price Index; Lawrence J. Hanley, "A Maximum Wage Law?" Huffington Post, 8/3/2012; raisetheminimumwage.com, a project of the National Employment Law Project.

This article was originally published in Too Much, *a weekly newsletter edited by Sam Pizzigati.* Too Much *is a project of the Institute for Policy Studies' Program on Inequality and the Common Good. <toomuchonline.org>*

While politicians in Washington and state governments complain that the country can't afford to give aid to families in financial crisis, economist Randy Albelda presents a bold proposal for rebuilding our outdated "social safety net."

BAIL OUT THE SAFETY NET

BY RANDY ALBELDA
January/February 2009

Even before the financial crisis and the recession, a substantial proportion of working families were not making it in America. The recession and the sluggish recovery have only made matters much worse. Poverty rates have increased. More and more families are facing severe economic hardships—finding themselves in need of the social safety net.

And what about that safety net? In the 1990s, the Clinton administration ended "welfare as we know it," but at the same time promised work supports as low-wage workers moved up the ladder. Since then, employment rates for poor and low-income mothers have indeed soared, and so has the demand for affordable housing and child care assistance. But funding for them has not, with long waiting lists for both. As a result, by the early 2000s, these government work supports helped only 10% of the population in working families that couldn't meet their basic needs to actually meet them.

Despite expansions in the Earned Income Tax Credit and public health insurance for children in the 1990s, the public support programs for low-income families provide inadequate help, and even that to only a fraction of those who need it. And for workers who lose their jobs: today, only about a third of all unemployed workers receive unemployment benefits.

The safety net is not only tattered; it is nearly obsolete.

Rising unemployment is beginning to take its toll, as are draconian state budget cuts. Congress and President Obama enacted a large stimulus package to spur the economy and create jobs in 2009. Their focus was mostly on infrastructure, on "rebuilding our crumbling roads and bridges, modernizing schools, ... building wind farms and solar panels," as Obama said.

But bridge repair and even green jobs are not enough. Our physical infrastructure needs work, but so does our social infrastructure. And it's not just the safety net. Quality care for children and long-term care for disabled and elderly people are in short supply—and unaffordably expensive for many families. Moreover, women are disproportionately employed in these sectors, many at low wages that barely enable them to support their own families. In contrast, the construction and green-energy jobs that often pay decent wages with benefits are overwhelmingly filled by men.

So let's enact a bold recovery plan that promotes employment but also reconstructs the safety net and jump-starts the process of upgrading our social infrastructure.

Here are four suggestions:

First, provide federal funding to states to prevent reductions in essential services. Now is not the time to reduce public health investments, stop transportation projects, cut higher education and lay off K-12 and early-education teachers.

Second, recreate our housing infrastructure. In exchange for buying up bad loans, secure foreclosed properties and develop an affordable housing stock.

Third, expand help for families who are struggling to pay for care for children and elders. Doing so will not only help the families struggling to care for their loved ones. It will also provide the job-creation stimulus for women workers that dollars for bridge repair will provide for men.

Fourth, replace our outdated and arbitrary poverty measure with a realistic measure of what it takes to afford basic needs and participate fully in society. This measure should be used to gauge whether the eventual economic recovery is reaching all Americans.

Economic recovery will require bold, public action. Such action isn't limited to reforming our financial system or to traditional stimulus spending. It also means upgrading our social infrastructure in ways that ensure our economy works for all. ❑

The current battle to increase the estate tax—which applies to fewer than the wealthiest 1%—is related to the movement to reduce inequality. Chuck Collins and Dedrick Muhammad propose tying the estate tax to a bold set of asset-building initiatives in order to mobilize support for wealth taxation.

CLOSING THE RACIAL WEALTH GAP FOR THE NEXT GENERATION

BY MEIZHU LUI
October 2012

It was only after the civil rights movement opened up new opportunities for people of color that Judith Roderick, an African-American woman, landed a union job in the defense industry. For quite a few years, she earned high wages and enjoyed health and retirement benefits.

Judith saved her money and bought a home in a predominantly black neighborhood. When the bank denied her a conventional loan to rehab the house even though her income was high, she resorted to a sub-prime, high-interest loan. She set to work on the home repairs and began making loan payments.

Unexpectedly, with defense contracting down in the early 1990s, Judith's employer laid her off. She struggled unsuccessfully to find a job with a similar wage. Meanwhile, her sub-prime loan had her spiraling into ever deeper debt. A few years later, with her neighborhood gentrifying, the bank foreclosed. Judith's home would sell for more than four times what she originally paid.

By this time, Judith had taken over the care of first one and then another grandchild. Life had become a constant struggle to pay bills and keep a roof over her family's heads. Her brief encounter with asset building had now ended, leaving her unable to provide any funds to jumpstart her grandchildren on their own economic life journey.

Judith's story is not unusual for a single woman of color. Better economic times and civil rights victories had allowed her to earn higher pay and begin to acquire financial assets. But when times turned hard, she was knocked back to square one in nothing flat. Last hired, first fired: In the United States, people of color, especially women, are the last on the boat—and the first to be dumped overboard.

The Effects of Racial Wealth Inequality on Future Generations

Women of all races, taken together, have less than half as much wealth as men. But single black and Latino women have only one penny of wealth for every dollar owned by their male counterparts—and only a tiny fraction of a penny for the dollar owned by a single white woman. According to a 2010 study by Mariko Chang, the median wealth of black and Latino single men is less than $10,000. Single white women have more than four times more, or $41,000, while black and Latino single women have a paltry $100 and $120 to cover emergencies and their future retirement!

These numbers for women of color represent the median, or the woman in the middle of the wealth spectrum. Nearly half of women of color have negative wealth, or debt.

Women of color have so little because they are the most likely to work in service occupations that do not provide pensions, paid sick days, health insurance, or any other wealth-enhancing benefits. They are also the most likely to be unmarried, the most likely to be primary caretakers for elders or children, and the most likely to support other family members as well. And, as in Judy's case, they have been the most likely to be inappropriately saddled with predatory loans.

Some 14.2% of white households with young children have no assets, notes a study by the University of Michigan's Trina Shanks, compared to 40% of black and Latino households. Some 60% of white children live with parents who are homeowners, compared to only 22% of black families. Life in an asset-poor household does real damage to children. In her groundbreaking research, Shanks found that household wealth links to school readiness and health. At nine months, all babies in her study had similar scores on child development tests. By the time they turned two, racial disparities—that correlate to wealth gaps—had emerged.

In 2011, for the first time, the majority of babies born in the United States were not white. By 2042, the majority of the nation's population will be of color. Increasing racial economic disparities and demographic trends are racing on a collision course. Either we focus seriously on the needs of all today's children or we will suffer a horrific crash.

'You Have to Work Twice as Hard to be Equal'

In non-white households, one maxim often gets repeated: "You have to work twice as hard to be equal." Why? The rules of the game for economic success have been fixed against people of color. One early example: the nation's first major wealth-building program, the Homestead Act of 1862. This legislation made free land available to those eligible for citizenship. At the time, that meant white.

Another example, from more modern times: Starting in the 1930s, numerous new public policies helped Americans build wealth. The federal government, for instance, backed $120 billion in low-cost home loans through the Federal Housing Administration. These loans enabled millions of families to attain homeownership. But FHA rules had the impact of tying mortgage eligibility to race. Between 1934 and 1962, 98% of FHA-backed loans went to whites in newly constructed suburbs, abandoning people of color to inner city ghettoes, barrios, and Chinatowns that deteriorated as lenders disinvested in them.

The original Social Security, for its part, left out the two occupations—domestic and agricultural work—that supplied the most jobs to women and men of color. After World War II, all veterans were supposed to benefit from the G.I. Bill provisions that paid for higher education. But many colleges and universities had white-only policies. Few non-white veterans could take advantage of G.I. Bill higher education benefits.

Some policies down through the years have been openly discriminatory. Others have been "universal"—that is, designed to apply equally to all regardless of race or ethnicity—but in practice shut out non-whites. Giving a tax deduction for college savings, for example, comes across as a "universal" benefit. But such deductions benefit the higher-income, disproportionately white people who can afford to save, in the process widening the wealth race gap.

The good news? Policies created the racial wealth divide, so policies can also close it. Universal policies, appropriately designed, can help people of color build wealth. Programs specifically targeted to different races and ethnicities will also be needed. Clearly focused interventions can give people of color the boost needed to get everyone to the same starting line. We can help Judith's grandchildren avoid the problems their grandmother faced—if we provide them wealth-building opportunities at every stage of their lives.

Five Policy Ideas to Close the Gap

In 2011, 30 experts of color in the asset-building field convened through the Closing the Racial Wealth Gap Initiative of the Insight Center for Community Economic Development to pinpoint specific life-stage initiatives that could help close the racial wealth divide. These five ideas emerged from their collaboration.

A Wealth Account for Every Baby

Babies cannot choose their parents. The children of parents of color are far less likely than white children to receive financial gifts in their lifetime, or to inherit at their parents' death. One in four white Americans will receive an inheritance, while only one in twenty African Americans will inherit anything—and the amount black inheritors do inherit will typically run only 8% of the bequest that goes to white inheritors.

But we as a nation, if we considered all babies the nation's own, could choose to put a silver spoon into the mouth of every newborn. A government-funded saving account could create an endowed trust at birth for every American baby, with a progressive structure of contribution based on household asset levels. To close the race gap, children would need accounts that yield $50,000 by the time they turn 18. These yields could be used to prepare young men and women for productive and stable lives. The funds could help them attend college, start a business, or put a downpayment on a home.

Using parental asset levels, rather than income, as the criteria for the amount of the public contribution to these accounts would close the racial inheritance gap and provide economic opportunity for all children. A form of this idea with lower contributions was proposed by Senator Hillary Clinton when she was running for President in 2008.

If implemented, this asset-building program would help local communities experience an immediate positive impact. In the UK, after a similar "Baby Bond" program hit the ground in 2005, banks began to develop products to meet the needs of low-income, low-asset families traditionally left out in the financial cold. The collective sums of money in these accounts made low-wealth communities players in the financial marketplace for the first time.

Would this program's cost be too high in a time of deficits? The cost could be offset by the savings from a decreased need for government grant and loan programs for education, business development, and home ownership.

Early Education for All Children

Universal high quality early education would enable all children to get a head start on developing to their full potential. Expanding public education down from age six to birth would boost school readiness and help build the skilled workforce we need for the 21st century.

Such a reform would also better accommodate the new shape of the American family. Single and working motherhood has been growing across every demographic. A public early education system would relieve mothers from the financial stress and the hassle of finding appropriate child care in a private child care system where costs can range up to $20,000 per child per year. Early education would allow mothers to stay in jobs, accrue the benefits brought by seniority, and save for their own and their children's futures. Poor mothers could rest assured that their children have the same developmental opportunities as the children of wealthier mothers.

Candidate Barack Obama proposed expanding early education in 2007. The benefits from this expansion have been noted in global economic circles. World Bank economists have concluded that universal early education can be "the most cost-effective strategy to break the intergenerational transmission of poverty," a move that "improves productivity and social cohesion in the long run." The returns from early childhood education, these researchers note, run "much higher than the returns generated by investing in financial capital," as much as $8 of benefit, one classic study found, for every $1 of preschool investment.

Guaranteed Jobs for Youth and Adults

Unemployment continues to be the problem most on the minds of the American public. Young people in particular are hard put to find a job, at a time in their lives when they should be becoming financially independent, contributing members of society.

In 2012, the jobless rate for white youth was 14.9%, but 28.6% for blacks, 14.4% for Asians, and 18.5% for Latinos. The private sector has not been able to cough up the jobs needed to close the racial income and employment gap. Only a permanent federal guaranteed jobs program, with the government as the employer of last resort providing jobs to all who want to work, will bring the "hard to employ" into the economic fold.

We certainly have the work that needs doing. A jobs program could help tackle the critical issues our country faces. We could be restoring our deteriorating physical infrastructure and addressing unmet human needs. This jobs effort could add in, for young adults between 16 and 24, additional education and training components, everything from college prep to and entrepreneurial skill building.

Full employment would improve wages and benefits in all jobs, since employers would no longer have a pool of desperately unemployed workers willing to take any job regardless of wages and working conditions.

But can we afford to guarantee jobs? We already know that unemployment increases drug and alcohol addiction, depression, domestic violence, and illegal activity. We pay now for these problems through our health care, criminal justice, and social service systems.

The U.S. incarceration rate currently stands at the highest in the world. According to Michelle Alexander in The New Jim Crow, three out of four young black men in Washington, D.C. can expect to serve time in prison. We spend as much per year to keep a young person in prison as we would spend to send them to Harvard. No more throwing money away: We can invest in bringing young people toward a positive adulthood.

Home Ownership

More than any other asset, home ownership symbolizes stability and security. But discriminatory policies past and present have left a wide racial gap in home ownership. Three of four white families own their own homes, only two out of three Asian and Native American families and only one out of two black and Latino families.

Fair lending rules that protect against discrimination and deceptive practices should be at the core of reshaping the housing finance market. The principles embedded in the Community Reinvestment Act of 1977 should be extended to all financial institutions, not just banks, but mortgage companies and other non-bank lending institutions, Wall Street investment and securities firms, insurance companies, and credit unions. All of these must be required to provide "safe and sound" mortgage and home equity products designed to meet the unique needs of our diverse populations and to serve all without bias.

The original Community Reinvestment Act required banks to offer low- and moderate-income people equal access to conventional loans that have predictable payments, such as the 30-year fixed rate mortgage. As a result, lending increased to all low-income borrowers. Between 1993 and 2002, home mortgage lending increased 79.5% to African Americans, 185.8% to Latinos, and 90.6% to low-income borrowers overall, compared to a 51.4% increase among middle-income borrowers. This helped narrow the inequality gap between low and middle-income people and between whites and people of color.

But the foreclosure crisis has wiped out much of the gain in communities of color, since many of the loans were made by financial entities not covered by the CRA. Those snake-oil marketers of the home lending market—and the banks that financed them—should be required to cover loan-forgiveness programs, payment reductions, and payment waivers.

Maintaining and increasing home ownership, especially in communities of color, would have positive ripple effects in the housing market, spurring the construction of affordable homes and the rebuilding of neighborhoods left to decay during the foreclosure crisis.

A Modernized Social Security

People of color are less prepared for retirement than their white counterparts. A stable retirement typically requires a "three-legged stool": personal savings, private retirement plans, and Social Security. A 2005 study by the Center on Budget and Policy Priorities found that only 29% of Latino workers participate in an employer-sponsored retirement plan, while 45% of African American and 53% of white workers do. Three out of four African Americans do not have a private IRA. In terms of financial assets overall, African Americans and Latinos now have only a nickel to the white family's dollar.

People of color, consequently, rely on Social Security more than white Americans. In fact, Social Security amounts to the biggest asset people of color own. If they were to try to buy an insurance policy with a similar payout in the private sector, that policy would cost $433,000.

But Social Security was never meant to be the only source of retirement income. A one-legged stool can never be stable! By itself, Social Security does not lead to economic security in old age. In fact, 30% of retired beneficiaries living in poverty have worked at least 30 years of work qualifying toward Social Security. In 2007, among African Americans receiving Social Security benefits, 30% of elderly married couples and 57% of unmarried elderly relied on Social Security for 90% or more of their income. For Latinos and Asian Pacific Islanders, 39% and 29% of elderly married couples and 63% and 60% of unmarried elders did.

To meet the needs of the growing populations of color, Social Security needs modernizing. A higher minimum benefit would, for starters, help ensure that working people don't spend their twilight years in the shadow of poverty, Social Security's stated goal.

Second, for those—usually women—who have to leave the workforce to care for family members without pay, we need a caregiver credit to help close the gender gap. These women often lack the years of creditable work they need to avoid extremely low benefits. A caregiver wage credit set at one-half of the average wage, awarded for up to five years, could help these women to more secure retirements.

Again, the cost question: Can we afford these reforms? We certainly can. Higher-income people currently pay less of their income in Social Security tax than low- and moderate-income people pay. According to the Commission to Modernize Social Security, raising revenues by lifting the income cap on the payroll tax — by half a percent over 20 years—and including all new public sector workers in Social Security would both allow for benefit expansion and secure the stability of the Social Security trust fund for all Americans.

The Imperative of Racial Economic Justice

When Dr. Martin Luther King Jr. traveled to Washington, D.C., in 1963, he didn't make the trip to tell people about a dream. He went to "cash a promissory note"— the Constitution's promise of life, liberty, and the pursuit of happiness for all, a promise that requires funding to back it.

Cashing this note today, as in Dr. King's time, requires government investment in all people. This investment for all has not been made. The "waters of righteousness" have not rolled down on people of color. Negative waves of institutional disadvantage have hit them instead. If, as a society, we truly believe in equal opportunity for all, then we cannot claim to have a fair race when some people find themselves forced to start well behind the starting line.

Call the investment we need reparations or restitution or a chance to catch up. Or simply call it justice. Whatever we call the goal, racial parity remains not just a moral imperative, but an economic and democratic imperative that will determine our position on the world stage.

In this day and age, an economy that marginalizes large segments of its population cannot be viable. In the United States, the twin engines of equal opportunity and economic growth have stalled. Moving our nation forward will require a bold and comprehensive policy agenda to get both engines firing.

The proposals briefly outlined have the potential to unleash the power of our nation's squandered human resources. If we do nothing, then we slouch inexorably toward American apartheid as our future. But if we provide Judith Roderick's grandchildren a financial nest egg, a quality education beginning at birth, a decent job, affordable homeownership, and a secure retirement—a wealth building opportunity at every stage of life—then this nation will regain its economic stability and global leadership and at last be on the road toward a truly democratic, post-racial society. ❑

Many small farmers have lost their land to big developers. Conservation land trusts provide an option for tenant farmers to take more control over their land, resist corporate consolidation of agricultural production, and help to protect communities and the environment. Michelle Sheehan reports on efforts to help small farmers while rethinking the nature of property ownership.

THE LAND TRUST SOLUTION

BY MICHELLE SHEEHAN
March/April 2005; revised October 2012

It was back in the early 1970s that Steven and Gloria Decater of Covelo, Calif., first started farming an unused plot of land belonging to a neighbor. Over many years, they turned the fallow plot into fertile farmland that yielded a bounty of organic vegetables. They named it "Live Power Community Farm" and launched California's first successful community supported agriculture (CSA) program there in 1988. But the Decaters' hold on the land was vulnerable. Without ownership rights, they risked losing the farm to encroaching development. The couple wanted to buy the property but could not afford the land into which they had poured their lives.

The Decaters found a solution to their land-tenure challenge that gave them ownership rights *and* ensured the land would remain an active organic farm. Their solution creates an important precedent—and a possible path for other small tenant farmers.

With the help of Equity Trust Inc., a Massachusetts-based organization that promotes property ownership reform, the Decaters gained ownership rights to the land in 1995—without having to pay the full value themselves. The couple purchased just its "agricultural use value," while Equity Trust, acting as a conservation land trust (a nonprofit institution that controls land for the benefit of current and future generations), purchased "easements," or deed restrictions, that were equal in value to the land's development rights. Together, the two payments amounted to the original asking price.

Agricultural easements are a good way for small farmers to gain ownership control over land when they're not looking to develop or sell it anyway, because they limit the property's market price to its working agricultural value, making it more affordable—while conserving it.

In transferring development rights to the conservation land trust, the Decaters forever forfeited their rights to subdivide or develop the land for anything other than farming; the terms cannot be changed unless both parties agree through a court process. The transaction unpacked the bundle of property rights associated with land ownership, dividing ownership between two entities and placing deliberate restrictions on how the land could be used in the future.

Ramped Up Land-Use Rules

This approach made sense for the Decaters, because they were interested in more than just owning the farm for themselves. "We wanted to have some sort of relationship where it wasn't merely privatized ownership," Gloria explains, "but a socially and economically responsible form of land tenure." They also wanted to make certain that the land would continue to be cultivated by resident farmers with sustainable methods well into the future.

Their vision for the farm was secured by designing easement provisions that went beyond any existing precedent. For example, most easements on farmland define agriculture rather loosely. As Equity Trust's Ellie Kastanopoulos notes, "anyone willing to put a few cows on their property and call it a farm" could exploit many agricultural easements. The Decaters and Equity Trust built in a "ramped up" agriculture requirement: Live Power Community Farm must be farmed continually by resident farmers and remain organic or "biodynamic" (a farming philosophy that treats the land as a balanced and sustainable unit and uses the rhythms of nature to maintain the health of the farm).

The Decaters' other major concern was the affordability of their land for future farmers. They see a lot of young farmers for whom "one of the biggest stumbling blocks is getting access to land," Gloria says. While traditional conservation easements ban developers, they do not curb the upward pressure on the price of the land from individual home or estate buyers. Steve worried that when he and Gloria were ready to pass on the land, market forces could "spike the cost of the land so high that any farmer would be bid clear out of the picture." To prevent this, the Decaters and Equity Trust crafted limitations on the resale price of the land into the easement.

What Are Conservation Land Trusts?

Conservation land trusts are nonprofit organizations designed to protect ecologically fragile environments, open space, or small farms. According to the Land Trust Alliance's 2010 National Land Census, there are 1,723 local and national conservation land trusts in operation nationwide which have protected approximately 47 million acres of land, an area larger than New England. This is twice the acreage protected by conservation land trusts in 2000. New conservation land trusts are formed at the rate of two per week, according to the Land Trust Alliance. They exist in every state; California leads with 197 land trusts, followed by Massachusetts (159) and Connecticut (137). While land trusts protect land in a variety of ways, two of the most common approaches are acquiring land and acquiring conservation easements, legal agreements that permanently restrict the use of land, shielding it from development to ensure its conservation.

For more information on land trusts, see: Land Trust Alliance <www.lta.org>, Equity Trust, Inc. <www.equitytrust.org>, and Vermont Land Trust <www.vlt.org>.

Today, Live Power is an active 40-acre horse-powered community supported agriculture (CSA) farm, thriving amidst encroaching development and the huge corporate farms that dominate California agriculture. Not only do the Decaters own their land, but their unique conservation easement ensures that it will permanently remain an affordable, active, and ecologically sustainable farm. The Decaters are true stewards of the land, and the land trust's easement provisions reflect their commitment.

New Ways of Looking at Land Ownership

In addition to conservation land trusts, Equity Trust and others have implemented a second land trust model. So-called "community land trusts" usually focus on low-income housing in urban areas, but have in some cases included agricultural interests. They operate by purchasing tracts of land and then leasing them on a long-term basis to tenants who agree to a detailed land-use agreement. Although a farmer who enters into such a relationship would not own the land, he or she would have agricultural control and would own any improvements made to the land. In the tenant contract, the land trust would retain a purchase option for those improvements so that when the farmer was ready to move on, the land trust could ensure the lands remained affordable for new farmers. The land-use agreement could also include provisions to ensure the land remains in production. This option works well in areas where land is exorbitantly expensive, prohibiting the farmer from purchasing even restricted land, or when easements are not available.

In both land trust models, Equity Trust stresses, there is flexibility in how the relationship between the land trust and farmer is defined. Key to the definition is the land use agreement, which can be tailored for the particular situation according to either party's wishes. Kastanopolous notes that these are complex arrangements and "there is no black and white way of doing things." Indeed, one of Equity Trust's missions is to "change the way people think about and hold property." Their goal is to provide models that can be replicated and adapted to varied situations.

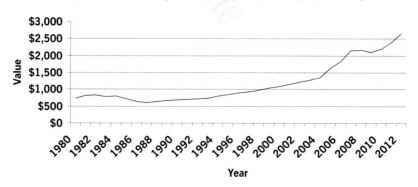

TOTAL VALUE OF U.S. AGRICULTURAL LAND, INCLUDING BUILDINGS, MEASURED IN $/ACRE (U.S. TOTAL)

SOURCE: US Department of Agriculture, National Agricultural Statistics Service, nass.usda.gov

These partnerships and new ways of looking at land ownership acknowledge that there are diverse interests in a piece of land. The farmers, the community, the environment, and future users are all considered. Steven Decater is excited by the prospect of agricultural land trusts catching on. "We'll have permanent farms," he says, "and they're going to be needed." He's right about that. From 2000 to 2008 farm real estate values more than doubled (see figure). Across the country, massive mechanized and chemically sustained corporate-controlled farms are rapidly replacing small-time farmers.

The most vulnerable small farmers are ones who sink tremendous energy and resources into improving their soil but are unable to afford the market value of the land they work. Their lack of ownership control puts their land, and their investment, in jeopardy. This is a particularly common experience for operators of CSA farms, in which producers sell "shares" directly to consumers who receive regular harvest portions during the growing season. According to an informal survey conducted by Equity Trust in the late 1990s, 70% of CSA farms operated on rented land.

Land trusts allow small tenant farms to access land, resist rising property values, and conserve small agricultural tracts. They provide an alternative to unchecked development and farm consolidation, while helping to preserve communities, shield the environment from development, and protect the livelihoods of small farmers. But they are underutilized—in part because the strategy poses certain challenges. It requires:

- resources to purchase the agricultural value of the land;
- willingness by current landowners to sell or donate the land to a land trust;
- technical expertise; and,
- in the conservation land trust model, the presence of a conservation land trust with enough resources to pay for easements—which has become more difficult with skyrocketing property values.

Yet thanks to the hard work of the Decaters, Equity Trust, and other organizations including the Vermont Land Trust (VLT) and the Institute of Community Economics (ICE), this innovative approach to land ownership has taken hold in several parts of the country (see "What Are Conservation Land Trusts?"). The VLT oversees many similar transactions every year; it has conserved more than 500,000 acres of land, including 745 farms. The group is successfully managing to preserve large areas of farmland in Vermont—and it is beginning to address the high demand for affordable farmland across the state through its Farmland Access Program. The VLT purchases farms and resells them to qualified farmers, it purchases conservation easements on farmland to reduce its underlying real estate value, and it ensures the farms they have protected are transferred to other farmers.

Steve Getz, a dairy farmer assisted by the VLT through an easement purchase, says, "We would not have been able to afford the land without the VLT." He and his wife Karen say they respect how the land trust model challenges the "it's my land and I'll do whatever I please with it" mantra that reflects the dominant conception of private land ownership in this country. They now own a successful pasture-based dairy farm in Bridport that will be forever preserved. ❏

Sources: Cynthia Nickerson, Mitchell Morehart, Todd Kuethe, Jayson Beckman, Jennifer Ifft, and Ryan Williams, Trends in U.S. Farmland Values and Ownership, EIB-92, U.S. Dept. of Agriculture, Econ. Res. Serv., February 2012; 2010 National Land Trust Census Report, www.landtrustalliance.org; Vermont Land Trust, www.vlt.org.

Americans are constantly exhorted to save—but also to spend! Social Securty alone is not enough to fund even a modestly comfortable retirement—but many families cannot save enough to fill the gap or meet a financial setback. How should the nation understand and address these dilemmas? Economist Ellen Frank looks at how we can both meet individuals' need for economic security and maintain the stability of a modern market economy.

NO MORE SAVINGS!
The Case for Social Wealth

BY ELLEN FRANK
May/June 2004

Pundits from the political left and right don't agree about war in Iraq, gay marriage, national energy policy, tax breaks, free trade, or much else. But they do agree on one thing: Americans don't save enough. The reasons are hotly disputed. Right-wingers contend that the tax code rewards spenders and punishes savers. Liberals argue that working families earn too little to save. Environmentalists complain of a work-spend rat race fueled by relentless advertising. But the bottom line seems beyond dispute.

Data on wealth-holding reveal that few Americans possess adequate wealth to finance a comfortable retirement. Virtually none have cash sufficient to survive an extended bout of unemployment. Only a handful of very affluent households could pay for health care if their insurance lapsed, cover nursing costs if they became disabled, or see their children through college without piling up student loans. Wealth is so heavily concentrated at the very top of the income distribution that even upper-middle class households are dangerously exposed to the vagaries of life and the economy.

With low savings and inadequate personal wealth identified as the problem, the solutions seem so clear as to rally wide bipartisan support: Provide tax credits for savings. Encourage employers to establish workplace savings plans. Educate people about family budgeting and financial investing. Promote home ownership so people can build home equity. Develop tax-favored plans to pay for college, retirement, and medical needs. More leftish proposals urge the government to redistribute wealth through federally sponsored "children's development accounts" or "American stakeholder accounts," so that Americans at all income levels can, as the Demos-USA website puts it, "enjoy the security and benefits that come with owning assets."

But such policies fail to address the paradoxical role savings play in market economies. Furthermore, looking at economic security solely through the lens of personal finance deflects focus away from a better, more direct, and far more reliable way to ensure Americans' well-being: promoting social wealth.

The Paradox of Thrift

Savings is most usefully envisaged as a physical concept. Each year, businesses turn out automobiles, computers, lumber, and steel. Households (or consumers) buy much, but not all, of this output. The goods and services they leave behind represent the economy's savings.

Economics students are encouraged to visualize the economy as a metaphorical plumbing system through which goods and money flow. Firms produce goods, which flow through the marketplace and are sold for money. The money flows into peoples' pockets as income, which flows back into the marketplace as demand for goods. Savings represent a leak in the economic plumbing. If other purchasers don't step up and buy the output that thrifty consumers shun, firms lay off workers and curb production, for there is no profit in making goods that people don't want to buy.

On the other hand, whatever consumers don't buy is available for businesses to purchase in order to expand their capacity. When banks buy computers or developers buy lumber and steel, then the excess goods find a market and production continues apace. Economists refer to business purchases of new plant and equipment as "investment." In the plumbing metaphor, investment is an injection—an additional flow of spending into the economy to offset the leaks caused by household saving.

During the industrial revolution, intense competition meant that whatever goods households did not buy or could not afford would be snatched up by emerging businesses, at least much of the time. By the turn of the 20th century, however, low-paid consumers had become a drag on economic growth. Small entrepreneurial businesses gave way to immense monopolistic firms like U.S. Steel and Standard Oil whose profits vastly exceeded what they could spend on expansion. Indeed expansion often looked pointless since, given the low level of household spending, the only buyers for their output were other businesses, who themselves faced the same dilemma.

As market economies matured, savings became a source of economic stagnation. Even the conspicuous consumption of Gilded Age business owners couldn't provide enough demand for the goods churned out of large industrial factories. Henry Ford was the first American corporate leader to deliberately pay his workers above-market wages, reasoning correctly that a better-paid work force would provide the only reliable market for his automobiles.

Today, thanks to democratic suffrage, labor unions, social welfare programs, and a generally more egalitarian culture, wages are far higher in industrialized economies than they were a century ago; wage and salary earners now secure nearly four-fifths of national income. And thrift seems a quaint virtue of our benighted grandparents. In the United States, the personal savings rate—the percentage of income flowing to households that they did not spend—fell to 1% in the late 1990s. Today, with a stagnant economy making consumers more cautious, the personal savings rate has risen—but only to around 4%.

Because working households consume virtually every penny they earn, goods and services produced are very likely to find buyers and continue to be produced. This is an important reason why the United States and Europe no longer experience the devastating depressions that beset industrialized countries prior to World War II.

Yet there is a surprisingly broad consensus that these low savings are a bad thing. Americans are often chastised for their lack of thrift, their failure to provide for themselves financially, their rash and excessive borrowing. Politicians and economists constantly exhort Americans to save more and devise endless schemes to induce them to do so.

At the same time, Americans also face relentless pressure to spend. After September 11, President Bush told the public they could best serve their country by continuing to shop. In the media, economic experts bemoan declines in "consumer confidence" and applaud reports of buoyant retail or auto sales. The U.S. economy, we are told, is a consumer economy—our spendthrift ways and shop-til-you-drop culture the motor that propels it. Free-spending consumers armed with multiple credit cards keep the stores hopping, the restaurants full, and the factories humming.

Our schizophrenic outlook on saving and spending has two roots. First, the idea of saving meshes seamlessly with a conservative ideological outlook. In what author George Lakoff calls the "strict-father morality" that informs conservative Republican politics, abstinence, thrift, self-reliance, and competitive individualism are moral virtues. Institutions that discourage saving—like Social Security, unemployment insurance, government health programs, state-funded student aid—are by definition socialistic and result in an immoral reliance on others. Former Treasury Secretary Paul O'Neill bluntly expressed this idea to a reporter for the *Financial Times* in 2001. "Able-bodied adults," O'Neill opined, "should save enough on a regular basis so that they can provide for their own retirement and for that matter for their health and medical needs." Otherwise, he continued, elderly people are just "dumping their problems on the broader society."

This ideological position, which is widely but not deeply shared among U.S. voters, receives financial and political support from the finance industry. Financial firms have funded most of the research, lobbying, and public relations for the campaign to "privatize" Social Security, replacing the current system of guaranteed, publicly-funded pensions with individual investment accounts. The finance industry and its wealthy clients also advocate "consumption taxes"—levying taxes on income spent, but not on income saved—so as to "encourage saving" and "reward thrift." Not coincidentally, the finance industry specializes in committing accumulated pools of money to the purchase of stocks, bonds and other paper assets, for which it receives generous fees and commissions.

Our entire economic system requires that people spend freely. Yet political rhetoric combined with pressure from the financial services industry urges individuals to save, or at least to try to save. This rhetoric finds a receptive audience in ordinary households anxious over their own finances and among many progressive public-interest groups alarmed by the threadbare balance sheets of so many American households.

So here is the paradox. People need protection against adversity, and an ample savings account provides such protection. But if ordinary households try to save and protect themselves against hard times, the unused factories, barren malls, and empty restaurants would bring those hard times upon them.

Social Wealth

The only way to address the paradox is to reconcile individuals' need for economic security with the public need for a stable economy. The solution therefore lies not in personal thrift or individual wealth, but in social insurance and public wealth.

When a country promotes economic security with dependable public investments and insurance programs, individuals have less need to amass private savings. Social Security, for example, provides the elderly with a direct claim on the nation's economic output after they retire. This guarantees that retirees keep spending and reduces the incentive for working adults to save. By restraining personal savings, Social Security improves the chances that income earned will translate into income spent, making the overall economy more stable.

Of course, Americans still need to save up for old age; Social Security benefits replace, on average, only one-third of prior earnings. This argues not for more saving, however, but for more generous Social Security benefits. In Europe, public pensions replace from 50% to 70% of prior earnings.

Programs like Social Security and unemployment insurance align private motivation with the public interest in a high level of economic activity. Moreover, social insurance programs reduce people's exposure to volatile financial markets. Proponents of private asset-building seem to overlook the lesson of the late 1990s stock market boom: that the personal wealth of small-scale savers is perilously vulnerable to stock market downswings, price manipulation, and fraud by corporate insiders.

It is commonplace to disparage social insurance programs as "big government" intrusions that burden the public with onerous taxes. But the case for a robust public sector is at least as much an economic as a moral one. Ordinary individuals and households fare better when they are assured some secure political claim on the economy's output, not only because of the payouts they receive as individuals, but because social claims on the economy render the economy itself more stable.

Well-funded public programs, for one thing, create reliable income streams and employment. Universal public schooling, for example, means that a sizable portion of our nation's income is devoted to building, equipping, staffing, and maintaining schools. This spending is less susceptible than private-sector spending to business cycles, price fluctuations, and job losses.

Programs that build social wealth also substantially ameliorate the sting of joblessness and minimize the broader economic fallout of unemployment when downturns do occur. Public schools, colleges, parks, libraries, hospitals, and transportation systems, as well as social insurance programs like unemployment compensation and disability coverage, all ensure that the unemployed continue to consume at least a minimal level of goods and services. Their children can still attend school and visit the playground. If there were no social supports, the unemployed would be forced to withdraw altogether from the economy, dragging wages down and setting off destabilizing depressions.

In a series of articles on the first Bush tax cut in 2001, the *New York Times* profiled Dr. Robert Cline, an Austin, Texas, surgeon whose $300,000 annual income still left him worried about financing college educations for his six children. Dr. Cline himself attended the University of Texas, at a cost of $250 per semester ($650 for medical school), but figured that "his own children's education will likely cost tens of thousands of dollars each." Dr. Cline supported the 2001 tax cut, the *Times* reported. Ironically, though, that cut contributed to an environment in which institutions like the University of Texas raise tuitions, restrict enrollments, and drive Dr. Cline and others to attempt to amass enough personal wealth to pay for their children's education.

Unlike Dr. Cline, most people will never accumulate sufficient hoards of wealth to afford expensive high-quality services like education or to indemnify themselves against the myriad risks of old age, poor health, and unemployment. Even when middle-income households do manage to stockpile savings, they have little control over the rate at which their assets can be converted to cash.

Virtually all people—certainly the 93% of U.S. households earning less than $150,000—would fare better collectively than they could individually. Programs that provide direct access to important goods and services—publicly financed education, recreation, health care, and pensions—reduce the inequities that follow inevitably from an entirely individualized economy. The vast majority of people are better off with the high probability of a secure income and guaranteed access to key services such as health care than with the low-probability prospect of becoming rich.

The next time a political candidate recommends some tax-exempt individual asset building scheme, progressively minded people should ask her these questions: If consumers indeed save more and the government thus collects less tax revenue, who will buy the goods these thrifty consumers now forgo? Who will employ the workers who used to manufacture those goods? Who will build the public assets that lower tax revenues render unaffordable? And how exactly does creating millions of little pots of gold substitute for a collective commitment to social welfare? ❑

Most proposals to address today's yawning wealth gap aim to rechannel more of the world's privately held wealth into the hands of people who now have little or none of it. That is necessary. But in this visionary article, Working Assets founder Peter Barnes reminds us that there is another, vast source of wealth that people are barely aware of and that institutions neglect and abuse: the commons. And in it, he sees the potential to restore a modicum of both equity and ecological sanity to modern capitalist economies.

SHARING THE WEALTH OF THE COMMONS

BY PETER BARNES
November/December 2004

We're all familiar with private wealth, even if we don't have much. Economists and the media celebrate it every day. But there's another trove of wealth we barely notice: our common wealth.

Each of us is the beneficiary of a vast inheritance. This common wealth includes our air and water, habitats and ecosystems, languages and cultures, science and technologies, political and monetary systems, and quite a bit more. To say we share this inheritance doesn't mean we can call a broker and sell our shares tomorrow. It *does* mean we're responsible for the commons and entitled to any income it generates. Both the responsibility and the entitlement are ours by birth. They're part of the obligation each generation owes to the next, and each living human owes to other beings.

At present, however, our economic system scarcely recognizes the commons. This omission causes two major tragedies: ceaseless destruction of nature and widening inequality among humans. Nature gets destroyed because no one's unequivocally responsible for protecting it. Inequality widens because private wealth concentrates while common wealth shrinks.

The great challenges for the 21st century are, first of all, to make the commons visible; second, to give it proper reverence; and third, to translate that reverence into property rights and legal institutions that are on a par with those supporting private property. If we do this, we can avert the twin tragedies currently built into our market-driven system.

Defining the Commons

What exactly is the commons? Here is a workable definition: *The commons includes all the assets we inherit together and are morally obligated to pass on, undiminished, to future generations.*

This definition is a practical one. It designates a set of assets that have three specific characteristics: they're (1) inherited, (2) shared, and (3) worthy of long-term preservation. Usually it's obvious whether an asset has these characteristics or not.

At the same time, the definition is broad. It encompasses assets that are natural as well as social, intangible as well as tangible, small as well as large. It also introduces a moral factor that is absent from other economic definitions: it requires us to consider whether an asset is worthy of long-term preservation. At present, capitalism has no interest in this question. If an asset is likely to yield a competitive return to capital, it's kept alive; if not, it's destroyed or allowed to run down. Assets in the commons, by contrast, are meant to be preserved regardless of their return.

This definition sorts all economic assets into two baskets, the market and the commons. In the market basket are those assets we want to own privately and manage for profit. In the commons basket are the assets we want to hold in common and manage for long-term preservation. These baskets then are, or ought to be, the yin and yang of economic activity; each should enhance and contain the other. The role of the state should be to maintain a healthy balance between them.

The Value of the Commons

For most of human existence, the commons supplied everyone's food, water, fuel, and medicines. People hunted, fished, gathered fruits and herbs, collected firewood and building materials, and grazed their animals in common lands and waters. In other words, the commons was the source of basic sustenance. This is still true today in many parts of the world, and even in San Francisco, where I live, cash-poor people fish in the bay not for sport, but for food.

Though sustenance in the industrialized world now flows mostly through markets, the commons remains hugely valuable. It's the source of all natural resources and nature's many replenishing services. Water, air, DNA, seeds, topsoil, minerals, the protective ozone layer, the atmosphere's climate regulation, and much more, are gifts of nature to us all.

Just as crucially, the commons is our ultimate waste sink. It recycles water, oxygen, carbon, and everything else we excrete, exhale, or throw away. It's the place we store, or try to store, the residues of our industrial system.

The commons also holds humanity's vast accumulation of knowledge, art, and thought. As Isaac Newton said, "If I have seen further it is by standing on the shoulders of giants." So, too, the legal, political, and economic institutions we inherit—even the market itself—were built by the efforts of millions. Without these gifts we'd be hugely poorer than we are today.

To be sure, thinking of these natural and social inheritances primarily as economic assets is a limited way of viewing them. I deeply believe they are much more than that. But if treating portions of the commons as economic assets can help us conserve them, it's surely worth doing so.

How much might the commons be worth in monetary terms? It's relatively easy to put a dollar value on private assets. Accountants and appraisers do it every day, aided by the fact that private assets are regularly traded for money.

This isn't the case with most shared assets. How much is clean air, an intact wetlands, or Darwin's theory of evolution worth in dollar terms? Clearly, many shared inheritances are simply priceless. Others are potentially quantifiable, but there's no current market for them. Fortunately, economists have developed methods to quantify the value of things that aren't traded, so it's possible to estimate the value of the "priceable" part of the commons within an order of magnitude. The surprising conclusion that emerges from numerous studies is that *the wealth we share is worth more than the wealth we own privately.*

This fact bears repeating. Even though much of the commons can't be valued in monetary terms, the parts that *can* be valued are worth more than all private assets combined.

It's worth noting that these estimates understate the gap between common and private assets because a significant portion of the value attributed to private wealth is in fact an appropriation of common wealth. If this mislabeled portion was subtracted from private wealth and added to common wealth, the gap between the two would widen further.

Two examples will make this point clear. Suppose you buy a house for $200,000 and, without improving it, sell it a few years later for $300,000. You pay off the mortgage and walk away with a pile of cash. But what caused the house to rise in value? It wasn't anything you did. Rather, it was the fact that your neighborhood became more popular, likely a result of the efforts of community members, improvements in public services, and similar factors.

Or consider another fount of private wealth, the social invention and public expansion of the stock market. Suppose you start a business that goes "public" through an offering of stock. Within a few years, you're able to sell your stock for a spectacular capital gain.

Much of this gain is a social creation, the result of centuries of monetary-system evolution, laws and regulations, and whole industries devoted to accounting, sharing information, and trading stocks. What's more, there's a direct correlation between the scale and quality of the stock market as an institution and the size of the private gain. You'll fetch a higher price if you sell into a market of millions than into a market of two. Similarly, you'll gain more if transaction costs are low and trust in public information is high. Thus, stock that's traded on a regulated exchange sells for a higher multiple of earnings than unlisted stock. This socially created premium can account for 30% of the stock's value. If you're the lucky seller, you'll reap that extra cash—in no way thanks to anything you did as an individual.

Real estate gains and the stock market's social premium are just two instances of common assets contributing to private gain. Still, most rich people would like us to think it's their extraordinary talent, hard work, and risk-taking that create their well-deserved wealth. That's like saying a flower's beauty is due solely to its own efforts, owing nothing to nutrients in the soil, energy from the sun, water from the aquifer, or the activity of bees.

The Great Commons Giveaway

That we inherit a trove of common wealth is the good news. The bad news, alas, is that our inheritance is being grossly mismanaged. As a recent report by the advocacy group Friends of the Commons concludes, "Maintenance of the commons is terrible, theft is rampant, and rents often aren't collected. To put it bluntly, our common wealth—and our children's—is being squandered. We are all poorer as a result."

Examples of commons mismanagement include the handout of broadcast spectrum to media conglomerates, the giveaway of pollution rights to polluters, the extension of copyrights to entertainment companies, the patenting of seeds and genes, the privatization of water, and the relentless destruction of habitat, wildlife, and ecosystems.

This mismanagement, though currently extreme, is not new. For over 200 years, the market has been devouring the commons in two ways. With one hand, the market takes valuable stuff from the commons and privatizes it. This is called "enclosure." With the other hand, the market dumps bad stuff into the commons and says, "It's your problem." This is called "externalizing." Much that is called economic growth today is actually a form of cannibalization in which the market diminishes the commons that ultimately sustains it.

Enclosure—the taking of good stuff from the commons—at first meant privatization of land by the gentry. Today it means privatization of many common assets by corporations. Either way, it means that what once belonged to everyone now belongs to a few.

Enclosure is usually justified in the name of efficiency. And sometimes, though not always, it does result in efficiency gains. But what also results from enclosure is the impoverishment of those who lose access to the commons, and the enrichment of those who take title to it. In other words, enclosure widens the gap between those with income-producing property and those without.

Externalizing—the dumping of bad stuff into the commons—is an automatic behavior pattern of profit-maximizing corporations: if they can avoid any out-of-pocket costs, they will. If workers, taxpayers, anyone downwind, future generations, or nature have to absorb added costs, so be it.

For decades, economists have agreed we'd be better served if businesses "internalized" their externalities—that is, paid in real time the costs they now shift to the commons. The reason this doesn't happen is that there's no one to set prices and collect them. Unlike private wealth, the commons lacks property rights and institutions to represent it in the marketplace.

The seeds of such institutions, however, are starting to emerge. Consider one of the environmental protection tools the U.S. currently uses, pollution trading. So-called cap-and-trade programs put a cap on total pollution, then grant portions

THE MARKET ASSAULT ON THE COMMONS

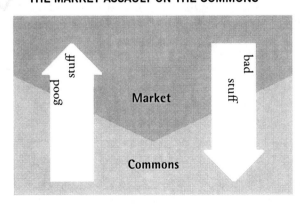

of the total, via permits, to each polluting firm. Companies may buy other firms' permits if they want to pollute more than their allotment allows, or sell unused permits if they manage to pollute less. Such programs are generally supported by business because they allow polluters to find the cheapest ways to reduce pollution.

Public discussion of cap-and-trade programs has focused exclusively on their trading features. What's been overlooked is how they give away common wealth to polluters.

To date, all cap-and-trade programs have begun by giving pollution rights to existing polluters for free. This treats polluters as if they own our sky and rivers. It means that future polluters will have to pay old polluters for the scarce—hence valuable—right to dump wastes into nature. Imagine that: because a corporation polluted in the past, it gets free income forever! And, because ultimately we'll all pay for limited pollution via higher prices, this amounts to an enormous transfer of wealth—trillions of dollars—to shareholders of historically polluting corporations.

In theory, though, there is no reason that the initial pollution rights should not reside with the public. Clean air and the atmosphere's capacity to absorb pollutants are "wealth" that belongs to everyone. Hence, when polluters use up these parts of the commons, they should pay the public—not the other way around.

Taking the Commons Back

How can we correct the system omission that permits, and indeed promotes, destruction of nature and ever-widening inequality among humans? The answer lies in building a new sector of the economy whose clear legal mission is to preserve shared inheritances for everyone. Just as the market is populated by profit-maximizing orporations, so this new sector would be populated by asset-preserving trusts.

Here a brief description of trusts may be helpful. The trust is a private institution that's even older than the corporation. The essence of a trust is a fiduciary relationship. A trust holds and manages property for another person or for many other people. A simple example is a trust set up by a grandparent to pay for a grandchild's education. Other trusts include pension funds, charitable foundations and university endowments. There are also hundreds of trusts in America, like the Nature Conservancy and the Trust for Public Land, that own land or conservation easements in perpetuity.

If we were to design an institution to protect pieces of the commons, we couldn't do much better than a trust. The goal of commons management, after all, is to preserve assets and deliver benefits to broad classes of beneficiaries. That's what trusts do, and it's not rocket science.

Over centuries, several principles of trust management have evolved. These include:

- Trustees have a fiduciary responsibility to beneficiaries. If a trustee fails in this obligation, he or she can be removed and penalized.
- Trustees must preserve the original asset. It's okay to spend income, but don't invade the principal.
- Trustees must assure transparency. Information about money flows should be readily available to beneficiaries.

Trusts in the new commons sector would be endowed with rights comparable to those of corporations. Their trustees would take binding oaths of office and, like judges, serve long terms. Though protecting common assets would be their primary job, they would also distribute income from those assets to beneficiaries. These beneficiaries would include all citizens within a jurisdiction, large classes of citizens (children, the elderly), and/or agencies serving common purposes such as public transit or ecological restoration. When distributing income to individuals, the allocation formula would be one person, one share. The right to receive commons income would be a nontransferable birthright, not a property right that could be traded.

Fortuitously, a working model of such a trust already exists: the Alaska Permanent Fund. When oil drilling on the North Slope began in the 1970s, Gov. Jay Hammond, a Republican, proposed that 25% of the state's royalties be placed in a mutual fund to be invested on behalf of Alaska's citizens. Voters approved in a referendum. Since then, the Alaska Permanent Fund has grown to over $28 billion, and Alaskans have received roughly $22,000 apiece in dividends. In 2003 the per capita dividend was $1,107; a family of four received $4,428.

What Alaska did with its oil can be replicated for other gifts of nature. For example, we could create a nationwide Sky Trust to stabilize the climate for future generations. The trust would restrict emissions of heat-trapping gases and sell a declining number of emission permits to polluters. The income would be returned to U.S. residents in equal yearly dividends, thus reversing the wealth transfer built into current cap-and-trade programs. Instead of everyone paying historic polluters, polluters would pay all of us.

Just as a Sky Trust could represent our equity in the natural commons, a Public Stock Trust could embody our equity in the social commons. Such a trust would capture some of the socially created stock-market premium that currently flows only to shareholders and their investment bankers. As noted earlier, this premium is sizeable—roughly 30% of the value of publicly traded stock. A simple way to share it would be to create a giant mutual fund—call it the American Permanent Fund—that would hold, say, 10% of the shares of publicly traded companies. This mutual fund, in turn, would be owned by all Americans on a one share per person basis (perhaps linked to their Social Security accounts).

To build up the fund without precipitating a fall in share prices, companies would contribute shares at the rate of, say, 1% per year. The contributions would be the price companies pay for the benefits they derive from a commons asset, the large, trusted market for stock—a small price, indeed, for the hefty benefits. Over time, the mutual fund would assure that when the economy grows, everyone benefits. The top 5% would still own more than the bottom 90%, but at least every American would have *some* property income, and a slightly larger slice of our economic pie.

Sharing the Wealth

The perpetuation of inequality is built into the current design of capitalism. Because of the skewed distribution of private wealth, a small self-perpetuating minority receives a disproportionate share of America's nonlabor income.

Tom Paine had something to say about this. In his essay "Agrarian Justice," written in 1790, he argued that, because enclosure of the commons had separated so many people from their primary source of sustenance, it was necessary to create a functional equivalent of the commons in the form of a National Fund. Here is how he put it:

> There are two kinds of property. Firstly, natural property, or that which comes to us from the Creator of the universe—such as the earth, air, water. Secondly, artificial or acquired property—the invention of men. In the latter, equality is impossible; for to distribute it equally, it would be necessary that all should have contributed in the same proportion, which can never be the case. ... Equality of natural property is different. Every individual in the world is born with legitimate claims on this property, or its equivalent.

Enclosure of the commons, he went on, was necessary to improve the efficiency of cultivation. But:

> The landed monopoly that began with [enclosure] has produced the greatest evil. It has dispossessed more than half the inhabitants of every nation of their natural inheritance, without providing for them, as ought to have been done, an indemnification for that loss, and has thereby created a species of poverty and wretchedness that did not exist before.

The appropriate compensation for loss of the commons, Paine said, was a national fund financed by rents paid by land owners. Out of this fund, every person reaching age 21 would get 15 pounds a year, and every person over 50 would receive an additional 10 pounds. (Think of Social Security, financed by commons rents instead of payroll taxes.)

A Progressive Offensive

Paine's vision, allowing for inflation and new forms of enclosure, could not be more timely today. Surely from our vast common inheritance—not just the land, but the atmosphere, the broadcast spectrum, our mineral resources, our threatened habitats and water supplies—enough rent can be collected to pay every American over age 21 a modest annual dividend, and every person reaching 21 a small start-up inheritance.

Such a proposal may seem utopian. In today's political climate, perhaps it is. But consider this. About 20 years ago, right-wing think tanks laid out a bold agenda. They called for lowering taxes on private wealth, privatizing much of government, and deregulating industry. Amazingly, this radical agenda has largely been achieved.

It's time for progressives to mount an equally bold offensive. The old shibboleths —let's gin up the economy, create jobs, and expand government programs—no longer excite. We need to talk about *fixing* the economy, not just growing it; about *income* for everyone, not just jobs; about nurturing *ecosystems, cultures,* and *communities,* not just our individual selves. More broadly, we need to celebrate the commons as an essential counterpoise to the market.

Unfortunately, many progressives have viewed the state as the only possible counterpoise to the market. The trouble is, the state has been captured by corporations. This capture isn't accidental or temporary; it's structural and long-term.

This doesn't mean progressives can't occasionally recapture the state. We've done so before and will do so again. It does mean that progressive control of the state is the exception, not the norm; in due course, corporate capture will resume. It follows that if we want lasting fixes to capitalism's tragic flaws, we must use our brief moments of political ascendancy to build institutions that endure.

Programs that rely on taxes, appropriations, or regulations are inherently transitory; they get weakened or repealed when political power shifts. By contrast, institutions that are self-perpetuating and have broad constituencies are likely to last. (It also helps if they mail out checks periodically.) This was the genius of Social Security, which has survived—indeed grown—through numerous Republican administrations.

If progressives are smart, we'll use our next New Deal to create common property trusts that include all Americans as beneficiaries. These trusts will then be to the 21st century what social insurance was to the 20th: sturdy pillars of shared responsibility and entitlement. Through them, the commons will be a source of sustenance for all, as it was before enclosure. Life-long income will be linked to generations-long ecological health. Isn't that a future most Americans would welcome? ❑

One of the nation's leading poverty experts has written a new book in which he asks some honest questions about the rich.

AN ANTI-POVERTY AUTHORITY CHANGES HIS MIND

SAM PIZZIGATI
August 2012

Peter Edelman has been battling against poverty for nearly half a century, first as an aide to Senator Robert Kennedy, later as a state and federal official, and currently as a key figure at a top law and public policy center in Washington.

Over his years in and out of government, Edelman has probably earned as much respect as anyone in the public policy community, not just for his obvious smarts and experience, but for his conscience and courage.

Back in 1996, Edelman did what few high-ranking government officials ever do. Then an assistant secretary in the U.S. Department of Health and Human Services, he resigned that position when President Bill Clinton signed into law legislation Edelman considered an unconscionable attack on the nation's poor.

The "welfare reform" that Clinton signed into law, Edelman publicly warned, would leave millions of America's most vulnerable children unprotected. He turned out to be right. The number of children living in deep poverty—in families making under half the official poverty threshold—rose 70% from 1995 to 2005 and another 30% the next five years.

America's elected leaders didn't listen to Edelman in 1996. Now they have another chance. Edelman, currently a co-director at the Georgetown University Law Center, has just released a new book, *So Rich, So Poor*, that aims "to look anew at why it is so hard to end American poverty."

You get the feeling from these pages that Edelman would be astonished if our elected leaders actually paid attention to the poverty-fighting prescriptions he lays out in *So Rich, So Poor*. He seems to be aiming at a different audience, the millions of decent Americans from across the political spectrum who share his outrage over our continuing horrific poverty in the world's richest nation.

These Americans have a special reason for paying close attention to Edelman's new book. The author, one of the nation's most committed and thoughtful anti-poverty thinkers, has changed his mind—not about poverty and the poor, but about wealth and the rich.

"I used to believe," Edelman writes candidly, "that the debate over wealth distribution should be conducted separately from the poverty debate, in order to minimize the attacks on antipoverty advocates for engaging in 'class warfare.' But now we literally cannot afford to separate the two issues."

Why? The "economic and political power of those at the top," Edelman explains, is "making it virtually impossible to find the resources to do more at the bottom."

Figuring out how we can achieve a more equal distribution of income and wealth has become, writes Edelman, "the 64-gazillion-dollar question."

"The only way we will improve the lot of the poor, stabilize the middle class, and protect our democracy," he notes, "is by requiring the rich to pay more of the cost of governing the country that enables their huge accretion of wealth."

What about those anti-poverty activists and analysts who still yearn to keep poverty—the absence of wealth—separate from wealth's concentration, those who argue that the rich as a group have no vested interest in opposing efforts to help end poverty? *So Rich, So Poor* addresses these Americans directly.

Some "might ask why the rich and powerful would oppose measures to help lower-income people—what difference does it make it to them?"

Edelman's answer? "More than anything else," he notes, the wealthy "want low taxes," and they know maintaining those low taxes will become ever more difficult "if government is going to spend money to help people who do need it." At America's economic summit, "selfishness trumps selflessness."

"The wealth and income of the top 1% grows at the expense of everyone else," Edelman goes on to observe. "Money breeds power, and power breeds more money. It is a truly vicious cycle."

Only average Americans, Edelman believes, have the wherewithal to end this cycle. Average- and low-income Americans need to join in common cause. If they don't, he notes bluntly, "we are cooked."

SOURCE: Peter Edelman, *So Rich, So Poor: Why It's So Hard to End Poverty in America*. The New Press, 2012.

This article was originally published in Too Much, a weekly newsletter edited by Sam Pizzigati. Too Much is a project of the Institute for Policy Studies' Program on Inequality and the Common Good. <toomuchonline.org>

Alejandro Reuss calls on workers to reunite to fight the war that's been waged against them, to reverse the tide of rising inequality, and to build a more egalitarian society.

THE 99%, THE 1%, AND CLASS STRUGGLE

BY ALEJANDRO REUSS
November/December 2011

Between 1979 and 2007, the income share of the top 1% of U.S. households (by income rank) more than doubled, to over 17% of total U.S. income. Meanwhile, the income share of the bottom 80% dropped from 57% to 48% of total income. "We are the 99%," the rallying cry of the Occupy Wall Street movement, does a good job of calling attention to the dramatic increase of incomes for those at the very top—and the stagnation of incomes for the majority.

This way of looking at income distribution, however, does not explicitly focus on the different *sources* of people's incomes. Most people get nearly all of their incomes—wages and salaries, as well as employment benefits—by working for someone else. A few people, on the other hand, get much of their income not from work but from ownership of property—profits from a business, dividends from stock, interest income from bonds, rents on land or structures, and so on. People with large property incomes may also draw large salaries or bonuses, especially from managerial jobs. Executive pay, though treated in official government statistics as labor income, derives from control over business firms and really should be counted as property income.

Over the last 40 years, the distribution of income in the United States has tilted in favor of capitalists (including business owners, stock- and bond-holders, and corporate executives) and against workers. Between the 1940s and 1960s, U.S. workers' hourly output ("average labor productivity") and workers' real hourly compensation both grew at about 3% per year, so the distribution of income between workers and capitalists changed relatively little. (If the size of a pie doubles and the size of your slice also doubles, your share of the pie does not change.) Since the 1970s, productivity has kept growing at over 2% per year. Average hourly compensation, however, has stagnated—growing only about 1% per year (see figure below).

As the gap between what workers produce and what they get paid has increased, workers' share of total income has fallen, and capitalists' share has increased. Since income from property is overwhelmingly concentrated at the top of the income scale, this has helped fuel the rising income share of "the 1%."

The spectacular rise in some types of income—like bank profits or executive compensation—has provoked widespread outrage. Lower financial profits or CEO pay, however, will not reverse the trend toward greater inequality if the result is only to swell, say, profits for nonfinancial corporations or dividends for wealthy shareholders. Focusing too much on one or another kind of property income distracts

GROWING GAP BETWEEN PRODUCTIVITY AND PAY, 1947-2010

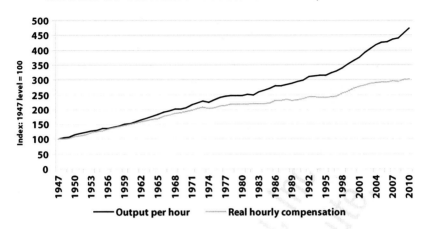

from the fact that the overall property-income share has been growing at workers' expense.

Workers and employers—whether they like it or not, recognize it or not, prepare for it or not—are locked in a class struggle. Employers in the United States and other countries, over the last few decades, have recognized that they were in a war and prepared for it. They have been fighting and winning. Workers will only regain what they have lost if they can rebuild their collective fighting strength. In the era of globalized capitalism, this means not only building up labor movements in individual countries, but also creating practical solidarity between workers around the world.

A labor resurgence could end workers' decades-long losing streak at the hands of employers and help reverse the tide of rising inequality. Ultimately, though, this struggle should be about more than just getting a better deal. It should be—and can be—about the possibility of building a new kind of society. The monstrous inequalities of capitalism are plain to see. The need for an appealing alternative—a vision of a cooperative, democratic, and egalitarian way of life—is equally stark. ❑

Sources: Bureau of Labor Statistics, Real Hourly Compensation, Private Business Sector, Series ID number: PRS84006153; Bureau of Labor Statistics, Output Per Hour, Private Business Sector, Series ID number: PRS84006093; Congressional Budget Office, Trends in the Distribution of Household Income Between 1979 and 2007 (October 2011) (www.cbo.gov); James Heintz, "Unpacking the U.S. Labor Share," *Capitalism on Trial: A Conference in Honor of Thomas A. Weisskopf*, Political Economy Research Institute, University of Massachusetts-Amherst (September 2011).

*The Occupy Movement inspired activists, analysts, and the general public to public-
ly question capitalism and propose real alternatives. Inspired by Occupy, economist
Richard Wolff offers a proposal for a system in which workers control the means of
production collectively and democratically.*

TURNING TOWARD SOLUTIONS
It's time to occupy and reorganize production.

BY RICHARD D. WOLFF
January/February 2012

Since last September, the 99% have been wielding the weapon of criticism against the 1%. They are effective because they act in a new, collective, and organized way. Occupy Wall Street (OWS) and its many offshoots expose basic truths and demand basic changes. They struggle peacefully to reach, inform, and mobilize public opinion. They keep winning huge numbers of hearts and minds. In reaction, the U.S. 1% copied their counterparts in Tunisia, Egypt, Syria, and Bahrain. They limited media access needed by the movement to reach its growing audience. That failed. Their police intimidated, but that failed. Democratic Party operatives tried to convert Occupiers into Obama enthusiasts for the 2012 election. That failed, too.

Then, the 99%'s weapon of criticism suffered the counter-criticism of weapons. The 1%— frequent preachers of non-violence to others—resorted to coordinated police violence in cities across the country. As elsewhere, to cover up its failure to win hearts and minds, the U.S. government resorted to violence. Chickens raised abroad returned home to roost. Internet images flashed of New York Police Department machines and personnel bulldozing the free library in Zuccotti Park. Many recalled the famous 1930s photographs of police burning the books of those the Nazis feared or hated and therefore demonized.

New York's newly renamed billionaire mayor—*Mubarak* Bloomberg—gave the order to "clear and clean" Zuccotti Park. Having presided over some of the world's filthiest subway tunnels and stations, Bloomberg suddenly became obsessed with cleanliness. In New York, where income distribution is even more unequal than in the nation as a whole, the 1% mayor tried to silence OWS criticisms of that inequality and its capitalist roots. As OWS matures into a national movement, will that lead to renaming the President—as *Mubarak* Obama?

The conditions causing OWS include deepening economic inequality, the money-eyed corruption of politics, and the collapsing fortunes and prospects of the mass of Americans. Neither Bloomberg nor Obama are changing them. The U.S. Census Bureau recalculated poverty last November (as requested and reported by the *New York Times,* Nov. 19, 2011). The new calculation divided poverty into three types: "deep" (earning 50% or less of the official poverty level), "poor" (earning 50-100 % of the poverty level) and "near poor" (earning 100-150% of the poverty level). The new calculation took into account regional cost of living differences, government benefits (transfer payments) and income lost to taxation, health care and work expenses.

The Census Bureau's conclusion: *one-third of the United States was in or near poverty.* Over 100 million of our fellow citizens live at poverty levels hard to imagine, let alone endure. What this capitalist system delivers contradicts most Americans' notions of fairness, expectations of "middle-class" rewards for hard work, and hopes for their children. Business and political leaders had refused to see, debate, or change these conditions for decades. Most mainstream media and academics were similarly in denial. The system thus kept reproducing the causes of poverty (unemployment that precluded wage increases, "deficit reductions" that cut government transfer payments to the needy, foreclosures yielding more homeless people alongside more abandoned homes, etc.). The capitalist system became increasingly intolerable to increasing numbers of people. It produced a mass movement like OWS that shook and disrupted the national consensus on denial. Today, the criticism of weapons (police) risks losing to the weapon of criticism (OWS).

For the last half-century, it was taboo in the United States to criticize, debate, or propose changes to the economic system. We could question and alter our educational, transportation, health and other basic systems. However, Cold War anxieties and hysterical anti-communism dictated that the economic system be celebrated. Criticism of capitalism was branded as disloyalty to the United States. Journalists and academics followed the politicians in giving capitalism a free pass. Behind that celebratory veil, a protected capitalism performed ever more poorly for ever more people. As average real wages stopped rising since the 1970s, Americans borrowed more than they could sustain. As flat real wages and rising worker productivity made for huge profits, executives paid themselves astronomical salaries, stock options, and bonuses. Inequality has mushroomed since the 1970s and has contributed considerably to this crisis's depth and duration.

American capitalists took full advantage of their exemption from basic criticism. They widened the distance between employers and employees to produce a new "Gilded Age" now targeted by the 99% vs.1% slogan. It is stunningly effective because it rings so true to most Americans.

The Occupy movement keeps developing and now turns increasingly toward finding solutions for the problems it exposed. One emerging perspective holds that the capitalist economic system itself is the problem and movement to another system is the solution. The goal is not to transition to traditional socialist alternatives (e.g., the old Soviet Union or modern China). Rather, these alternatives too seem flawed systems needing basic change.

The solution for them too is to reorganize production from the ground up. Wherever production of goods or services occurs, the workers there should collectively and democratically function as their own board of directors. An exploitative and conflicted capitalism (employer versus employee) should be abolished much as our ancestors abolished slavery (master versus slave) and feudalism (lord versus serf). The solution is a system of workers' self-directed enterprises—where those who do the work also design and direct it and distribute its fruits. The basic goal of democracy—that all those affected by any decision participate equally in making it—would finally arrive inside production itself. No longer would a tiny elite minority—major shareholders and the corporate boards of directors they choose — make all the basic decisions: what, how and where to produce and how to use the surpluses/profits. Instead, the workers themselves—in shared democratic partnership with the residential communities interdependent with their enterprises—would make all those decisions.

Only then could we avoid repeating capitalist cycles. Those begin when capital accumulation and competition generate a crisis. When sustained mass suffering follows, movements for reform arise and sometimes succeed. Capitalists use their profits to block reforms and, when unsuccessful, to undo the reforms. This sets the stage for the next period of accumulation and competition and the next crisis: the U.S. pattern since the 1929 crash.

To break such truly vicious cycles, we need now to transform capitalism by internally reorganizing enterprises. Then, those who most need and benefit from reforms would be the self-directed workers who dispose of as well as create the profits of enterprises. No separate class of employers will exist and use the profits to undo the reforms won by workers. Self-directing workers would pay taxes to a state only insofar as it secures those reforms. More basically, our best hope of ending history's legacy of 99% against 1% lies in establishing new enterprises where democratically self-directed workers would no longer distribute incomes in capitalism's grotesquely unequal ways.

Workers' self-directed enterprises are a solution to problems shared by both capitalism and socialism. Establishing workers' self-directed enterprises moves further in the modern democratic movement beyond monarchies and autocracies. Democratizing production in this way can finally take political democracy beyond being merely an electoral ritual facilitating the same old rule by the 1% over the 99%. ❑

Sam Pizzigati finds visionary activists fighting for pay equity, strict regulations on corporate finance, and wealth redistribution in Britain, where the general public has a better understanding of the effects of inequality on quality of life.

WHY GREATER EQUALITY STRENGTHENS SOCIETY

What US progressives can learn from British efforts to fight inequality.

SAM PIZZIGATI
December 2011

For American progressives, looking at Britain can sometimes seem like looking in a mirror. The British face essentially the same economic crisis we do. A never-ending recession—and never-ending windfalls for CEOs. Austerity budgets. Rising poverty. Young people without a future. Old people without security.

But this mirror analogy cracks as soon as we start comparing progressive agendas. Some top priorities on America's progressive to-do list simply don't show up on the British version. There's no mystery why: British progressives already have in place a good chunk of what we're still desperately seeking. A healthcare system that ices out profiteering insurers? Britain has one. Progressive tax rates up to 50% on income over $250,000? Check. A financial transactions tax on stock trades? The British even have that, too.

These contrasts should give us pause. If the British are hurting even after achieving so much of what we're seeking, we're clearly not seeking enough.

Maybe our transatlantic colleagues can help us here. What are they seeking? Can their visions—and strategies—inform and embolden ours?

I spent some time in London just after Occupy Wall Street launched in Manhattan—and just before British Occupiers set up shop at St. Paul's Cathedral—posing these questions to an array of thoughtful campaigners against Britain's top 1%. I didn't expect these activists to have any "secret" for plutocracy-busting success. But I was hoping to find some emphasis that I hadn't expected, and I found plenty.

Take orientation, for instance. Unlike us, British progressives are not looking backward for ideas and inspiration. We do that all the time: contrasting Obama with Franklin D. Roosevelt, demanding a new version of FDR's Civilian Conservation Corps, coveting New Deal tax rates. Britain has a similar heroic progressive past— the years right after World War II, when the Labour Party, steeled by sacrifice and solidarity, laid the foundation for the modern British welfare state.

Conventional Labour Party politicos still try to "resuscitate that 1945 moment," notes Neal Lawson, the chair of Compass, Britain's largest independent progressive pressure group. But British progressives don't see that moment as a blueprint for the future, because the conditions that made it possible—an economy built on mass manufacturing, a heavily unionized working class, cold war rivalry—no longer exist.

British progressives also have a deeper point to make: the basic blueprint of their heroic past may be inherently flawed. The activists I met, young and old alike, sprinkled their analyses with dismissive—and disconcerting—references to "tax and spend" policies. How could they, I wondered, so casually accept a basic conservative frame? Didn't they realize they were legitimizing a right-wing epithet?

I eventually caught on. British activists don't consider "tax and spend" any sort of social engineering outrage. They simply consider "tax and spend" policies inadequate to the task of creating the just and sustainable society our future demands. Such policies take the corporate economy as a given—and accept that it will help some and hurt others. The tax-and-spend antidote to this inequality: tax the fortunate to fund programs that boost the disadvantaged.

This notion of the "redistributive state" drove Labour Party policy from the mid-20th century to the 1990s, when New Labour added a perverse twist. To regain power in Thatcherite Britain, Tony Blair and friends argued, Labour would have to soothe the City, Britain's Wall Street. New Labour, they insisted, could comfort the bankers and help poor people at the same time—by freeing the City to rev up the economy. If the City boomed, even modest levies on the rich would raise enough revenue to end child poverty. In effect, Blair was positioning British high finance as "a cash cow for an improved welfare state," says Stewart Lansley, an award-winning analyst of British poverty.

Once elected in 1997, New Labour followed through on this City soothing. "Light touch" regulation soon had the economy roaring—and made the rich phenomenally richer. Growing inequality didn't seem to matter, so long as poor people were getting some help. As Blair strategist Peter Mandelson famously put it: "We are intensely relaxed about people getting filthy rich, as long as they pay their taxes."

Of course, growing inequality did matter. In Britain, as in the United States, the chase after grand fortune would crash the economy. The poor would be worse off. The rich, after a brief dip, would rebound.

The lesson in all this? "We need to attack inequality at its roots—and not depend on redistribution at the end," says Faiza Shaheen, a young economist at London's innovative New Economics Foundation. Shaheen makes a medical analogy. Over time, she explains, viruses can develop resistance to antiviral medications. The rich, over time, develop resistance to redistributive taxes. They use their wealth and power to carve out loopholes and lower rates. Their fortunes balloon. Inequality grows.

Smart public health officials stress prevention. Smart social and economic policy, says Shaheen, would stress prevention, too. We shouldn't rely on our ability to tax income that concentrates at the top. We should prevent that income from concentrating in the first place. And the front line of any prevention struggle should be the corporate enterprise, where power-suited "one-percenters" are raking off a fantastically disproportionate share of the wealth our economies generate. Inequality simply matters too much, sums up Shaheen, to let it dig in.

British progressives were never comfortable with New Labour's "intense relaxation" about people getting rich. But they now have much more evidence to back up their instinct—and a renewed sense of egalitarian confidence. Both the evidence and the confidence come in large part from a remarkable 2009 book, *The Spirit*

Level: Why Greater Equality Makes Societies Stronger, by British epidemiologists Richard Wilkinson and Kate Pickett.

The authors explore the impact of inequality on modern societies and demonstrate in graphic detail that people in more equal nations live longer, healthier and happier lives. Wilkinson and Pickett took their stunning data slides to cities across Britain. If Britain had levels of inequality as low as those of Scandinavia and Japan, they explained, British murder rates would drop by half, mental illness by two-thirds, teen births by 80%.

The Spirit Level became a bestseller, and two advocacy groups have formed to deepen its impact. One Society reaches out to policy-makers; the Equality Trust helps inspired readers organize locally. The campaigns seem to be having an impact. In the run-up to the May 2010 general election, the leaders of Britain's three major parties jostled to claim the fairness mantle. Conservative Party leader David Cameron even favorably cited *The Spirit Level*. "We all know in our hearts," he opined, "that, as long as there is deep poverty living systematically side by side with great riches, we all remain the poorer for it."

After the elections, Cameron, the new prime minister, moved quickly to burnish his fairness credentials. He tabbed Will Hutton, a respected journalist and foundation executive, to conduct an official policy review of pay disparities within the public sector.

British progressives, meanwhile, had already started down a different road. In August 2009, Compass rallied 100 progressive leaders and called on the then-ruling Labour Party to establish a "High Pay Commission" that would aim to help ensure that "out of control" private-sector rewards could never again fuel the "excessive risk taking" that can melt an entire economy.

Labour ignored the call, and after the elections Compass decided to move ahead on its own. With foundation support, the group filled an independent High Pay Commission with a blue-ribbon cross-section of British civil society, business, and labor. The new commission, chaired by a former *Financial Times* editor, quickly gained a high media profile.

In both Britain and the United States, the commission noted, the executive pay debate has essentially revolved around protecting and empowering shareholders—so "poorly performing" CEOs don't walk away rich while share prices plummet.

British lawmakers gave shareholders "say on pay"—the right to take advisory votes on executive pay—nearly a decade ago. U.S. shareholders didn't get that right until the Dodd-Frank financial reform legislation passed in 2010. But "say on pay" hasn't ended runaway compensation in Britain, where executive bonuses have nearly tripled over the past decade. Top executive pay at banking giant Barclays has gone from 13 times the average British worker pay in 1980 to 169 times the worker average today.

Such "stratospheric" increases, the High Pay Commission final report charges, are "damaging the UK economy"—undermining productivity, distorting markets, draining talent from key sectors. Expecting only shareholders to end this executive excess makes no sense, the commission suggests, not when the excess imperils more than shareholders. We have all become stakeholders in the decisions that determine the distribution of corporate rewards.

HEALTH AND SOCIAL PROBLEMS ARE WORSE IN MORE UNEQUAL COUNTRIES

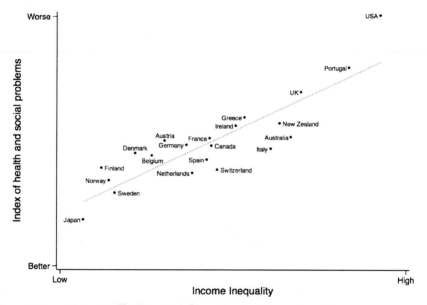

Source: Wilkinson and Pickett (2009), *The Spirit Level*; chart and more information at http://www.equalitytrust.org.uk/why.

The report recommends a series of steps to empower this broader community of stakeholders. Real employees, not just CEO cronies, should sit on corporate board remuneration committees. And full disclosure must accompany every facet of the process—not just so shareholders can protect their investment but so that workers and consumers can mobilize and press against enterprises that contribute to greater inequality.

How can stakeholders gauge corporate contributions to inequality? The commission recommends that every British corporation be required to publish the ratio between top executive and median worker compensation. Pay ratios have been floating around British egalitarian circles for quite some time. Various progressive groups have called for a "maximum wage" set as a multiple of worker pay. David Cameron even asked his Hutton review panel to consider limiting top pay in the public sector to 20 times bottom pay. That review, in the end, rejected ratio limits but endorsed disclosure, in both the public and private sectors.

Progressive groups like One Society see much more organizing potential in pay ratios than in traditional "tax and spend," mainly because three decades of right-wing pounding against government have left the public deeply wary about expanding the welfare state. Polls, by contrast, show widespread interest in limiting pay gaps.

British activists have begun building a pay-ratio politics at the local level. Last year the Greater London Authority pledged to reduce the high-to-low pay gap "to no more than 20 times, with a long term goal of no more than 10 times."

Another locality is moving more boldly. Islington, a London borough that sits next to the financial district, formally adopted a 10-times pay commitment late in 2011. A local government, Labour Party activists in Islington acknowledge, has limited clout. It can't force private employers to narrow pay differentials. But Islington as a public employer can ensure its lowest-paid employees a living wage, establish pay ratios between top and bottom, and encourage local private employers to adopt similar fairness benchmarks.

In Islington, local employers who honor this "fairness agenda" now earn a "kitemark," a recognition symbol they can publicly display.

Other localities are ramping up fairness campaigns on the Islington model. The wage ratios that emerge from these efforts, Equality Trust's Bill Kerry believes, will help stimulate an ethical consumer movement that champions "narrow gap" employers. Every consumer, in effect, will be able to become an advocate for more equitable workplaces.

Maybe every taxpayer, too. The pounds paid in taxes by average British families regularly pour into the coffers of private contractors that lavish windfalls on their top execs. Public bodies can end these taxpayer subsidies for inequality by giving preferential treatment to "narrow gap" contractors, and by denying tax dollars to those with overpaid executives. They can even extend this denial to corporations that line up for tax incentives and subsidies.

Leveraging the public purse in this way would require, as a first step, the mandatory disclosure of corporate pay gaps that progressives have been pressing for and the High Pay Commission report has recommended. Ironically, that mandate already exists, at least on paper, in the United States. In 2010, New Jersey Senator Bob Menendez outflanked corporate lobbyists and slipped into the Dodd-Frank bill a provision that requires publicly traded companies to reveal their CEO-median worker pay ratios every year. The Securities and Exchange Commission hasn't yet articulated how it will enforce this mandate, and embarrassed corporate shills are pushing hard to get it watered down or repealed in Congress.

So Americans have a ratio disclosure mandate with no political momentum behind it—and no vision for making the most of it. Brits have no mandate but momentum and vision. They see how organizing consumer and procurement battles over pay ratios could help bring about a sea change in Britain's polite political culture. "Excessively high incomes," as the British Archbishop of York John Sentamu recently wrote, have to become as socially "unacceptable" as racism and homophobia.

That's not to say that British progressives feel they can tame inequality one enterprise at a time. "I'm patient," Compass chair Neal Lawson says with a smile, "but not that patient."

Compass has released a plan that sets forth not just an alternative to austerity, but an alternative "to business as usual and all that means for growing inequality, climate change, and people's well-being." The plan demands national action on everything from creating a publicly accountable British investment bank to forging a new progressive tax structure. British activists don't see these reforms as imminent. But most share a feeling that the public must begin to see some indication that progressive approaches can actually curb the inequalities so rampant around them.

Without this sense of progress, the danger remains that growing social cynicism—particularly among the young—may erupt in more outbreaks of looting and burning, as London experienced in 2011. And then what?

"The response to crisis doesn't have to be left-wing," notes George Irvin, a British economist steeped in European history. "It can be right-wing as well."

And incredibly ugly. Unless we get our acts together—on both sides of the pond. ❑

This article was originally published December 6, 2011, by The Nation magazine, www.thenation.com. Reprinted with permission.

CONTRIBUTORS

Randy Albelda is a professor of economics at the University of Massachusetts-Boston and a *Dollars & Sense* associate.

Sylvia A. Allegretto is a labor economist and co-chair of the Center on Wage and Employment Dynamics at the Institute for Research on Labor and Employment, University of California, Berkeley.

Gar Alperovitz is a professor of political economy at the University of Maryland, president of the National Center for Economic and Security Alternatives, and a founding principal of the Democracy Collaborative.

Peter Barnes is a successful entrepreneur who co-founded Working Assets and has served on several business boards. He is a senior fellow at the Tomales Bay Insitute.

Chuck Collins is a senior scholar at the Institute for Policy Studies and directs IPS's Program on Inequality and the Common Good. His most recent book is *99 to 1: How Wealth Inequality is Wrecking the World and What We Can Do About It* (2012, Berrett-Koehler). He co-edits www.inequality.org, a portal of data, commentary and analysis.

James Cypher is profesor-investigador, Programa de Doctorado en Estudios del Desarrollo, Universidad Autónoma de Zacatecas, Mexico, and a *Dollars & Sense* associate.

Ryan A. Dodd is a Ph.D. student in economics at the University of Missouri-Kansas City, and a visiting instructor at Gettysburg College.

Ellen Frank teaches economics at the University of Massachusetts, Boston.

Amy Gluckman is a former co-editor of *Dollars & Sense.*

Howard Karger is Head of School at The University of Queensland School of Social Work & Human Services in Queensland, Australia, and the author of *Short-Changed: Life and Debt in the Fringe Economy* (Berret-Koehler, 2005).

Meizhu Lui is the co-author of *The Color of Wealth: The Story Behind the U.S. Racial Wealth Divide*, as well as numerous articles, reports, and book chapters. She is a member of Freedom Road Socialist Organization.

Arthur MacEwan is an emeritus professor of economics at the University of Massachusetts-Boston. He is a *Dollars & Sense* associate and founding member of the magazine.

John Miller, a member of the *Dollars & Sense* collective, is a professor of economics at Wheaton College.

Dedrick Muhammad is senior director of the Economic Department and executive director of the Financial Freedom Center of the NAACP.

Linda Pinkow is development and promotions director of *Dollars & Sense,* and a member of the D&S collective.

Alejandro Reuss is co-editor of *Dollars & Sense* and an instructor at the Labor Relations and Research Center at UMass-Amherst.

Sam Pizzigati edits *Too Much,* an Institute for Policy Studies weekly on inequality and excess. His latest book is *The Rich Don't Always Win: The Forgotten Triumph Over Plutocracy That Created the American Middle Class* (Seven Stories, 2012).

Michelle Sheehan is a former member of the *Dollars & Sense* collective.

Chris Tilly is director of the Institute for Research on Labor and Employment and professor of Urban Planning at UCLA. He is a *Dollars &Sense* associate.

Jeannette Wicks-Lim is an assistant research professor at the Political Economy Research Institute, UMass-Amherst.

Richard D. Wolff is professor of economics emeritus at University of Massachusetts, Amherst, and a visiting professor in the Graduate Program in International Affairs of the New School University.

CPSIA information can be obtained at www.ICGtesting.com
Printed in the USA
BVOW080125081212

307607BV00003B/8/P